C000119642

BETTER OFF DEAD

A SORDID TRUE STORY OF SEX, SIN AND MURDER

BY MICHAEL FLEEMAN

WILDBLUE PRESS

WildBluePress.com

BETTER OFF DEAD published by:

WILDBLUE PRESS
P.O. Box 102440
Denver, Colorado 80250

Publisher Disclaimer: Any opinions, statements of fact or fiction, descriptions, dialogue, and citations found in this book were provided by the author, and are solely those of the author. The publisher makes no claim as to their veracity or accuracy, and assumes no liability for the content.

Copyright 2017 by Michael Fleeman

All rights reserved. No part of this book may be reproduced in any form or by any means without the prior written consent of the Publisher, excepting brief quotes used in reviews.

WILDBLUE PRESS is registered at the U.S. Patent and Trademark Offices.

ISBN 978-1-947290-43-3 Trade Paperback
ISBN 978-1-947290-42-6 eBook

Interior Formatting/Book Cover Design by Elijah Toten
www.totencreative.com

BETTER OFF

DEAD

A SORDID TRUE STORY OF
SEX, **SIN** AND **MURDER**

Table of Contents

1.

An hour before sunset, Shaun Ware swung his white work truck right off Goodrick Drive into the Summit Industrial Park, a complex of metal buildings with tall garage doors. It was Sunday, Aug. 17, 2014, a warm summer evening in the high desert. Shadows enveloped the Tehachapi Pass, the mighty turbines in the windmill farm standing still in the light western breeze. Traffic roared by on Highway 58, cars and trucks shuttling between Bakersfield and the Mojave Desert. Every half hour, a long freight train from Burlington Northern Santa Fe Railway would rumble behind the complex.

Arriving for his overnight shift, Shaun pulled his truck up to a space with "BNSF" stenciled on the concrete parking block and immediately felt something was wrong. The metal door to the work area was closed. The day-shift responder, Robert Limon, would have kept it open to ventilate the stuffy garage during the 89-degree afternoon. Robert would have told him if he were out on a service call or making a food run.

Shaun raised the door with a remote opener. Robert's BNSF utility truck was parked next to his personal car, a silver Honda. Shaun walked into the garage along the right side of the truck. He nearly stepped on broken glass that appeared to have come from one of the fluorescent fixtures hanging from the 18-foot ceiling.

To his right, the door to the small office was wide open. That was wrong, too. The office door always stayed closed. The office appeared to have been ransacked. File drawers had been yanked open and papers strewn across the floor. A BNSF-issued Toshiba laptop was missing.

Shaun walked around the front of the work truck, which pointed toward the kitchenette against the back wall. The door of the small refrigerator was flung open. So was the door to the bathroom.

That's when he saw him.

Robert Limon was on the floor, his back slumped against the driver's side tire of the truck.

Shaun kneeled.

"Rob, what happened?" Shaun said. "Wake up, buddy."

Robert had a vacant look on his face, one eye closed, the other half opened. Blood had pooled beneath him. He didn't respond.

Panic gripped Shaun. He called 911 on his cell phone. He told the operator that he had found his coworker on the ground around a lot of blood and that he wasn't moving.

The operator asked if Shaun was willing to try CPR. He said yes. Following the operator's instructions, Shaun pulled Robert down flat on his back. He put his face close to Robert's. There was no breath. The operator asked Shaun to push his hands against Robert's chest to begin compressions.

One push and blood oozed out of Robert's mouth.

The operator told Shaun to get out of the building, now. He did, in a daze. The cell phone still to his ear with the 911 operator on the line, he wandered out to the asphalt parking area.

A man approached—somebody who worked in a neighboring unit—and asked Shaun what was going on.

"I think Rob's dead," Shaun told him.

Then it hit him. Shaun dropped to his knees and his body convulsed. He felt tears coming.

How long he was like this, he couldn't remember. The next thing he knew, he heard cars approaching. Sirens. Lights. He looked up and saw a woman in a sheriff's uniform.

Shaun pointed to the garage and said, "He has two kids."

2.

Two deputies from the Kern County Sheriff's Office fielded the 911 call at 6:46 p.m. for a "male found bleeding and not breathing" at 1582 Goodrick Drive, Tehachapi, Calif. They arrived in separate one-deputy patrol cars. Both had often seen the facility from the 58, but had never been on call there.

Goodrick Drive took them to a cul-de-sac with a driveway leading into the five buildings of the complex. Since it was a Sunday night, all of the garage doors were shut—save for one—and the place empty, except for the man crouched on the pavement.

Kern County Senior Deputy Marcus Moncur got there first. The 10-year veteran cop approached the man, who was shaking but saying nothing. A second, deputy, Anna Alvarez, a rookie patrol officer, arrived in her patrol car. Moncur asked her to stay with the man and talk to him while he checked out the garage 50 yards away.

There, the deputy saw the silver Honda and the white Chevy work pickup with the utility bed. On the ground next to the driver's side door, he spotted a man flat on his back. He was a big, strong man, about 6 feet tall, with a shaved head and tuft of beard on his chin. He wore an orange safety shirt, black tank undershirt, gray pants and black shoes.

Moncur could see that the man had a lump on his eye and blood around his mouth and right cheek. A large pool of blood congealed beneath his head and upper body. His right arm extended from his body as if hailing a cab. The body showed signs of lividity, the purple discoloration caused by blood pooling under gravity at low points in the body after the heart stops. Just behind the man, red spots were splattered on an open refrigerator door. A sign on the wall read: "A culture of commitment to safety to each other."

Moncur radioed for a paramedic and walked carefully out of the garage so as not to step on any evidence. He asked Alvarez to cordon off the area as a crime scene.

Within minutes, an ambulance and a paramedic truck raced into the complex. Two emergency medical technicians took the man's vital signs and ran a field EKG reading. No signs of life. The EMTs called a physician at the Kern Medical Center in Bakersfield, recited their findings.

At 7:06 p.m., the man was officially declared dead. Over the next half hour, phone calls went out to supervisors and investigators, plus crime scene technicians and the coroner. Moncur started a crime-scene log to keep track of what would be a small invasion of law enforcement personnel overnight.

He then waited an hour and a half.

Covering more than 8,000 square miles, Kern County is just smaller than the entire state of New Jersey. But with 880,000 people, it has only a tenth of its population. Kern County is vast and in most places, empty. The rectangular-shaped county is made up of sprawling farmland, rugged mountains and wide swaths of desert.

The closest detective was more than an hour's drive away in the county seat of Bakersfield. Randall Meyer of the robbery homicide division got the call at home from the Kern County Sheriff's Office Communication Center at about 7:30 p.m. A former patrol deputy, training supervisor and investigator in the sex crimes unit, Meyer had been transferred to robbery-homicide six months earlier. He put on a suit and tie and headed east for Tehachapi.

He got to the top of the pass at 8:30 p.m. Pulling off Highway 58, he made his way on side streets to Goodrick Drive to the industrial complex. He flashed his ID, got logged in and was directed to the crime scene through two checkpoints, one at the outer perimeter near the entrance to the facility, the second the taped-off inner perimeter closest to the garage.

Darkness had come to the high desert. At an elevation of more than 4,000 feet, even on this summer night the temperature would plunge more than 40 degrees to the mid-50s. The complex was ablaze with emergency lights and full of cops.

Meyer received a briefing from another Kern County detective, Mitchell Adams, who was in charge of processing the crime scene. Adams had phoned another detective with instructions to seek a search warrant from a night-duty judge. In the meantime, Adams had an evidence tech videotape the exterior of the garage. He walked around to the back of the building, looking for any signs of evidence. Behind the garage, in the hard-parked dirt, he spotted what looked like footprints near the back door. He had the tech photograph those. About 15 feet west of the corner while walking southeast, he found another shoe track, also photographed.

After 90 minutes, Adams had a search warrant and for the first time entered the garage. Adams told Meyer that he followed the same path as Shaun Ware along the right side of the truck, stepping over the glass shattered into a powder. The fixture above was missing one of its two fluorescent bulbs and Adams could see some damage to the metal frame.

On the ground, directly below the fixture, he spotted a bullet. It was mangled from apparently hitting the light fixture. It appeared to be a larger caliber, .44 or .45, from a big, powerful gun.

To his right, through the office door, he could see a television, sofa, desk and office chair, exercise machine, photocopy machine, whiteboard, calendar and two desks against the wall. The bottom desk drawers were open and items, including file folders, had been removed and thrown on the floor. Behind the bookcase on the northwest wall were several binders on the ground that Adams believed had been hastily removed from their previous location. Two cell phones sat on the desk.

Walking around the front of truck, Adams saw the body for the first time, the blood on the face and a bump on the back of the head. Behind the man, red dots from blood spatter were on the doors of the refrigerator.

An evidence technician photographed the interior of the office, the bullet fragment on the ground, the tiny blood spatter on the interior of the refrigerator door, the door of the truck—everything Adams pointed out.

That was the extent of the physical evidence. Beside the footprints, Adams found nothing that a killer or killers would have left behind. An evidence tech dusted for fingerprints, but analysis would take days.

"I immediately started thinking that it was possibly a staged scene," Adams later said in court, repeating what he told Meyer. "In numerous investigations, with burglary and robberies and such, I've never seen items placed as those were and the amount of items."

How the victim died would remain a question mark. The bullet on the ground and the blood on and around the body suggested he was shot. The bump on the head could have come from a blow. An autopsy would sort that out.

No gun or other weapon was found. Nor did they find spent brass ammunition shells, suggesting the shooter used a revolver or picked up the ejected shells from a semi-automatic.

Meyer was led to the "reporting party," Shaun Ware. A burly man with a shaved head, Shaun could have been the victim's brother. Shaun explained that the garage was leased by Burlington Northern Santa Fe Railway as a repair shop.

He and the victim, whom he identified, worked as "rapid responders," going into the field when trains break down, which they had a habit of doing on the Tehachapi Pass.

From the flat San Joaquin Valley, the trains strain up the grade, so steep in one spot that the tracks form a circle, like a spiral staircase, that takes the trains up 77 feet in a mile. Train buffs flock from around the world to see the famed Tehachapi Loop. YouTube is full of scenes of the loop.

Some 20 trains a day labor up the pass, making it one of the busiest stretches of single track in the country and one of the hardest on engines. Metal cracks, hoses blow, wires short circuit. That's when the phone rings in the BNSF garage in Tehachapi. A rapid responder jumps in a truck and races out to the scene of the breakdown, diagnosing the problem and making repairs.

Shaun told the detective the Tehachapi responders work 12-hour shifts. They always work alone. The 7 p.m. to 7 a.m. shift the night before belonged to Shaun, that day's 7 to 7 to Robert Limon.

The last time he'd spoken to Robert was that morning during the 7 a.m. shift change. They talked about Robert's iPad, which was not working. Shaun slept all day before his overnight shift and had no idea what Robert had done during the day shift.

Meyer asked Shaun how well he knew Robert. He said he'd worked with him off and on for about two years. "He was a very friendly guy, very outgoing," Shaun later said in court, repeating what he told Meyer.

Robert was married with two kids and lived in a community called Silver Lakes, in the town of Helendale, in San Bernardino County, about an hour-and-half drive away toward Barstow. Shaun had never known Robert to use drugs or have been involved in any illegal activities. He couldn't think of anybody who'd had an argument with Robert, much less want to harm him.

Then Shaun said something that Meyer found particularly intriguing. Robert did not usually work in Tehachapi. He was based far across the Mojave Desert to the east at Barstow Yard, BNSF's sprawling rail classification yard where rolling stock is changed between engines along a labyrinth of tracks. According to Shaun, Robert was filling in that Sunday for the regular responder, who was either out sick or taking vacation time. Shaun didn't know which employee was out but he knew that Robert had taken the shift at the last minute.

Shaun told him something else: the BNSF work truck in the garage, like all trucks, was equipped with a forward facing camera that activates during accidents. It may have captured something.

When the processing of the scene was complete, the body was released to the coroner's investigator, who put bags over the hands to preserve evidence and pulled the wallet from the victim's back pocket. The driver's license confirmed what Shaun Ware had said. The victim was Robert Limon, age 38, with a home address on Strawberry Lane in Helendale.

The coroner investigator and two other body removal assistants placed the corpse into a blue body bag and sealed it with a tag. Robert Limon—husband, father and railroad worker—was now coroner number C01615-14.

One of the cell phones in the office belonged to Robert. It had several missed phone calls and text messages. The last text came at 8:30 p.m.: "Babe I'm worried about you. Call me. Leanna wants to say goodnight."

Det. Randall Meyer would find out that the text had come from Robert's wife, now widow.

It was never returned.

3.

"Detective, what happened to my husband?"

The woman's voice sounded tired and stressed.

"I do want to give you some information real quick," Det. Randall Meyer told her, but then the cell reception got fuzzy, and she told him to call her landline. "This is Detective Meyer again," he told her when he called back. "I just have some questions for you, and then we'll talk a little bit about what's going on."

It was 1:30 a.m. when Det. Meyer called Sabrina Limon. She was at home in Silver Lakes. In the background, Meyer could hear adults talking and the voices of children. The house on Strawberry Lane was full of relatives, friends and the two Limon children, son Robbie, 11, and daughter Leanna, 8. Death draws a crowd.

He called her after what could only have been the worst night of her life. When Sabrina's husband didn't come home, didn't answer his phone and didn't reply to her texts, she called her older sister, Julie Cordova, and their parents. They all lived in Silver Lakes and came over immediately—Julie accompanied by her husband and one of her two sons and his wife.

Then at about 8:30 p.m., a white BNSF Jeep pulled up to the house. Two men from the railroad came to the house to tell Sabrina that her husband had died at work in Tehachapi. All they knew was that it appeared to be an injury to his head. Police were investigating.

Julie watched as her sister collapsed on the porch in tears. Robbie and Leanna started crying.

Julie's husband demanded more information, but they said they didn't know anything more. Her husband wasn't so sure. He once worked for BNSF—he was the one who had helped Robert get hired there back in 2000. Then he suffered an injury on the job. The Cordovas tangled over a settlement. "They did not take care of him," Julie later claimed. Her husband told them he wanted to drive to Tehachapi and find out for himself what was going on. The railroad men urged him to stay away and not interfere with police. He reluctantly agreed.

Julie started making phone calls.

"Julie called me probably about 10:30 in the evening," Robert Limon's sister, Lydia Marrero, recalled in an interview. "She had told me there had been a terrible accident and my brother was gone. I said: 'What happened to my brother?' And she couldn't tell me. The next thing, I just lost it."

All Julie knew was that Robert had died at work. Lydia, who lives with her husband, Reyes, in the San Bernardino Valley community of Rialto, wanted to make the 120-mile drive to Tehachapi that night, but Julie talked her out of it. "She said we probably couldn't talk to anybody there, so we waited until the next morning."

After 1 a.m. the Kern County coroner's office called the house and an investigator officially notified Sabrina that her husband was dead. The investigator had little more information than the railroad men. Sabrina heard her say something about Robert still having his wallet.

Then Sabrina's cell phone rang. It was Det. Meyer. She ended the call with the coroner investigator and asked Meyer to call her back.

"Your husband," Meyer said, "his first name was Robert, correct?"

"Robert, yeah."

"What time did he leave to go to work yesterday?"

"He leaves about 5 o'clock."

"In the morning?"

"Uh-huh."

"And why was he coming to work here in Tehachapi?"

"He's a responder. He relieves when guys go on vacation."

"Does he normally work somewhere else?"

"He's a car inspector in Barstow Yard."

"Do you know why he was working over here yesterday?"

"He got called. A guy asked if he could work. One of the guys needed him to cover. I'm not sure why."

"What's his normal shift he works in Barstow?"

"He has Thursday, Fridays off. He works 7 to 3 p.m. in Barstow Yard."

"From what you're aware, he was coming in to cover for somebody here in Tehachapi? He left Sunday morning at 5 a.m.?"

"Yes."

Meyer would later find out that Robert was filling in for a responder named Cory Hamilton. A railroad employee for only a year, Cory had met Robert when Cory was hired in the fall of 2013. He knew Robert only through work, chatting during shift changes. More important, Cory was the responder who had been scheduled to work that Sunday day shift. With family visiting from out of town, Cory took sick days for that Saturday and Sunday. Another fill-in employee, John Justus, covered the Saturday shift, but couldn't do Sunday. It was Justus who got in touch with Robert Limon on Saturday and arranged for him to go to Tehachapi on Sunday.

"Did you speak to him in the morning before he left?" Meyer asked Sabrina.

"I hugged him goodbye. He always wakes me up before he leaves for work."

"Did you have a chance to talk to him throughout the day yesterday?"

"I talked to him a little after 1. And then I talked to him

again. He was on a call and he said he was stuck on a train and he said it was—he called it 'A Million Dollar Train.' It was a UPS train where they carry, they call—how did he tell me?—he called it a hot train. He said he was getting it going and he said he got a sandwich and he just had to pick it up. … I talked to him and he was back in the shop."

As Sabrina was starting to ramble, Meyer said, "Let's back up a little bit. When you talked to him at 1 p.m., is that when he said he was working on the train?"

"Uh-huh."

"And he got lunch? Where did he go to lunch at?"

"He ordered a sandwich from a bakery. He has a favorite place he always goes to."

"And do you know the name of that place?"

"It's just, like, the only one in town. He always gets a tuna melt, he tells me about it."

"So you talked to him at 1 o'clock. How long was your conversation?"

"Not long. I told him I would call him back."

She recalled that he called her cell phone, reaching her shortly after she had come out of church, which would have been around 1:30 p.m.

"I called him back from the landline and talked to him for a little bit," Sabrina said. "He said he was tired and he said he was going back to the shop. He said he had been chasing trains. He was going to go back and take a nap."

"What time was that call?"

"I'm going to say about 2:30, about 2 maybe. I have my girlfriend here. She said her husband talked to him about 1:30. I talked to his mom, and his mom talked to him today. I asked her what time it was and I can't remember what she told me."

"About 2:30, you talked to him and he said he was little bit tired and heading back to the shop. And you said you also talked to him while he was at the shop, correct?"

"He was at the shop. I said, 'Lay down and take it easy,'

and then usually, he'll call me after he wakes up. But I got busy around here. And I called him about probably about 4:30, maybe even closer to 5, and I was going to go to my mom's and see her. And I called him, and he didn't answer. I also sent him a text to say call me on my cell phone; I'm going to go over and see my mom."

Her parents also lived in Silver Lakes. She was visiting her mother to see how she was doing while recovering from a broken hip.

"I stayed over there until about 6, little after 6," Sabrina said, "and the kids and I came home. And our kids are supposed to start school tomorrow. So I was getting them ready. I called him on the way home on my cell phone. No answer. And then called him again from the home line. No answer. And then I thought he must be on call."

She kept calling Robert because it was getting later and the children would be going to sleep soon to rest up for school.

"Our daughter wanted to talk to him, she started saying, 'Why isn't Daddy answering?'" said Sabrina, who told her daughter he was probably on a repair call. "Then it got closer to 7, and no answer. That was weird, because he'll always call me on his way home. So I just started calling him after that, 7, after 7, 7:30 until it was 8 o'clock. I figured, I was worried about him. I sent him a text. I said call me. Leanna wants to say goodnight to you and I never ..." Her voice trailed off.

Meyer asked, "At what point in time did you hear something from someone?"

It was when the two railroad supervisors came to the house. "I was looking out the window, and they pulled up in a white Jeep," said Sabrina. She then began crying. It was two supervisors from BNSF railroad who came to her house between 8 and 8:30 p.m. They told her only that Robert was dead and that he had a head injury. They said nothing about him being killed, and for much of the night, Sabrina would say, she assumed that Robert had suffered an accident.

Meyer now made it clear that was not the case.

"As far as Robert goes," asked Meyer, "do you know of him having any trouble with anybody?"

"Never."

"Never?"

"Never. Everybody loves Robert."

"Everything going pretty normal with your guys' relationship? There are no issues or anything like that?"

"No, I love him so much."

"There was nobody you can think of that might have been upset with him?"

"No."

"How about his coworkers? How does he get along with his coworkers?"

"Great. Everybody loves Robert," said Sabrina. "Everybody."

"He had never told anybody that he had any issues with coworkers at all whatsoever?"

"No."

Meyer turned to the detective. "Anything you can think of, Detective Robins?"

He said nothing.

"Right now, Sabrina, we're at the very preliminary stages of this whole investigation," Meyer explained. "We don't have a lot of information right now."

"What happened?" Sabrina asked in a pleading tone. "What happened to him?"

"That's it," said Meyer. "We don't know. We don't really have any information yet. We're still working on it right now."

"Where was he? What happened? Did they take his car? She said they didn't take his wallet," said Sabrina, referring to the coroner investigator. "Like, why?"

"Obviously, I can't answer that stuff," said Meyer. He changed the subject. "What type of cell phone does he have?"

"Nothing fancy, but maybe like a 'droid."

She gave him his cell number. "Did you find his phone?"

"I think we did find the phone," said Meyer. It was one of the two phones recovered from the office. "We don't really have a lot of info to go on. We're working on the scene right now. I'm actually away from the scene. … So I don't even know what's going on yet. What we're going to do, when we're done here, we'll basically do a detective briefing and get everybody up to speed. When I find more information, I'll give you a call and let you know."

"Please," she pleaded, "because I want to know. I want to know. I don't understand. I just don't understand. I don't understand. My brain is not putting this together at all. It isn't even possible. I don't understand. I just want to know what happened. I don't understand. I just want to know."

"As soon as I find out some information, I'll let you know."

"Thank you so much."

"We are working our best right now.

"Thank you."

"I'll call you when I get more information."

"Thank you."

"You have my phone number, call if you ha—"

Sabrina asked: "And you're a detective?"

"Yes," he said.

"Detective Meyer?"

"With the Kern County Sheriff's Office."

"Okay, thank you so much."

The call ended 2:14 a.m. and Meyer would later say that it went about the way he expected. His experience in patrol and sex crimes had him speaking to many people under similar traumatic circumstances. He investigated dead baby cases. And nothing in Sabrina's demeanor raised red flags. She struck him as a suitably upset and confused woman who had no idea what she was going do next for the rest of her life.

Meyer had been calling from a management office at the industrial complex. He had barely seen the crime scene. His ignorance about the circumstances of Rob's death was not invented, though he'd invent plenty before it was over.

One of the investigators had tracked down the landlord and asked if the facility had any surveillance cameras. There were several, in fact, including one at the entrance on Goodrick Drive pointed toward the garage where Robert was killed.

The next day, Meyer would see that footage. Meyer hoped for the best. Unless a witness materialized, it was all he would have to go on.

4.

Later that Monday morning, Sabrina got another visitor from the railroad. Daniel Flatten Jr., the general director of claims for the Burlington Northern Santa Fe Railway, is based in Fort Worth, Texas. By sunrise, Flatten was at the front door with a folder full of paperwork.

Railroad employees don't have Social Security benefits or workers compensation. If injured or killed on the job, they and their families get money from BNSF's own insurance and from a pool of money from the Railroad Retirement Board, an agency established in the 1930s.

Flatten was there to hand deliver the BNSF railroad benefits. Sitting at the kitchen table with Sabrina and her sister, Flatten explained to her the covered details of the insurance, retirement plan and the company 401(k). He also made arrangements to return whatever personal property of Robert's the police had not seized and to make sure Sabrina got Robert's last paycheck. He said the company would also pay funeral expenses up to $15,000.

It was a short meeting and nothing was decided. He gave her his business card and left. The visit seemed to rankle Julie, still bitter over her husband's experience with BNSF. "He was out there the very next day after Rob passed away," said Julie, "and Brina couldn't process it."

Flatten would later say he didn't remember how it came to be, in his words, he simply "showed up" at the Limon's house. Though there was the matter of money. The railroad stood to lose a bundle off of Robert's death. In addition to the usual injury and death benefits, Sabrina could seek an additional direct settlement. For workers who are maimed or die on the job in accidents, the settlements can reach into the millions of dollars.

The Limon case was uncharted territory. Flatten had never handled a case in which a worker was murdered while on the clock. Depending on what police found, this one could be a record payout.

Over the next two months, Flatten kept in touch by phone, sometimes speaking to Sabrina, but mostly dealing with Julie. "I would tell her, 'Brina you have to take care of these kids and yourself,' " Julie said. "It was unsafe where Robert was."

Working all night in remote garages like the Tehachapi shops, some BNSF workers were rumored to carry handguns, in violation of company policy. Their calls took them into wild country at all hours. Robert once told his wife about encountering a bear during a call. He said the Tehachapi area was considered particularly dangerous because so many trains broke down around the Loop, leaving them vulnerable to old-fashioned train robbers seeking valuable cargo.

Within weeks, Flatten broached the subject of a settlement with Sabrina. BNSF had classified Robert as a "high wage earner" whose extra pay for doing relief work put his salary at more than $100,000. Had he worked another 20 years until retirement, he would have made $2 million—a number that would be a logical starting point in settlement talks with BNFS.

It was one of the hallmarks of this case that at critical junctures, Sabrina declined to seek the advice of a lawyer. Early on, BNSF abruptly canceled health insurance for Sabrina and the children, an apparent mistake that Julie worked out on her own. The only advice Sabrina received outside her family came from representatives of the railroad union.

According to Julie, Robert and Sabrina were never tightfisted with money—they loaned Julie and her husband money, voicing no expectations that it would have to be repaid. They also helped cover the student loans for Julie's son. It was Julie who rifled through Sabrina's financial papers and found that Robert had a life insurance policy with a $300,000 payout. Sabrina had said nothing about it. "I was really on her about it," she recalled. "I was so concerned that the kids would be taken care of."

In phone calls from Texas, Flatten went over the settlement process with Sabrina and her sister, but urged them to give BNSF more time. Robert's death was still under investigation by both the Kern County Sheriff's Office and the railroad's in-house police department. Its investigators were working closely with the sheriff's detectives, interviewing witnesses and reviewing records. At least twice, Flatten recalled, he told Sabrina, "We needed to pump the brakes and allow the process to work."

The work was going slowly. From the police standpoint, the whole thing seemed stuck in neutral. Police had no witnesses, little evidence save for a single bullet and some faint shoeprints beside the BNSF building and no apparent motive. Detectives couldn't find anybody who had a bad word to say about Robert. He was financially secure, had no known substance abuse issues, no pending litigation and had not so much as raised his voice at any anyone who police could find. Obviously, a bear didn't kill him.

From a BNSF coworker, Meyer confirmed Sabrina's account that her husband had gone on a service call at around 1 p.m. Robert Garnas, a road foreman based in Bakersfield, met Robert Limon at a train breakdown at a place called Cable Cross Over Station, a few miles west of the Tehachapi garage. They diagnosed the source of the problem—the dynamic brakes on a locomotive—and got to work. Within an hour, the train was up and rolling. The men talked shop. They both knew the new terminal manager in Bakersfield, a guy who had previously "worked up on the hill," as Tehachapi was known, but who now seemed to enjoy life in the city. Robert Garnas liked Robert Limon—nearly everybody did, a big teddy bear of a man. "He always seemed very happy, a big smile," Robert Garnas would say.

The state of the early part of investigation was reflected in the first news accounts. "Helendale Man Found Dead at BNSF Yard," read the headline in the *Daily Press* based in Victorville, 15 miles south of Helendale. The story appeared on Tuesday, Aug. 19, two days after Robert's body was found, and provided scant details. It said deputies were investigating the murder of BNSF employee Robert Limon, 38, of Helendale, who was found "unconscious" with "obvious signs" of trauma to his upper body, at 6:46 p.m. that previous Sunday in a BNSF maintenance facility in Tehachapi.

Kern County Sheriff's spokesman Ray Pruitt said no arrests had been made and detectives had no possible suspects. "One of the potential motives we're looking at is that he interrupted a burglary or a theft in progress on the property. That's a possible scenario that we're certainly looking at," he said. "There's somebody out there in the community that committed this crime, and we want to identify that person as soon as we can and get that person into custody. This is obviously a very high priority case, and it's a case that we want to solve."

To juice the investigation, BNSF offered a $100,000 reward for information leading to the arrest and conviction of the killer. "Mr. Limon was a valued BNSF employee for 13 years and all those who worked with him are shocked by this tragedy," BNSF said in a statement. "BNSF Railway extends its deepest condolences to his family and friends. … BNSF Police are working closely with the Kern County Sheriff's Office to investigate this senseless crime and ensure the security of BNSF's employees at this location." BNSF spokeswoman Lena Kent told Bakersfield TV station KBAK that Limon was liked and respected. "Everyone is shocked," Kent said. "It's really devastated our community."

The Sheriff's Office then revealed one of the few breaks in the case. As Randall Meyer was talking to Sabrina Limon, an evidence tech was downloading the security video from the five cameras at the Summit Industrial Complex. Most of the footage showed nothing on this lazy Sunday.

But the entrance-mounted camera captured a person, probably a man, wearing bulky clothes and carrying a dark bag. The hunched-over figure was limping left past some trees in the direction of the BNSF garage at 5:21 p.m. Eighteen minutes later, at 5:39 p.m., the person could be seen limping back the opposite way.

The face was too far from the camera to be seen and none of Robert's coworkers or other tenants in the complex recognized the person. So two days after the murder, Det. Meyer released the video to the media and posted it on the Kern County Sheriff's Office YouTube page.

A press release gave Meyer's phone number as well as the number and texting information for the Secret Witness anonymous tip line. That night, the video was all over the Bakersfield and Los Angeles news stations and posted on the websites of the local newspapers. "Hopefully, somebody in the community will recognize the person of interest and we can talk to that person," Pruitt told the media. "Or, somebody will hear something, or has some information that points us in the right direction."

The next day, Meyer would have even more information with which to work. On the morning of Aug. 20, 2014, the remains of Robert Limon arrived in a pouch at the lab of Dr. Robert Whitmore, a forensic pathologist working under contract for the Kern County Sheriff–Coroner, at his offices in Bakersfield down the street from a Home Depot and Walmart.

A graduate of the St. Louis University School of Medicine, Whitmore toyed with psychiatry before changing his specialty to anatomic pathology. After a residency in New York, he got a fellowship with the San Diego County medical examiner's office. He's also a regular doctor, licensed to practice medicine on the living in California and Florida. But on this day, his patient was no longer among the living.

The ID tag was cut and the bag opened, revealing a shrouded corpse; the body had been wrapped in three white sheets at the crime scene. A small group would witness the external and internal examinations: two autopsy aides to assist Whitmore, two evidence technicians shooting photographs and bagging evidence, and one of the sheriff's investigators, Deputy David Hubbard, who took notes.

The removal of the sheets showed that Robert's body was still wearing an orange safety shirt, black tank top undershirt, gray pants, gray boxer briefs, black belt, black socks and black shoes. The clothing was removed and stored for inspection, as were the sterile white evidence-preservation bags that had been placed on his hands at the scene. From Robert's right rear pocket, Whitmore found a note that "appeared to be a note left for him regarding his work." Apparently innocuous, the note warranted no other mention.

The body was photographed clothed and nude, then weighed and measured. At death, Robert was 201 pounds and 5-foot-11½ inches.

As Whitmore examined the outside of the body for trauma and signs of medical procedures, he recited his findings into a handheld Dictaphone and made sketches. He swabbed both hands with sterile wipes for possible DNA evidence and clipped the fingernails. He then sliced open the body for the internal examination, removing each organ one by one, weighing them, looking for evidence of disease or injury and taking tissue samples, before returning the organs to the body cavity. Although lab tests would still be conducted, it appeared that Robert was a perfectly healthy

38-year-old man at the time of death.

Next, Whitmore examined the wounds to the body. First, where a bullet entered the left side of the chin. He could tell it was an entry wound from the skin pushed inward. The bullet shattered the left side of the jawbone, went into the mouth, grazed the left side of the spinal column at the neck, punctured a muscle in the back of the neck, and went out through the back of the neck, leaving a nasty exit wound.

This may have been from the bullet that struck the light fixture and landed on the floor for Det. Adams to find. If so, that meant the gun was fired at Robert's head at a sharp upward angle. A second bullet wound was located on the upper right side of Robert's chest. This bullet also traveled in an unusual upward path. Whitmore had never seen anything like it. It was as if the shooter were lying on the floor at Robert's feet and aiming skyward. This second bullet pierced the body cavity, crashed into the right collarbone, exited the body near the shoulder and then re-entered the body through the right side of the neck. The bullet tore through the muscle that turns the neck, perforated both the right jugular vein and carotid artery, and traveled into the head. It hit against the inside of skull and rattled around inside the brain. That bump on Robert's head was likely caused by the bullet pushing up through the skull.

Whitmore removed the bullet. Like the one on the ground, it was a large-caliber, .44 or .45. Whitmore could not determine the order of the shots, though both would be fatal. The shot to the chin would have taken seconds, maybe minutes, to kill Robert; the one that ended up to the head would have caused instantaneous death.

Along with upward trajectories of the shots, the wounds showed signs the gun was fired at close range. Black-gray soot covered both entrance wounds from the burning gunpowder shooting out of the barrel along with the bullets. This meant the gun was inches away or closer. Had the shots come from slightly farther away, as an intermediary range shot, the wounds would have been surrounded by abrasions, known as tattooing, caused by the unexploded gunpowder grains.

On the chest wound, Whitmore saw what appeared to be a rectangular abrasion, perhaps caused by the barrel of a handgun pressed against the skin when fired.

Robert showed none of the traditional scrapes and cuts from defensive wounds. It also didn't appear that he did what many gunshot victims do—put up his hands in a reflexive effort to block the shots—due to the lack of any bullet wounds to the palms or fingers.

Cause of death: gunshot wounds. Manner of death: homicide.

As Whitmore sent his findings out to be transcribed into a written report, Deputy Hubbard briefed Det. Meyer.

Robert Limon was shot twice up close—from down low—and didn't put up a fight or even have time to raise his hands.

This raised two possibilities. He was taken completely by surprise, perhaps by somebody lurking on the ground. Or he was shot by somebody he knew and trusted enough to let them get close.

Which meant that not everybody loved Robert.

5.

It was a 125-mile drive from Bakersfield to Helendale. The trip took detectives Randall Meyer and Kevin Kimmel up the Tehachapi Pass. They emerged from the mountains, where the huge white turbines of the wind farms line the ridges like sentries, and entered Tehachapi, a former railroad town two hours due north from Los Angeles but a world away.

The air is thinner and the population is proudly eccentric, desert rats on the edge of the grid. Tehachapi's official website boasts of a "unique environment" that leaves the community "outside the mainstream and conventions of suburbia. It's original. More unconventional attitude attracts people with fresh ideas and energy."

The metal buildings of the Summit Industrial Park, where Robert Limon was killed, whizzed by the detectives' car on the right, a reminder that Tehachapi on one night at least attracted another element of the more dangerous kind.

The investigators followed Highway 58 as it skirted the dusty town of Mojave and down into the vast California desert by the same name. To the north lay Edwards Air Force Base, where the space shuttles landed. Otherwise, nothing but sand and rocks and desert scrub dominated the scenery for the next half hour until they got to the first sign of civilization, the exit for the old town of Boron, where the 20-mule trains used to haul away the solvent borax dug out of the surrounding hills.

The freeway ended and the road narrowed to two lanes, clogged with trucks hissing to a stop at the only traffic light for miles and miles in all directions. This was Kramer

Junction, locally known as Four Corners, a collection of gas stations, mini-marts and fast food joints at the intersection of 58 and Highway 395. The investigators took a sharp right onto 395 and went another lonely 30 miles to the turnoff for Silver Lakes.

This last leg took the detectives up a steady climb of nearly 1,700 feet, the low desert of Four Corners becoming the high desert. Out of nowhere a huge tract of stucco houses emerged. "I thought: 'Who in the hell would live here?' " recalled Meyer. "It is waaaay out there in the middle of nowhere.' "

Silver Lakes is charming as it is surreal, a tidy community of homes surrounding two manmade lakes surrounded by miles and miles of desert. It was as if somebody plopped a housing tract from the O.C. on the face of Mars.

Silver Lakes boosters call it "the happiest place on the high desert." With its two lakes, golf course, Olympic-sized pool, clubhouse and parks with playgrounds, the community lives up to its motto of "vacation where you live." Jobs can be found 30 miles away in the small desert cities to the south of Hesperia and Victorville, located on the very fringe of commuting distance to Los Angeles, or 30 miles to the northeast in Barstow, where Robert had been employed.

It was now 5:30 p.m. and as the bright desert sunshine turned to dusk, the detectives got their first look at the place Robert Limon had called home. The Limons lived in a neat single-story ranch house on Strawberry Lane with a two-car garage and a front yard of grass and one tree. The eastern shore of North Lake was a short walk away, as was the Silver Lakes Country Club golf course. Across the street was the elementary school.

The detectives were led into a living room brimming with activity. Some 30 people—all friends, relatives and children—were there, as was Sabrina Limon.

For quiet, they went into a bedroom. A pretty blonde with a warm smile, Sabrina appeared in person nothing like she had sounded just four days earlier on the phone. "We started to get kind of thrown off. There's something not right here. She was very put together," Meyer recalled. "She was dressed nice. She didn't look like she'd been a wreck."

Meyer turned on his recorder. This would be the official interview with Sabrina, filling in the gaps, retracing subjects covered from before.

"How long have you known Robert?" he asked.

"I've known Rob my whole life, since 18 years old," she said. "I've known Robert my whole life."

"And how long have you been married?"

"Married 14 years."

"And your kids are ages?"

"11 and 8."

"And their names?"

"Robbie and Leanna Limon."

The release of the surveillance video had generated a number of leads, many of them anonymous phone calls to the secret tip line. But it was too soon to get anything of value. Meyer had no idea who could have killed Robert or why. He had hoped the answer may lie somewhere in his personal or work life.

"He would change pinion gears, weld, he did it all," Sabrina said. As a railroad carman, Robert normally worked in Barstow, but took shifts as a rapid responder in Tehachapi "quite often," drawn by the money.

"If he got called on a sick deal, would he get paid extra?" asked Meyer.

"He would get supervisor pay, and he gets paid to drive up and there and gets food expenses."

"That was a far drive to work a shift."

"He worked it quite often, made a lot of money. They would pay for a room, but he would want to come home."

Sabrina said she had visited him at the Tehachapi shop a couple of years earlier with the children.

"I'm familiar with the shop. And if he would get a call,

we could stay and the kids could like play. I haven't been up there for a couple of years."

Meyer said, "So let's talk about this last weekend. Did he work last Saturday?"

"Yeah, he did."

"Did he work up in Tehachapi?"

"I'm trying to think."

"The incident occurred on Sunday."

"Saturday? No, he worked Barstow Yard on Saturday.

"Did he work Friday also?"

"Yes, he did."

She said Robert had been called by coworker John Justus, another carman in Barstow, to cover Cory Hamilton's Sunday shift. In a separate interview with police, John confirmed that. A 21-year veteran of BNSF, John knew Robert better than anyone at the railroad. They met in 2000 at Barstow Yard around the time Robert began working for the railroad. "He's a good guy, a nice friend," John told the investigator. They played golf, but John didn't socialize with anyone else in Robert's family. He had only met Sabrina when coming by the house to pick up Robert for a round of golf.

Meyer asked, "What time did he leave to go to work?"

"I'm going to say 5:15."

"How long does it take him to get to Tehachapi?"

"It would take, like, an hour and 20 minutes."

"Did you talk before he left?"

"No," she said, then to herself. "Did we? I was always: 'Call me when you get there. And call me when you get off,' " she said.

Sabrina was calmer than she had been during the first interview, though this time she tended to ramble and struggled to remember times and dates. Her sister would later say that Sabrina had barely slept that week. "She wasn't eating," said Julie. "I went over there every day. I took off work, and she was not doing well. She would collapse on the floor when the kids would be asleep. I would have to get her off the floor. I would dress her. She was a mess."

Meyer asked what time she had spoken to Robert after he left the house.

"I want to say 7."

"In the morning?"

"Around the time he gets up there, which would be a little bit before 7. If you want me to think really hard, maybe it was 8 or 8:30 or so. Church is at 10, 10:30, so somewhere between that time."

"Some time between 7 and 10?"

"Uh-huh."

"And you talked to him later that day?"

"We talked when I got back. It was one-ish."

Sabrina said she had gone to church that morning around 10, telling Robert in a phone call, "I'll call you when I get out of church." It was a typically busy day. Leanna had a friend over at the house, so Sabrina picked them up lunch on the way home. Robbie was at another friend's house. She was scrambling to get everybody home by late afternoon, so they would settle down and get to bed early for the start of school the next day.

"I was just ready to have both the kids home," she said. "Because we're always going."

She spoke to Robert around 1 or 2 p.m.

"What did you guys talk about?" asked the detective.

"I just said, 'I got back from church,' " she said. She then had to hang up because her daughter needed something. "I think something happened. It wasn't that long of a phone call. And then I talked to him again."

"Do you know what time it was, the second call?"

"I was trying to think about that, a lot. I'm going to say it was between 1 and 2. No, no, no. It was not 1 o'clock. I want to say it's between: let's say 2 and 3. He was on a call."

This was the call that took him to fix the UPS train.

"He said it was a million-dollar train that broke down

for some reason," she said. "Sometimes it was the silliest thing. A detector would go off. I didn't pay attention to everything he said. I was like, okay. He had to get that one back going. And then he said he was tired. He said he'd been going since he'd been there. I remember that. I remember he said he went to that sandwich shop."

She couldn't remember the name of the shop, but said, "He said he got a sandwich and he couldn't even take it back to the garage. He said he ate it in the truck. He said he was going to go and kick back. There were some times he wouldn't go out all, all day long. Some times where he would be going all day, call after call, non-stop."

"You talked to him again; how long was the conversation, do you think?"

"It was longer. I didn't talk to him a whole lot."

"Did he say he'd talked to his coworkers or anything that day?"

"He talked to Dax that day," she said. Dax and his wife were part of their circle of friends in Silver Lakes.

"He talked to his mom. I'm going to say for sure, now my … I know for sure, because I texted him. I tried calling him," she said, her voice trailing off. "I got up to my mom's around five-ish."

"What time was that?"

She thought it was close to 4:30 p.m. when she checked in on her mom with the broken hip. She recalled texting Robert around that time and calling him on her cell phone. She returned home around 6 p.m. and started the kids' dinner.

"So I called him, and he wasn't there," she said.

This would have been about an hour before his shift would end—and right around the time he was murdered.

She texted to say she was at home and getting the kids ready for school the next day and still didn't hear back. She kept calling, but couldn't reach him. She called at 7 and couldn't reach him.

"I was definitely concerned by 7:30," she said. "I'm

calling, and by 8, like, he would have been home, anywhere from 8 to 8:20, and I was concerned. I was thinking either he got on a late train call or he got in a car accident. But I wasn't, like, panicked out. I wasn't. I just kind of, like, thought—but I was looking for him. I was looking out the window."

She read to the kids and put them to bed. It was about 8:20 p.m. She thought if Robert didn't come home in the next 10 minutes, she'd call Barstow Yard and ask a supervisor or a coworker if they had heard from him.

Just about that time, the two men from the railroad came to tell her that Robert was dead.

Meyer abruptly changed the subject: "Now, some of the questions we ask people: this, marriage. How was your guys' marriage?"

"We had a great marriage," Sabrina said.

"You guys have any problem or anything or any issues with infidelity or anything like that on either half?

"No," she said. But then she added. "We, well, we kind of like to party. Nothing that would harm the kids or anything like that, but we like going to the river, drinking. Robert didn't drink a whole lot. He'd get buzzy. He always stayed in control. And I just told Robert just recently, after my mom fell and broke her hip, it's time to straighten out. Now mind you, we worked. I kept the house. I kept the children. But I started feeling it a little more when I would wake up in the morning; I need to chill a little bit. I'm tired. And we would keep going. We were super social."

Her answer had defensive edge to it. Meyer pressed: "You guys have never had any issues with infidelity or anything like that? At any point in time did you maybe think Robert may have had a girlfriend?"

"Never," she said.

"Have you ever looked at Robert's phone, gone through his text messages or pictures?" he asked.

"I've gone through his pictures," she said carefully.

"I'm embarrassed. So, I mean, I don't think, don't know."

"How about yourself?" Meyer asked. "Have you ever had a boyfriend or anything like that?"

"No," she said.

Meyer and Kimmel took the questions in another direction.

Kimmel asked, "Have you ever carried a gun?"

"No," said Sabrina. Her voice had a touch of shock.

Meyer said, "We're trying to figure out if the person who did this brought the gun, or if Rob introduced the gun into the situation."

It was the first time anybody had told her Rob was shot. She said, "I'll tell you what: I know Rob did not have a gun."

"Here's why I say that," Meyer explained, "because a lot of people with the railroad carry guns and they're not supposed to. If I worked with the railroad and I was working in those rural areas like that, I would have a gun with me, even if I wasn't supposed to."

"He carried a knife on him."

Kimmel interjected: "What kind of knife?"

"When I say carried it, I'll show you."

She went through drawers, but couldn't find the knife.

"Did he carry it, like, religiously?" asked Kimmel.

"Maybe it was, like, in his locker."

Kimmel brought the conversation back to Robert's telephone.

"Sabrina, there's another question that comes to mind," he said. "You said you looked through the pictures on Rob's phone. When was the last time you went through his phone?"

"I don't know."

"Within six months?"

"Yeah."

"The reason why I asked," said Kimmel, "there are several pictures of naked women on the phone. I haven't looked at them. Are they of you?"

Sabrina seemed momentarily stunned: "Well, this isn't

my best face."

Meyer said, "I didn't spend any time looking at them. I breezed through them really quickly. I was told it was pictures of other women. There were some family photos on there. And the detective that was looking at them said there were some family photos and then it looked like some photos that you can see you in and some other photos. We're not sure if those are some photos from the Internet or personal photos. That's why we're asking. There are some of you on there?"

Sabrina acknowledged, "Yeah."

"We're trying to eliminate if he did have a girlfriend, if that person had come to try to harm Robert," Meyer told her. He said the detective who had examined the phone found only a few risqué photos and that some of them could have been of Sabrina. "There was maybe like one here and one there. There wasn't a lot. So that's why we're asking. We're trying to eliminate the fact that maybe he had a girlfriend, if her husband or boyfriend found out and was trying to harm him. You know what I mean? We have to try to reach for everything that we can. That was it. That was why we're asking. That's our job. Try to find all the facts and try to put them together and try to eliminate every possibility."

Sabrina suggested that the women "might be some of my girlfriends, like."

Kimmel asked: "Did you guys have an open relationship then?"

"No," she insisted.

Meyer suggested: "Just party at the river?" Some of the photos showed topless women on a boat on what could be the Colorado River.

"Party at the river," Sabrina said. "Those were older. I could tell you."

Kimmel suggested that identifying the naked women in the pictures was not an investigative priority.

"If it comes down to it, and I may be wrong, we may have to cross that bridge," he said. "But right now we don't have to. We're just trying to eliminate certain things, okay."

Meyer asked, "Anything you can think of?"

"I know Robert didn't carry a gun. I know he did want a gun, and I know he wanted a handgun, but he would always say we'll get it in Arizona."

Sabrina started pacing.

Kimmel asked: "You want to sit down?"

"No," she said. Then she asked, "Who are these girls that … ?"

Meyer said, "I haven't even looked at them yet. It's just what the other detective told me."

"Oh, you guys," sighed Sabrina. "I don't know what to think."

Sabrina acknowledged she had seen naked pictures of herself when she went through his phone.

"This is, like, disgusting," she said of her reaction. "The kids—he didn't have a code. So I could totally look in his phone any time."

She said: "We just weren't jealous. Our personalities are kind of like: We live life. We were super close, so we knew, I would talk to him all day. I'm not saying that anything isn't possible, but I can't imagine that. That would be devastating to me."

Her words tumbling out, she told them of the mirror they had over their bed, and how embarrassing it was when her parents saw it. "We just have fun together, that's all."

Kimmel said: "If there's nothing there for you to suspect anything, then don't let us put other thoughts into your head."

"I can't even wrap my mind around it."

"There are questions that we have to ask," said Kimmel. "We cross stuff off so we don't spend time on it."

Meyer added, "We don't want your mind to go off and think something's happened."

"I don't like bad news," Sabrina said. "If I was to see the pictures, I would say, 'I know this girl.'"

She asked again about the gun.

Meyer said, "We wanted to know if Rob dropped the gun into the scenario."

"There was a bear on the tracks and he had a video and he showed everybody," Sabrina said.

"Are you okay?" asked Kimmel.

"Yeah, I haven't slept, either," she said, her voice now quiet and breathy. "I just, I don't know.

Meyer said: "I'll stop the recording right there."

But Sabrina kept talking: "I can't thank you enough. I really want to just bring you guys out. I hope everybody feels better. Rob's gone and there's no bringing him back. And there's been deaths in our family. It doesn't feel real. It just … I feel like I have to … Rob's gone. I don't know, just don't know what to think about. I don't know what to think now at all. I have to be strong for my kids, not that I wasn't a good mom. We were good parents."

The interview ended at 6:15 p.m. Meyer would later say that the interview followed his usual script. He had not been surprised to hear from another detective about the photos on Robert's phone. The women were actually topless, not fully nude. And it was not unusual for police to find all sorts of embarrassing things on people's phones that have nothing to do with the case at hand. "We asked her the normal questions about affairs and boyfriends and girlfriends and all that stuff," he said. "That is something you ask everybody. You're trying to get a baseline. And you're trying to eliminate stuff, trying to get rid of things if it doesn't make sense."

Sabrina's reaction did strike him as unusual. In her talk of partying and waking up hung over, she seemed to be dancing around something, but Meyer couldn't figure out what it was.

After the interview, Meyer handed out his business cards to the dozens of people in the house and asked them to call if they could think of something. He would have to dig a little deeper into the Limons' marriage. "I left there thinking: 'Wow, this is kind of strange,' " he said.

As he and Kimmel started the two-hour-plus drive back to Bakersfield, those thoughts were abruptly interrupted. A call came in from another detective.

They may have found the murder weapon—and a suspect.

6.

The gunsmith ran his shop out of his home in Tehachapi. On Aug. 18, a man called to set up an appointment to drop off a handgun. He was a repeat customer, having previously brought in a rifle to be fixed. The customer said it was urgent and wanted to see the gunsmith the next day.

When he arrived on Aug. 19, he presented a powerful piece of weaponry: a Ruger Super Blackhawk, .44 Magnum. The customer said the firing pin broke and needed to be repaired or replaced.

In the gunsmith's experience, this model of revolver had no history of firing pin problems. But he agreed to do the job and, as he filled out the paperwork, he talked to the customer. The customer said he'd recently purchased the gun for his son. Then he asked if the gunsmith knew the son.

"No, I never met him," replied the gunsmith. He thought it was an odd question.

The gunsmith took down the customer's phone number and address. It was a business on Goodrick Drive, located in the same industrial complex as that murder everybody was talking about in town.

But the customer never mentioned the killing, which the gunsmith also found strange.

When he inspected the gun, he discovered that the firing pin was completely fine. The gun operated properly. He told himself the whole thing was a "bizarre coincidence," but it weighed on him for days. Finally, he called the sheriff's department.

The lead was assigned to Deputy David Manriquez,

who visited the gunsmith, took down the gunsmith's story and asked about the customer's demeanor.

"He just seemed withdrawn," the gunsmith said.

Manriquez knew what the gunsmith didn't: that Robert Limon had been killed by bullets from a large-caliber gun like a .44 that may have been a revolver, based on the absence of shell casings at the scene.

Manriquez notified his sergeant, who contacted the robbery homicide division, which called Meyer in the car on the way home from Silver Lakes.

After obtaining a search warrant, Meyer and an evidence technician went to the gunsmith's shop. Photographs were taken of the work area and the Liberty safe in which he kept the gun. The gunsmith opened the safe. Wearing latex gloves, Meyer picked up the gun like it was a precious relic. He noted the name and address on the repair tag, and placed the weapon into a brown evidence bag. He left a search warrant receipt with the gunsmith and told him to call if he had any more information.

Three days later, another gloved detective, Deputy David Hubbard, checked the gun out of the property room at the sheriff's office in Bakersfield and recorded the weapon's serial number, then delivered the gun to the Technical Investigations Unit.

After taking more photos, evidence tech Nicole Townsend dusted it for latent prints and swabbed the trigger and hammer for DNA. Next, Hubbard brought the gun to the Kern Regional Crime Laboratory, a modern-looking building covered in blue-tinted windows in downtown Bakersfield. There, a technician would compare a bullet test fired from the evidence gun to the slug found in Robert Limon's head.

Meyer was hopeful. "The guy who brought in the gun is in the same complex, so maybe he had some beef with Rob or his son had a beef with Rob for some reason," he later said. "The wheels started to turn. This is good. This could be the gun. I was waiting anxiously."

In the meantime, Meyer did "book work" on the gun owner, searching every official database at his disposal "to figure out about this guy and his background." A search of the Criminal Information System got a hit. A person with the same last name was wanted on an active felony warrant for second-degree burglary.

Deputies were assigned to conduct surveillance on the gun owner.

"He had a limp!" Meyer said. And while the gun owner appeared heavier than the person of interest on the security video, "things were starting to match up."

This was not the only lead. Another promising one came from anonymous tipsters reporting that a man who lives near the murder scene had been recently spotted in the past walking across a drainage ditch toward the industrial complex.

What's more, this man also walked with limp. Meyer could barely believe it.

The night of the murder, police had found and photographed foot tracks behind the BNSF garage. They returned and discovered more tracks. This brought them to the address of the man identified by the tipsters. It was his parents' house located a couple hundred yards from the industrial complex.

"We snatched him up and brought him into the office," said Meyer. "He has a limp. And the shoes he's wearing are the same ones that left the tracks in the dirt."

The man was read his rights and agreed to talk to Meyer. He lived about a mile from the murder scene and said he worked odd jobs. Earlier that day, the man said, he had been walking into town when he blacked out and fell to the ground. The next thing he knew he was in the hospital. He said after walking out of the hospital he went to a grocery store and bought a couple of beers.

Meyer asked him how many alcoholic beverages the

man had consumed that day. He said he had a couple of beers.

On the day of the murder, he said he awoke at 9 or 10 a.m. to get a ride into town and hang out. He bought beer and got a ride home, where he drank the beer, watched TV and did nothing else. At 7 p.m., he had dinner with family members and went to bed. He said he often walked near the industrial complex, looking for cans and bottles to sell for recycling, but that he hadn't been there in about four days.

He was told about the murder and said he didn't know anything about it. He was told about shoe prints matching his shoes behind the complex. He said he sometimes goes back there to urinate in the bushes. He said he had a limp from a bad knee. He'd also been hit by a car recently, which left him with a big bruise on his side.

Asked if he could tell Meyer anything about the murder investigation, he said, "Um, I didn't have anything to do with it."

They showed him the security video of the person walking through the complex.

"Looks like the Mexican guy," the man said.

He asked who that was. The man didn't have a name.

Meyer had heard enough. "We're thinking, this isn't going to work," he said later. "We talk to him and it just seems impossible for him to have done this as far as his abilities. He just didn't seem physically capable of overcoming a guy as large as Rob."

Meyer ruled the man out as the killer and hoped that the ballistics examination on the .44 would bring good news. On Sept. 10, three weeks into the investigation, detectives Darin Grantham and Kevin Brewer interviewed the gun owner. They began by asking the man if he was familiar with the murder case. He said he was because it happened in the same complex where he had his business. The man had also seen the surveillance footage released to the media, but said he didn't recognize the person. His business and others were closed on Sunday. It would be unusual for someone who didn't work there to walk through, particularly on a weekend.

Grantham asked if he owned any firearms. He said he did. He described himself as an avid shooter who loads his own ammunition. He said he always obeys the law and adheres to gun safety. He showed the detectives a binder with the paperwork for his guns, receipts for repair service, serial numbers and other documentation. He also had a bag containing four handguns, each packed in their own soft cases that were padlocked.

One gun was not there. Grantham told the man that detectives knew all about the .44 Ruger and said that was in the possession of the Kern County Sheriff's Office. Grantham asked him why he took it to the gunsmith two days after the murder. The man said the firing pin was not depressing the ammunition far enough, causing the gun to malfunction. He thought a new firing pin would fix the problem.

He admitted that given the circumstances, it seemed suspicious and he wasn't surprised that the sheriff had seized the gun. But he insisted that he had told the same gunsmith six months earlier that the Ruger needed a new firing pin and that the gunsmith must have forgotten.

The detectives then asked him about the man with the same last name with an outstanding felony warrant. The man said that was his son. The son had gone to Florida in July for a substance abuse program and had not returned to California. At the time of the shooting, the son could prove he was at the other end of the country.

"I asked (him) several additional questions related to the homicide investigation," Grantham wrote in his report. "During my questioning, (he) displayed no deceitful behavior and was willing to assist in any way. After my interview with (him), it was my belief that he had been honest. This was also the belief of Detective K. Brewer."

Much to Meyer's distress, their instincts proved correct. The forensic analysis showed that the slugs found in

Robert Limon's head and on the floor of the BNSF garage were .45 caliber bullets. The Ruger fired .44s. It could not have been the murder weapon.

The gun was ultimately returned to the gunsmith, whose name and that of the gun owner were redacted from police reports.

Two limping men, two dead-ends. The Ruger implosion was the toughest to swallow. "It was upsetting," he later said. "I had been thinking this was it."

Then Meyer got a phone call. It was from one of the people to whom he'd given a business card that night at Sabrina's house.

The caller said his name was Jason Bernatene and he had a voicemail he wanted the detective to hear.

7.

In her eulogy at Robert Limon's funeral, Kelly Bernatene described Robert and Sabrina Limon as "two of a kind." The same could be said for the Bernatenes and the Limons.

Kelly and Jason and Sabrina and Robert were the closest of friends. Living a couple of miles apart, they got together two or three times a week, sometimes more, for birthday parties and picnics, rounds of horseshoes, holiday celebrations and barbecues. The lights came out at Christmas. Halloween meant elaborate costume parties. The costumes were coordinated—superheroes, '50s greasers and good girls, pimps and 'ho's.

For nightlife, they'd rent a sleek black bus, round up friends and family from the neighborhood and raise hell in the high desert at their favorite bars. Every few months, they'd line up babysitters, Robert would hitch up his powerboat—the *Limon Tree*—to the SUV and they'd caravan off to Lake Havasu or the Colorado River for sun-baked fun. The beer and wine flowed and the parties raged all day and all night under the bright Arizona stars.

They could be loud and obnoxious and not everybody in Silver Lakes approved. But they lived the life and made no apologies. This was a rowdy, loving group of friends bound by family and good times. They jokingly called themselves the Wolf Pack. And the Bernatenes and Limons were the leaders.

When Robert was killed, the Bernatenes were despondent. Kelly dedicated a Pinterest page to him with photos and poems and messages including, "The hardest thing is not talking to someone you're used to talking to every day." She set up a GoFundMe page to raise money for Sabrina and the children while the family waded through the insurance company and BNSF benefits paperwork. Kelly took charge of the funeral arrangements. Kelly picked out the music, lined up speakers and made a slide show, a heartbreaking series of photos of Robert from childhood through his recent 38th birthday.

The service drew hundreds of people to the Grace Bible Church in Helendale on the Saturday after Robert's death. The turnout surprised even Sabrina. In the slide show, Robert's smile radiated, and in many photos, he was shirtless and sunburned on the water, giving a thumb's up or Hawaiian shaka sign. A video clip had him doing a goofy dance for Sabrina that ended in peals of laughter and a high-five from his pal, Jason Bernatene.

"Rob was a kind-hearted, loving father, husband and friend. Rob truly did live by his father's command to 'love one another,' " read his obituary, which appeared in local California newspapers and in the *Daily Courier* in his former hometown of Prescott, Ariz. "Rob spread sunshine everywhere he went and touched the hearts of everyone he met."

The obituary ended on a whimsical note: "In honor of Rob, buy a new pair of Vans shoes and a bright shirt, and go out and treat someone Rob's way."

Robert lived his entire life in the desert surrounded by railroad men. Born in Lake Havasu, Ariz., in 1976, he was the youngest of five children, his siblings all sisters or half-sisters. "He was spoiled rotten," said Lydia, his oldest sister, laughing. "He was the only boy, and we couldn't pick on him. He was a good kid, though. When we had family picnics and family reunions at the park, Robert would wander off and go to other people's picnics. He was a little social butterfly and always adventurous."

It was a big blended family that moved around a lot.

His father, Robert Sr., worked for the railroad on the "tie gang," repairing and replacing railroad ties. When Robert was a baby, the family moved to Cadiz, Calif., a tiny unincorporated town along the Atchison, Topeka and Santa Fe Railroad tracks east of Barstow. Then to Twentynine Palms, a Marine Corps community on the northern edge of Joshua Tree National Park. Then back to Arizona when Robert was about 8.

The family went first to Prescott, northwest of Phoenix, for Robert's elementary and junior high school years, then to Mojave Valley near Lake Havasu. By now, Robert Limon stood nearly 6 feet tall—a big, strong kid who played defensive back for River Valley High School.

The moves reflected troubles at home. By the time Robert was in Arizona, his older sisters had moved out. (Lydia and her sister are from Robert's father's first marriage.) "He was alone with his parents at the time," said Lydia. "My dad was pretty abusive. He was an alcoholic. I think Robert was having a difficult time with mom and dad's relationship."

Robert's parents separated, reunited, then divorced when Robert was in high school. Robert stayed with his mother. They would always be close. After graduation, Robert worked in construction and had a job with the Prescott Fire Department. He dreamed of joining the Granite Mountain Hotshots, the department's elite unit that would lose 19 members in a 2013 wildfire. "Those boys who were killed in Prescott, Robert knew most of them," his brother-in-law, Reyes, said.

At a family barbecue around 1999, Robert met a beautiful 18-year-old daycare center worker named Sabrina SanMillan. "We had been passing through Prescott one day and he brought her by," recalled Lydia. "When I saw them come up the driveway and walk into the house, I thought, 'Wow, I think he's going to marry her.'"

She was right. Robert and Sabrina were married on Aug. 19, 2000, in a big church wedding in Prescott. By now, Lydia was living in California and didn't know much about Sabrina except that she had grown up in Barstow and moved to Prescott around her high school years. She seemed friendly and outgoing and very much in love with Robert. After Robert got a job at BNSF with the help of Julie's husband, he spent a couple of months in Kansas City at welding school, then packed up and moved to Silver Lakes, where Sabrina's parents were now living.

Kelly first met Sabrina in 2007 when she came into Kelly's hair salon as a referral. They quickly became friends and after a few months, Kelly introduced Jason to Robert and the men hit it off. The women were especially close, two outgoing blondes who loved throwing back some drinks and getting wild with their husbands. When the couples weren't hanging out together, Sabrina spent hours in Kelly's salon chair, the two women talking, laughing, gossiping, confiding.

In the fall of 2012, Sabrina told Kelly she was ready for a change. With both kids in school, Sabrina went back to work. She donned a red apron and handed out food samples at Costco in Victorville. The job demanded about 20 hours a week—allowing time to get the kids off to school and pick them up—and fit her people-person personality. Sabrina called herself a "sample girl" and was excited to be back working and to have money of her own. She was so friendly. Some customers came into the store just to talk to her and left without buying anything.

Around December of 2012, one of her more attentive customers was a young man wearing a fire department T-shirt. He had come in to load up on food and supplies for his station house. Sabrina and the firefighter were chatting and she casually mentioned that one of her close friends, Jason Bernatene, was also firefighter. The customer knew Jason; they had worked together briefly. She asked him his name. He said Jonathan.

Sabrina told the Bernatenes about him. Kelly vaguely recalled meeting a young fireman named Jonathan at her husband's station. "I remember being introduced to him casually, like he was working on his shift that day," she later said in court. "I asked Jason if he knew who he was."

At first, Jason couldn't place him. "I know a lot of Johns," Jason said. When Jason next spoke to Sabrina, he listed the guys named John he had worked with, but none seemed to be the one Sabrina had met. He told her next time to ask his last name and what station he worked for. A few days later, she said he was employed by the city of Redlands, 60 miles to the south near the city of San Bernardino.

Jason made the connection. About a year earlier, he had worked with a Jonathan Hearn. Only 21 years old at the time, Jonathan was classified as an LT. That's a limited term paramedic working part-time on an ambulance for the county of San Bernardino fire department. Jason was assigned to a different station, but worked about two dozen overtime and fill-in shifts at Hearn's station.

"I was very impressed with him," Jason recalled later in court. "To become a paramedic, you have to be 21. That means that he had planned all his life ahead of time to become a paramedic by 21, which is pretty hard to do. He was also very intelligent, very well spoken, very proper. Inside the fire station, he struck me as kind of sheltered. He didn't cuss very much."

Jason said that despite Jonathan's young age, he was a pro. "I was very impressed with how he treated patients. He was a very good paramedic," Jason said. "I told him on several occasions he was too smart to be a fireman, that he should become a doctor or lawyer. He told me he just loved being a fireman."

Then about three months after Sabrina mentioned Jonathan, the Bernatenes ran into him.

Every March, a bunch of friends from Silver Lakes celebrate several birthdays that month. They'd get a big SUV or bus and go out drinking. They called it March Madness. In 2013, the Limons, the Bernatenes and a bunch of others, including two of Sabrina's grown nephews, rolled up to a sports bar called Beef 'O' Brady's just off Interstate 15 in Hesperia. The restaurant had 15 TVs tuned to games mounted over the bar, which served up beer on tap. The kitchen dished up beef nachos and fish tacos.

The main attraction was a musical performance by a band that included one of Sabrina's coworkers.

As Jason Bernatene walked up to the bar, he saw a familiar face. It was Jonathan Hearn chatting up another firefighter. Jonathan wore a black shirt and jeans and had short hair molded with gel and hip, long sideburns. He had the same lean, fit build of Jason and other firefighters.

Jason told Kelly, who introduced herself and said, "Oh, you know my friend Sabrina from Costco."

Jonathan said that he did and then waved down Sabrina from another part of the bar.

Sabrina, in a short blue dress, bright pink nails, and long blond hair cut by Kelly, flashed a big smile and raced over. Sabrina threw both arms around Jonathan and hugged him tight, with her head pressed against his cheek.

Jonathan held his nearly empty mug of beer with his right hand and wrapped his left arm around Sabrina. Kelly snapped a picture, which would later be posted on Facebook.

More introductions were made. Jonathan met other people in Sabrina's group and posed for another picture taken by Kelly, this one a group shot with Jonathan at one end and Sabrina's husband at the other.

Jonathan mingled elsewhere and the Wolf Pack partied the night away, finally tumbling into the big SUV for a raucous ride home. Kelly didn't give much thought to Sabrina hugging Jonathan at the bar. "She was always very outgoing and friendly," Kelly said. "Maybe a little bit more, but not a lot."

It occurred to Jason that the Jonathan he saw at Beef 'O' Brady's wasn't the sheltered young paramedic he once knew. "Jonathan never struck me as a person who was very social in that type of sense; he was more reserved," Jason recalled. "So to see him go with his hand out and make friends that fast, I was really impressed with him."

But the Bernatenes would learn that Robert Limon wasn't happy. The next day, Sabrina told Kelly that the couple had argued. Robert didn't like how much attention Jonathan gave his wife. He had known nothing about Sabrina meeting him at Costco and didn't understand how he came to be at the same bar at the same time.

Robert asked her if something was going on between them. Sabrina denied it. Sabrina also assured Kelly there was nothing to worry about. Sabrina was 10 years older than Jonathan. They were just friends.

Then something weird happened. A few days later, Jason started getting text messages from Jonathan.

Jason wasn't put off by the fact that Jonathan knew his number; firefighters who've worked together always collect each other's contact information in case they need to swap shifts or call somebody in at the last minute. What was odd was Jason's tone.

"Hey, Jason, how's it going?" said one message, affecting a familiarity that Jason didn't think he had with Jonathan. They had worked maybe a dozen shifts together more than a year earlier. They had never socialized.

"You're somebody I really like," Jonathan wrote in another. "I miss you."

Jonathan mentioned that he'd met Sabrina and said it sounded like her circle of friends had a lot of fun out at Silver Lakes. He wanted to know if he could be invited to join them some time.

Jason ignored the question, texting back, "How's Redlands treating you?"

More texts arrived from Jonathan, many of them lavishing Jason with compliments. It got to the point, Jason said later, where "I felt a little weird."

Jason spent a lot of hours in close quarters with guys

at the fire station; he never knew them to compliment each other like that.

"I started having a joke with my wife: I think this guy likes me," Jason said. "It was odd."

He never invited him to Silver Lakes and did his best not to reply to the messages.

As these messages arrived, the Bernatenes noted a subtle change in Sabrina. Every so often, when Kelly would ask if her friend Jonathan had stopped by the store lately, Sabrina would snap at her and say she didn't want to talk about it.

Then one day in the spring of 2013, Jason got the strangest text yet from Jonathan: "Hey, Jason I need your buddy Rob's phone number. Call me."

Jason dialed Jonathan's number and asked, "Hey, Jonathan, what's up? Why do you need Rob's phone number?"

Jonathan didn't answer right away. Then Jason put it together. "Do you have something going on with Sabrina?"

Jonathan gave what Jason would later call a "song and dance" and "hemmed and hawed."

"It's not like that," Jonathan said. "We are just friends." Then he added, "She's really important to me."

Jason lost it. He started yelling at Jonathan: "That's my best friend's wife and you need to leave us alone!"

At the time of the phone call, Jason was doing work on a new house he'd purchased. He was putting up drywall.

Helping him was Robert Limon.

An enraged Jason gave Robert the phone. "Dude, I don't know what's up, but I have Jonathan Hearn on the phone and he wants to talk to you, and I think it's something bad."

Robert's response surprised him. "I know," he said. He wasn't mad. He seemed resigned.

Robert took the phone outside and he spoke to Jonathan for what seemed like a half hour. Jason couldn't hear what was said but surprisingly Robert didn't appear angry. It looked to him more like he was trying to work out a problem.

When Robert ended the call and gave the phone back to Jason, he explained that Sabrina and Jonathan had still been seeing each other at Costco. They had developed some sort of "intellectual relationship," as Robert called it. It had turned emotional. Robert knew this because he had recently looked at Sabrina's cell phone and found page after page of messages from Jonathan saying, "I love you."

At the time, Robert erupted and smashed Sabrina's phone. But they had made up, and Robert said that Jonathan was calling to apologize for his behavior and to assure him that he wouldn't have anything to do with Sabrina again.

Jason wasn't so sure.

"Do we need to do something about this?" he asked Robert.

"No, it's handled," Robert said. He asked Jason not to tell any of their other friends about the matter.

Nearly a year went by and the Bernatenes heard nothing about Jonathan Hearn. Then one day in early 2014, they stopped at the Costco on their way home from the doctor. Jason had been treated for a knee injury and needed to pick up his medication. He stayed in the car while Kelly went into the store pharmacy.

When she got back to the car, she was livid. She had seen Sabrina with Jonathan. They were hanging out in one of the cavernous aisles. Sabrina appeared to be on her break; she wasn't wearing her hair net. The two women made eye contact and Kelly made haste for the cash registers, with Sabrina following her. Kelly made her purchase and dashed out without talking to Sabrina.

Hearing this, Jason was outraged. He dialed Jonathan and shouted, "What the fuck!" He demanded that Jonathan stay away from Sabrina.

The tongue-lashing seemed to work. Jonathan drifted away again. Among the Wolf Pack, everybody remained friendly, going over to each other's houses, throwing backyard barbecues, hitting the bars. Kelly kept doing Sabrina's hair.

But there was a chill between the Bernatenes and Sabrina. The name Jonathan Hearn never surfaced, but it always seemed to lurk.

Then Robert got killed. Jason figured it for "tweakers" out in the desert looking for a few bucks for a fix. When they saw the security video on the news, the bulky limping figure looked like nobody they knew.

But a feeling nagged. Something about Sabrina was off. The night Robert died, the Bernatenes went to their house. Nobody knew anything except Robert was dead, and Sabrina wasn't Sabrina.

"Sabrina was crying, but she was very much in control," Jason recalled. "Being a fireman and being a paramedic, I've seen tragedy hit people suddenly. I've seen what people do. They lose control. That night she was answering the phone. She even told me she wanted to do it. She had to handle it. She had her kids on the couch. They had their dad's T-shirts on. She was in control."

Most disturbing: Sabrina didn't want anybody else to know that Robert had died. "She wanted everyone to have one last night of good, then she was going to tell everybody the next day," Jason recalled. "I was in a daze," he recalled. "I left to go over to some other friend's house."

He told people anyway about Robert.

Weeks passed and Jason thought more about Robert's unsolved murder. That's when he started thinking about Jonathan Hearn. Jason was still sore about Sabrina's— whatever it was—with Jonathan Hearn. Rob was his buddy.

Jason turned over in his head something unspeakably impossible. He chased it away. Not Jonathan. No way. It had to be tweakers.

Then Jason got a voicemail.

"Uh, Jason, um, I, uh …" the voice said, sighing, then, "I'd really like to talk to ya sometime tonight," the message began.

He recognized the voice. It was Jonathan.

"I, um, I just got back from San Diego and went into Costco and talked to Sabrina last night, yesterday afternoon, and heard about Robert. I'm a little just, uh …" another sigh, "and you know what I've been living so wrong, I've been living so wrong."

It was left on Friday, Aug. 29, 2014, less than two weeks after Robert's murder, a long stream-of-consciousness message.

After sighing once more, Jonathan said, "I just realized life is so short and …" another sigh, "short to have enemies and you were someone I've always admired and respected for your wisdom and you were, you've always been so kind to me, and I have repaid that kindness with offenses, and I'm hurting our friendship, and you know what I would like to, um, I know it's asking a lot, and I," he sighed again, "I am asking you now—though you know, I, I, I did not sleep last night. I just, I can't believe it. I, I am, I feel numb. And you know what I feel like: God has crushed me and he has gotten my attention."

On and on it went, the message more bizarre than any of the texts he had sent Jason.

"And you know what, Jason: There's only two people in this world that I? feel like, um, I have offended, and I have never taken care of that offense, and that is you and your wife," Jonathan continued. "And I am begging you on my knees right now that I could perhaps meet with you and your wife and say sorry for, um, the hurt that I caused you."

Jonathan said it hardly seemed like a year and half had passed since he subjected the Bernatenes to "my pride and my arrogance, my selfishness." He said he'd never considered their feelings and he'd never properly apologized.

"I did talk to Robert and I was able to apologize to him and that was something that was—I was certainly hoping he forgave me," said Jonathan. "But I just realized now life is so short and I am shaky right now, and I'm sorry."

He ended the message by saying, "I would really like to talk to you and …" a final sigh, "I'm at work today. But tomorrow, I'm off, and I don't know if there would be a time I would really like to either take you guys to dinner or meet with you and your wife. And I need, God needs me to have a clear and—I wanna, I wanna fix this with you. So if you could give me a call back, I would really appreciate it. Thank you so much."

The voicemail floored Jason. There was no way he was going to take Kelly to dinner with this nut job.

Jonathan followed up the creepy voicemail with a text.

"Jason, I hope my message doesn't make you angry, I cannot imagine what you and Kelly are going through right now. God has used this as a what-up [wake-up?] call for me though, and I need to make things right. Thank you!"

Jason sent him a terse reply. "I got your message. I do not want to talk to you right now."

"OK, Jason," he texted back, "I fully understand. Please forgive my timing. This is so overwhelming. Thank you for getting back to me. Please know that I beg your forgiveness."

Then he sent yet another text: "Jason, I have been feeling awful bad about what a dirtbag I was in how disrespectful I was of you and your wife, and as I realize how short life is. I am SO inspired to live life without sins or regrets. I know that there is so much that you are dealing with right now, and I don't want to intrude or upset you in the midst of your pain, so could I ask you for your mailing address? Can I please write a letter of apology and sent [sic] it to you so that you can read it in your own timing? Life is so short. I want to have a conscience that is clear of offenses. Jason, thank you. Last time I talked to you this much, it was to selfishly work my way into your group of friends to be closer to Sabrina. It was selfish and evil, and stupid. I won't use you for that ever again by God's grace. I need to stand ALONE and live for God. R will be my Forever reminder of this."

That night, Jason fished out a business card from Det. Randall Meyer.

They set up a meeting for the following Monday at Jason's house. Meyer had asked Jason to say nothing to Sabrina about being in contact with the police. Jason followed the orders, but felt uncomfortable about going behind Sabrina's back.

"I knew Sabrina would not want me to tell the detectives that she had had an affair with Jonathan Hearn, so I didn't now want to upset her, and I did not want her to freak out," Jason later said in court. "But I knew that they needed to know about Jonathan, and I thought the best person to tell them would be her."

So Jason tried to set up a surprise meeting between Meyer and Sabrina. He invited her over to the house at the same time that the detective would be there.

Jason heard nothing from Sabrina. When Meyer arrived at his home that night, she wasn't there and the interview started without her.

Jason gave Meyer the rundown on Jonathan Hearn, how he'd met Sabrina at Costco in 2012, how he'd turned up at Beef 'O' Brady's and how he'd sent those many messages from Jonathan attempting to join their social circle in Silver Lakes.

He told the detective about how Robert himself had spoken to Jonathan.

Despite it all, Jason refused to believe Sabrina had anything to do with Robert's murder, but now, he wasn't sure about Jonathan. Jason described Jonathan as the smartest person he'd ever met; he wouldn't put it past him to devise a way to kill Robert so that he could be with Sabrina.

Meyer listened to the long voicemail and read the text messages. He asked Jason to keep their meeting a secret. Meyer especially didn't want Sabrina to know that Jason was talking to police "as it may be harmful to the investigation."

Jason told Meyer nothing about inviting Sabrina over.

That night, he finally heard from her. She called at 10 p.m., apologizing for not coming by.

For the next few weeks, the Bernatenes acted in front of Sabrina as if everything was the same as it ever was, all things considered. Whatever suspicions they had about Jonathan did not extend to Sabrina. She continued to act like a widow in mourning, posting a long Facebook tribute to Robert on Sept. 8.

"Words can not begin to express my thankful heart. Robert showed his love, compassion, hardworking skills, and genuine kindness to everyone he met. Through this pain and unbelievable tragedy, Rob's love continues on. The love and kindness given back to me and OUR kids has been overwhelming.

We THANK YOU ALL SO MUCH for acts of random kindness that has been shown to us. Flowers. Gifts. Hugs. Food. All of the love that has come to us has been such a BEAUTIFUL tribute to the AMAZING man Robert was and will never be forgotten

"God blessed US with Rob for the time he did, and the love he gave was more than some ever will feel or show. I will never let Rob's love die or fade out. I will carry it with me wherever I go, and remind our children of it daily as they grow. We received something wonderful from Rob Limons life and the effects are truly overwhelming.

It's a feeling of joy, yet I'm totally numb to the fact that I'm left on earth now without him. I look towards God and the beautiful sky HE painted with colors that fill my heart with hope to see Rob again some day."

But through September, the Bernatenes' attitude toward Sabrina shifted. Kelly spotted a truck one day in Helendale and she could swear the driver looked like Jonathan. She couldn't be sure; neither she nor her husband knew what kind of vehicle Jonathan drove. They let it pass.

About three weeks later, on Friday, Sept. 19, Kelly drove by Sabrina's house and saw what looked like the same truck, a gray Ford pickup, parked in her driveway at 10 a.m.

When Kelly next saw Sabrina a couple days later at her home to help her fill out thank you cards to funeral guests, Kelly mentioned seeing the truck. She asked if it was Jonathan's.

"No," said Sabrina, smiling.

"Oh, okay," said Kelly. She asked whose truck that was.

Sabrina said it belonged to Dale Smith, an old friend. Kelly had known Sabrina for a long time; she felt she could tell when she was lying.

Kelly jotted down the truck's license plate number and gave it to Meyer.

Around this same time, Jason got another psycho communiqué from Jonathan. It came in the form of a two-page letter that arrived by mail, another rambling message of apology from Jonathan, who appeared haunted by Robert's death.

"Along with the tragic news came a wave of remembering sins that I have left undone in my life," Jonathan wrote. "I am sorry for being prideful, for being selfish and disrespectful, I showed such pride in not seeing my mistakes as having such horrible and dangerous consequences."

As he had said in the voicemail, Jonathan wrote, "I used our acquaintance from the past as an excuse to be better friends with Sabrina, knowing that you would say nice things about me, and vouch for my character.

"I ask your forgiveness. Will you each please forgive me? I am not wanting you to accept me and love me, I was absolutely untrustworthy, but I want to live right! I need to live my life without offense."

Jason called Meyer.

The next morning, Tuesday, Sept. 23, Kelly drove by Sabrina's house on the way to picking up her daughter from her mother-in-law's house and saw a motorcycle parked outside that she'd never seen before.

It was a black, vintage-looking bike with the word "Forgiven" painted on the gas tank. She wrote down the license number and gave it to Meyer.

Around this same time, Jason ran into Sabrina and her children at the local grocery, the Silver Lakes Store. "I hadn't seen her in a while. I was avoiding her on purpose. I was avoiding her house. I did not want to run into Jonathan," Jason later said in court. "I gave her a hug and told her I missed her. The kids gave me a big hug."

The kids then told him about their new friend named Jonathan.

"Sabrina just changed the subject and kind of hushed them away," Jason said.

He called Meyer.

On Sept. 26, Kelly and Sabrina took a morning walk. Sabrina said nothing about Jonathan, which Kelly thought was a little strange in light of Jason's encounter at the store. Sabrina did talk about Robert's murder. It was the first time Kelly ever heard her express any curiosity about who may have killed him and why.

Kelly said nothing about being in touch with the police. In fact, she had an interview with Meyer that afternoon.

Meyer showed up at the Bernatene house with Det. Kimmel. He flipped on the recorder and listened as Kelly described how her eight-year friendship with Sabrina was now in tatters, at least from Kelly's standpoint. A lot of what she said was reruns from her husband; then Kelly offered some news. She noted that Sabrina's new job at Costco triggered some concern in their social circle. "Great, now she's going to have an affair," Kelly said at the time. It seemed another woman friend of theirs got a job at Costco and then had an affair.

Something about the Victorville Costco.

Sure enough, Sabrina began seeing Jonathan on the side

and Kelly didn't think it was a casual relationship. On April 6, 2013, around the time of the blowup between Sabrina and her husband, Sabrina got drunk at a wedding and sent a group text to several friends. Kelly looked at Sabrina's phone and noticed several messages from Jonathan, saying things like, "You're so beautiful" and "I love you so much."

Kelly said nothing about it at the time. The next day, it was Sabrina who said she had something she had to speak about. But when asked what it was, she told Kelly she wasn't ready to discuss it. Kelly said that was fine, but wondered why she brought it up in the first place.

A few days after Robert spoke to Jonathan on the phone while working on the Benatenes' new house, Sabrina asked Kelly if she was mad at her. Kelly said the only concern she and Jason had was how Robert felt. This set off Sabrina. She started yelling at Kelly. They didn't talk for a week. Kelly got the impression Sabrina was brooding over the fact she couldn't see Jonathan.

They made up about a week later, telling each other they were such good friends that none of this should stand between them.

But tensions continued. Robert told Sabrina he didn't feel comfortable working on the Bernatenes' house anymore. The place gave him bad memories. For months, the two couples tiptoed around certain subjects—a "weird vibe" between them that never had existed before.

By early 2014, when Kelly saw Sabrina with Jonathan at Costco, she knew she could not fully longer trust Sabrina, though they continued to socialize.

Robert's death obviously made things worse. In early September, just weeks after Robert's murder, Sabrina told Kelly that Jonathan and his sister had come by the house with flowers. Jonathan also left a note and Sabrina read from it. Jonathan said something like "all the things he read in the paper and on Facebook about Robert was that he was such an amazing man." He went on to say something to the effect of: "I'm going to try to live my life like him and that he was an inspiration."

Kelly was stunned. Sabrina, however, said, "I don't feel he had any bad intentions."

After that, Sabrina played coy about Jonathan. Kelly didn't even bother asking Sabrina about the motorcycle in her driveway: "She had already lied to me once."

The detectives brought up the subject of the Limons' marriage. Kelly said that after she and Sabrina had been friends for a few years, Sabrina confided that she and Robert had an open relationship with another couple. They would sometimes swap spouses and stay in different motel rooms. Kelly wasn't sure how long that had gone on, but she knew that the other couple had divorced and the foursome was no more. Robert didn't mind; he always called the other wife a "bitch."

The couple was Dale Smith and his wife, the same Dale who Kelly claimed had parked his truck at her house. Sabrina said she had remained friendly with Dale. They spoke every day, and Kelly got the impression Dale had fallen in love with Sabrina. Robert got wind of the conversations and told them to stop, which as far as Kelly knew, it did.

This happened before Jonathan entered the picture.

The intel from the Bernatenes sent the investigation in a new direction, boomeranging to those early routine questions to Sabrina about her marriage.

She had denied having any issues, denied having a boyfriend, insisted Robert didn't have a girlfriend and specifically denied the question about whether they had an open marriage.

Now it was clear the truth about who killed Robert Limon likely was intertwined with the secrets of Silver Lake.

The investigation was circling back on itself, like the Tehachapi Loop.

Meyer believed the Bernatenes. "They were very

genuine people," he said later. "They were good friends of Rob and Sabrina. They were obviously upset about his murder, almost more upset than Sabrina was, which was very odd."

He asked both of them if they were involved in the swinging life with the Limons. "They said they partied and had a good time, but didn't swap partners," said Meyer. "I guess I believed them. I didn't get that intuition they were involved in that stuff. But it was still in the back of my mind going, 'Hmmm.' "

At least one of the photos found on Robert Limon's phone was of a topless Kelly Bernatene.

8.

Det. Meyer combed through the databases again. The DMV told him that Jonathan did, in fact, drive a diesel-powered Ford pickup and a Yamaha motorcycle. The license plate numbers from Kelly showed both were registered to Jonathan Hearn of Hesperia. Law enforcement databases showed that Jonathan owned several handguns, including a .45-caliber pistol. "This stuff is just building," said Meyer. "It's coming together."

The motorcycle proved important in another way. After finding the security video of the limping man, police searched for security footage from nearby businesses. A company down the street from the industrial complex called Patco Grinding Corp. had a camera trained on Goodrick Drive. Since the east- and west-running street dead-ends into the industrial complex, the camera recorded every vehicle and pedestrian going to and from the murder scene.

An evidence tech downloaded the footage from 3 to 8 p.m., covering several hours before and after the murder. The camera recorded enough cars, trucks and people to keep detectives busy. Working off still images, they tracked down the drivers of nearly all of the vehicles. Each provided convincing alibis. The only car driver they couldn't find was one at the wheel of a red compact. But another business owner reported seeing that car with some kids in it who were later playing in a dirt field.

The standout footage was of a motorcycle rider. Wearing a black helmet that hid the face, the motorcyclist rode what looked like an older model bike with a silver gas tank and silver tailpipe. It first appeared on the video at 4:12 p.m., traveling west away from the industrial park.

Three minutes later, at 4:15 p.m., the rider returned, heading east toward the complex, only to reappear two minutes later again driving away from the complex. At 4:21 p.m., the rider whisked past Patco toward the complex once again. And in another 50 minutes, at 5:11 p.m., the rider was again driving toward the complex, having either found another way out of the area or the camera simply missed the rider's return trips.

The last time the rider is seen is at 5:48 p.m., again heading toward the complex. The camera did not capture a motorcycle leaving the scene. If this was, in fact, Jonathan, and if he went straight home after the murder, the most direct route to Hesperia would have followed the same drive that Meyer had taken to Silver Lakes.

The halfway spot between the murder scene and Jonathan's house in Hesperia was an hour away, at Four Corners, with practically nothing for miles around. Meyer sent Thomas Gates, special agent from BNSF's police operation, there to check gas stations, stores and restaurants for security camera footage.

He hit pay dirt at a gas station/truck stop called Pilot Travel Center. On the day of the murder, one security camera shows a motorcyclist in a black helmet pull in at 6:51 p.m. and park next to pump number 3. The rider then walked into the mini-mart, which sells coffee, cold drinks, food and supplies. It has a Cinnabon kiosk and next door is a Subway sandwich shop. The driver kept his hand up toward his face as he looked straight up at the security camera. Inside, another camera showed the person still wearing a helmet, getting a water bottle and Gatorade from the cooler. The cash register showed that the items, along with enough gas for a motorcycle, were purchased with cash. The person then went back outside and gassed up the motorcycle. He drank something and walked toward the trash can, then returned to the motorcycle. The rider drove away from the gas station south on Highway 395 toward Silver Lakes and, beyond that, Hesperia.

The motorcyclist's face and plate could not be made out on any of the footage. But Jonathan Hearn owned a motorcycle. Jonathan Hearn had an apparent relationship with the victim's wife before and after the murder.

Those facts got Meyer a search warrant. Requested in October, the warrant sought phone company records for any cell phones or landlines in the names of Jonathan Hearn and Sabrina Limon. Every call, every text message from the time the two met at Costco to the present.

The records arrived about a month later. It was a voluminous amount of data: incoming and outgoing calls, the dates and times and numbers, whether the communications were voice calls, text messages or multimedia messages, such as photos or videos. As the detectives toiled to enter and sort the records on Excel spreadsheets, Jonathan's cell phone and Sabrina's cell and landlines made many, many connections.

Then it mostly stopped in late April of 2014. A new number pops up on Jonathan's cell phone records. It had a Kern County prefix of 760 and it dominated communications on Jonathan's phone records: a staggering 7,000 communications from April through October, to and from Jonathan's phone and this number.

Phone company records coughed up nothing on the number—no name or address, no phone company account.

In other words, a burner phone. Pay by the minute.

The records showed its user was in nearly constant contact with Jonathan before, during and after Robert Limon's murder.

From Aug. 1 to Aug. 16, 2014—the day before Robert was killed—there were 1,902 text messages between Jonathan's cell phone and this number, an average of more than 100 messages a day. There were another 117 multimedia messages, probably an exchange of photos.

And on Aug. 17, the day of the murder, there was a flurry of phone calls and texts between Jonathan's phone and the mystery number. His phone got texts from 1:26 to 5:04 p.m., then a gap until 6:57 p.m., covering the time when Robert was murdered. Then Jonathan's cell and this other phone exchanged voice calls at 7:50 and 8:37 p.m., followed by more than 50 text messages that went all night until 6:48 the next morning.

For all of August, Jonathan and the mystery number exchanged nearly 2,500 texts and 120 voice phone calls.

In all likelihood, the burner was being used by Sabrina.

There would be one way to find out for sure.

Det. Randall Meyer had never utilized a wiretap in an investigation. After this case, he vowed never to do one again. Getting the go-ahead from a judge requires police to prove they've exhausted all other avenues for getting the information. Once approved, police have only 10 days to tap the phones before they have go back to the judge to seek a renewal. In the interim, police must provide the judge with detailed updates of everything gleaned from the tap. Paperwork on top of paperwork.

The wire room where the calls are monitored must be monitored 24 hours a day, seven days a week. When a call is made or received on a tapped line, a screen lights up and a cop listens just long enough to determine if a call is pertinent to the investigation. If not—telemarketer or a meddlesome mother-in-law—the call has to be terminated. If it sounds pertinent, the cops listen in and then make a detailed report.

Already stretched thin with one murder a week to investigate, the eight members of the Kern County Sheriff's robbery homicide division would need help from other departments and other agencies. "It is a ton of work," Meyer said. "Most guys do one and say, 'I'm done.' "

In this case, he considered the wiretaps crucial. The

phone records could only take the investigation so far. They tracked the number of calls, when they were made and between which numbers. But they didn't reveal what was actually said or sent. Since a burner phone can be purchased for cash and the minutes purchased from any gas station or convenience store, it was impossible to prove for certain that all those communications Jonathan made were, in fact, with Sabrina.

If these two had conspired to murder Robert, and they were still together as the Bernatenes believed, Meyer needed to know what they were talking about.

In early November 2014, after the paperwork was duly filed and a judge approved the taps, detectives borrowed the Drug Enforcement Agency's wire room in Bakersfield and waited for a screen to light up.

The first call came at 10:39 p.m. on Nov. 7. It was Jonathan's cell phone calling the burner.

"Hi, baby," came a male voice.

"Hey," came a soft female voice. "How are you?"

"I'm good," the man said. "How are you, baby?"

A few seconds in and the conversation already oozed intimacy.

The detectives had infiltrated the private world of Jonathan Hearn and Sabrina Limon.

9.

The first call caught turned out to be one of the best.

"Um, I'm okay," said Sabrina, though her voice didn't sound like it.

"What's the matter?" Jonathan asked.

"Well, I don't know," Sabrina said. She explained that a friend who knew somebody in law enforcement told her on the down low that "they're getting ready to make the arrest or arrests."

Between Sabrina's soft voice and the poor cell coverage quality, much of the conversation was difficult to hear, though this statement from Sabrina came through loud and clear: "I'm just, oh my gosh, she just, like, scared me."

"What was that last thing you said?" asked Jonathan.

"Phone lines may be tapped."

Jonathan was calling from the car. "I'm going to come back to see you, is that okay?"

"Yeah."

"I would like to see you. I'm sorry, wow, crazy." Then he said: "I'm just going to pray right now. Oh, God, please help us."

The rest of the prayer got lost in bad phone service.

"I'm going to be there in about five or six minutes," Jonathan said, calling back. "I'll talk to you then. Please keep praying."

"I will," said Sabrina.

"I love you, baby."

"I love you, too, baby."

In only a few minutes, detectives had a gold mine

of circumstantial evidence, two lovers talking in soft conspiratorial tones about what had to have been the Robert Limon murder investigation.

But rather than celebrating the possible arrest or arrests in the slaying of her beloved husband, the supposedly grieving widow treated the development like a problem.

In the opinion of the detectives, this brief chat reeked of guilt.

There was, however, one thorny issue. Somebody from inside law enforcement may have been feeding information to Sabrina. While the sheriff's office was nowhere near to making an arrest, the possibility of a leak was troublesome.

Meyer suddenly had two investigations on his hands: one into Sabrina and Jonathan, the other into his own operation.

"We had another agency helping us," he said later. "It takes a lot of people to do a wire. Plus we have all the other moving parts that are happening. The other agency, we believe, leaked the information from the wire room."

Interagency politics kept Meyer from revealing the suspect agency, but he was clearly angry. "We had a lot on the line with the wire," he said. "We basically told them goodbye."

Back to the wire room.

While Meyer had never used wiretaps before, he knew somebody who did. "I had another officer who had done multiple wires, a DA investigator," said Meyer. "He was the guy who helped me in the wire direction."

The investigator suggested that if the operation hits a potential snag, as this one already had with Sabrina expressing concerns her phones tapped, the solution was to "tickle the wire"—say or do something that gets the targets talking.

On the morning of Sunday, Nov. 9, Meyer sent Sabrina a text message to call him, then waited to see what she did.

She immediately called Jonathan on her burner phone: "I just got a text message from Detective Meyer and he asked me to call him."

"Oh, great," said Jonathan. He did not sound like it was great.

"I just wanted you to pray," said Sabrina.

"God, please help us," Jonathan prayed. "Help Sabrina to have the right words."

The prayer was interrupted by one of Sabrina's children in the background trying to get her attention. "You have to give Mommy a few minutes for an important phone call," she said. "Go watch the movie, whatever is on, and just relax."

Then to Jonathan, she said, "I'm sorry."

"We have a purpose. We have a vision," Jonathan's prayer continued. "Please keep Sabrina's calmness and clarity of thought to not give too much information that doesn't need to be shared. God, please help, please give us wisdom. Amen."

"Amen," said Sabrina.

"I love you," said Jonathan.

"I love you, too."

Then Sabrina called Meyer at 10:15 a.m.

"Hi, Sabrina, how are you?" the detective said in a big, friendly voice. He effusively apologized for texting her on a Sunday, but said he wanted to update her. Detectives were considering re-releasing to the public the surveillance video of the man walking near the crime scene.

"We've kind of run into a dead-end spot right now," he said. He said he just wanted to give her a warning in case somebody saw it on the news.

"I've been wanting to talk to you," Sabrina said. "I'm just feeling really bad."

"I'm sorry," said Meyer. "I know that you probably have some good days and bad days and hope that initially, you'll be able to get through it and everything."

"There's no information at all?"

"Obviously, I don't have anything. I wish I did. I think we're kind of getting into a dead end and I was hoping that by re-releasing, that will spark something in somebody and give me Secret Witness tips. If something comes up, I will always call you. I didn't mean to bug you on a Sunday."

"I had talked to some friends. It's just like, so random, you know."

"And that's what we are discussing in the office. To us, it just seemed like a random kill."

"I was given details just the other day," she began, an apparent reference, to the friend with law enforcement connections. "I cannot believe that Robert was murdered, like it just seems so unreal that that could even happen. I feel like I'm just living, I guess, like, I don't know. I can't believe that that happened. So crazy. So crazy. It's one of those things, the timing and everything, you know, just so crazy to me."

"That's why it kind of seems random to us, too," Meyer agreed. "We've just run into a dead end and we don't have anything."

"Is the video better?"

"We don't have that back yet." He had told her police were trying to make an enhanced, clearer version, but that could take a couple of months. In the meantime, "It's the one we originally released. It's the only one I have right now. Did you have a chance to watch that video?"

"I did. I have watched it," she said. "It's weird. It's just like, what does that even mean. It's such a question mark."

"I'm just hoping that by reposting it, somebody has seen something and will call us back."

He said he was off to grab some lunch with his wife.

"Have a great Sunday," said Sabrina. "Thank you for keeping in touch with me."

Sabrina called Jonathan.

"Everything's fine," she told him. "I'll talk to you after church when I see you. Is that okay? He just said that they don't have anything and that they're re-releasing the same video because the other one won't be back for like two months. He sent it out to another detective."

"He asked you questions?"

"No questions at all, just a dead end."

Jonathan said, "Hmmm."

"He said there's a dead end."

"I'll talk to you after church," said Jonathan. "I'll keep praying."

"Thank you for praying. I appreciate that."

"God wants his name to be upheld," said Jonathan. "I want him to stand up for his own namesake. I just think we have such a ministry. I am going to be so willing to be his badge. I am Christian and this is my story. Let's get out there and enjoy the Sunday and get recharged."

"I'm so late," she said. "I don't think I've ever been this late, but there's a first time for everything. I'm still going to go. That's what's most important."

Sabrina said she was bringing the children to church and suggested Jonathan join them for a picnic in the park afterwards.

Jonathan said, "I'll see you later, baby. I love you so much."

The wire tickled; the ruse worked. Along with more of Sabrina and Jonathan's complicity, these calls showed how swiftly Sabrina could change personas, from dazed and confused on the phone with Meyer to clear and no-nonsense with Jonathan.

Not all of the calls were as revelatory. Soon a repetition set in. It was a lot of talk about love, God and their day-to-day routines. One call from early the morning of Monday, Nov. 10, started out in typical fashion.

"How's my girl this morning?" asked Jonathan. "You're up all bright-eyed and bushy-tailed?"

"Not really," a sleepy-sounding Sabrina said. "What about you? Praying you're okay?"

"Thank you, baby. I really appreciate your prayers today."

It went on like this, the two talking about their weekend and Jonathan eliciting giggles from Sabrina with an anecdote about a coworker. Both sounded much more relaxed.

"You are cracking me up this morning," she said. "I love you."

"I love you, too."

"You know what, I'm going to be aching about you tonight," she said.

They prayed together before the conversation suddenly took a new turn.

"Did you hear that weird thing on the phone right now?" Sabrina asked.

She thought she heard a click. She began to wonder again if the phone was tapped.

Hearing this, Meyer conferred with the investigators. Modern wiretaps don't click. The calls are intercepted remotely through a facility in San Francisco. The click was their imagination—an imagination fueled, Meyer hoped, by mounting anxiety. It was decided to try to make them more anxious.

Meyer stepped out of the wire room and called Sabrina.

"I've got some exciting news," Meyer said, his own words being monitored by the other detectives. "I just got an email from our crime lab. We got a good DNA sample from what we believe was a sweat sample from the floor. It looks good, the best."

"Really," said Sabrina, "that's great."

"I'm excited," he said. "We've been waiting and waiting to see if something would happen and I wanted to give you a call as soon as possible."

Sabrina said, "Detective Meyer, thank you."

He said the test results would be available in about a month. In the meantime, he wanted to know if Sabrina would be available for a follow-up interview. Normally, they would do it by phone, but his boss wanted this one done at headquarters in Bakersfield.

"My boss has been giving me a little pressure," Meyer said. "He's been kind of a jerk lately. Wondering if you're available Wednesday?" That was in two days. "Come over here and get the interview knocked out?"

"Sure," said Sabrina. "I can do that."

The sweat sample and the boss pressure was pure B.S. invented to rattle Sabrina.

It worked. She quickly called Jonathan.

"I just talked to Detective Meyer. He called me."

"Oh, really?" said Jonathan, a hint of worry in his voice.

"He asked me to come in on Wednesday for, like, a final statement."

"Okay."

"And so he said that the DNA isn't back, but the call from the lab was exciting news. He just said that there was a bit of DNA found and I don't know how it's not actually back yet. He said that was really good news. He said that was the only thing they had so far. He was super excited about that."

"Good," said Jonathan carefully.

"And then he also, he said that they're super excited to have that and that his boss is kind of being a jerk and he needs a final statement for me to come in."

"Good, good," said Jonathan. "So what time on Wednesday?"

"I said about 11."

"Good to know, well, wow, okay."

"That's what's new," said Sabrina, "and I just wanted to share it with you."

"Thank you, thank you, and I'll keep praying for the situation and hope it all goes well. I'm just trying to think if maybe I could, maybe I could, uh, see you before you go or something?

"Yeah, that would be good. Just pray," she said.

"Just pray, and get all your thoughts together, you know," said Jonathan.

"We'll talk maybe in a little bit."

"I wonder what they're—they don't have DNA back?" he asked.

"He said there was a drop of sweat."

"Okay."

"I don't know if you can (determine) if it's Robert's?"

"Yeah, I'm not sure."

"He said that he was really excited about that news, because that's the only thing they had to go on."

"Hopefully, it leads to the right person and everything," said Jonathan. "Good to know. I'll keep praying for that situation. Did he clarify 'final statement'?"

"He said it was all just legal—what word am I looking for?—how the order goes."

"Just a cursory part of the process," said Jonathan. "Okay, good to know."

"Should I ask my sister to go with me?" asked Sabrina.

"Yeah, probably, I mean maybe have some company, you know. That seems like a good idea."

"That's what I'm going to do. Can we talk later on?

"For sure."

Sabrina asked: "How are you feeling?"

"Good, good," he said. "It's crazy how everything's— you know—God is bringing—God has a plan. We have somebody. We have a DNA match. I don't know how that works, either. I think they have to be in the system."

"That's what he had said—that if there was a criminal."

"So, hmm, wow. Putting a face to a name, putting things all together, God has a purpose in that, too."

Once again, Sabrina's children interrupted the call. "Kids!" she said. "I'm sitting out here on the patio. I'm talking to Jonathan."

One of the children could be heard shouting, "Hi, Jonathan!"

Later that day, at 5:54 p.m., Sabrina called Meyer,

seeking more information about the DNA test.

"I'm sorry, I don't have a whole lot of information for you," he said. "The only thing I was told from the lab is they got a good profile from what they believe to be a sweat drop. That's kind of all they told me. I'm supposed to meet with them today. ... You have another question?"

"No, uh, I've heard stuff from people. Do you have an autopsy report?"

"There is an autopsy report. I haven't reviewed it, but there is one, yes."

"How was Robert shot?"

"I haven't read the autopsy report," Meyer repeated. "The only thing I've really looked at is the crime scene photos, but I haven't looked at the autopsy stuff yet."

He was now deep into a ruse. He'd been briefed on the autopsy immediately and had pored over Dr. Whitmore's report multiple times.

Sabrina said, "I don't want to think. I have to be so strong for my kids."

"If you're having a bad day, I'm sorry. It's horrible. You're going to have good and bad days for a time."

"I can't believe it. I don't understand how a crime scene like that—why?"

"We may never know why, just build the pieces back together, but we may never know. It's unfortunate."

Sabrina asked again about the DNA results. "That might lead to somebody?"

"That might lead to somebody."

"No one has come and talked?"

"No, not yet. I was so excited when I saw that email from the crime lab about the DNA. I was just ecstatic. I'm really stoked about it. I think it's going to be the break in this case, I'm hoping."

"Okay."

"I don't know that scientific crap. I'm just a cop. That stuff is very technical." "You haven't heard anything from like the railroad?"

"No, I haven't heard anything from those guys. Every once in a while, they would check in with me and ask if I knew anything. I haven't heard much from them. I know for a while, their police officers handed out fliers everywhere and that's where we got the majority of tips from. That went nowhere, which is unfortunate."

It was another falsehood for Sabrina's benefit. The Sheriff's Office had been working closely with BNSF's police officers, who were assisting with interviews and reviewing the cell phone records.

Meyer was now piling ruse upon ruse. It is a tactic allowed by law and commonly used by police, but one fraught with risks.

"You really have to be careful," Meyer said later, "because if you're providing them with a ruse, they may know the answer to that. So you have to be very careful in the way you word them."

Already, Meyer may have pushed it a little too far. In another wiretapped phone call that day, Jonathan wondered if the detective was toying with them.

"Honestly, it almost seems like, just because of how they're treating you, it's almost like they're suspecting you or something, or us," he said. "So I started to think they might be tapping into our phones. I don't know. If they suddenly came upon phone records, well of course, they're going to be suddenly suspicious."

"I just called Detective Meyer," said Sabrina. "I asked: 'If you have DNA, do you have a suspect?' And he said: 'No.' He said: 'I'm just a detective.' He said all the lab people do all that stuff. I was like: 'How does that work?' He said: 'I'm not really sure.'"

"To me, it's like, well why would he say he's not sure about it because he's the detective who investigates homicides," said Jonathan. "It's like: 'What do you mean, you're not sure?'"

"He said it's all the scientific stuff," said Sabrina. She was at home. In the background, one of her children was asking her if they could make popcorn in the microwave.

"There are just a couple of things that are bothering me about the way he's treating you," Jonathan continued. "You know, keeping you out of the loop. That doesn't seem right."

"Is it weird that he's having me come to the station?"

"He's using a couple of things, like watching our relationship, kind of like observing our patterns and stuff," said Jonathan. "Then probably his first thought is: 'Oh, well, obviously they're together, so they're involved.' I feel like this is going to be his effort."

"I can't even believe that," said Sabrina "It's, like, so crazy, you know?"

"Now that I think about it, it's almost like he's suspecting us of being involved. You know how officers are allowed to use a ruse. If you want to get information, you're allowed to lie to get information. So it seems like it's probably a ruse to get you to relax and open up and if you have some secrets. Honestly, I feel like that's what he's doing: bringing you out of your comfort zone and into his comfort zone."

"Oh, yeah, he's really nice right now."

"Obviously, you're driving to Bakersfield to just give a final statement: Why didn't you guys get all the final statements before? I was going to talk to you and see if you want to maybe kind of feel him out a little bit, and so then tomorrow call him and say: 'You know what, stuff has come up, family, I'm not going to able make it, and reschedule for Friday.' Feel him out, see if he's jerking you around. He's kind of been back and forth with you. He hasn't been straightforward. I understand what he's doing: He's just making sure you don't really have knowledge and involvement, but that's how he has to do it."

"I hope not," said Sabrina.

"That's kind of the feeling I'm getting," said Jonathan. "I don't know what you think of that. That was one of my thoughts: Let's reschedule."

"I can call him."

"I'll want to talk to my buddies, too, some of my investigator buddies and ask: 'Hey, what's the deal with this?' "

From Meyer's background checks on Jonathan, he knew that the firefighter was taking classes to become an arson investigator. Part of the instruction covered the basics of criminal investigation, including interviewing techniques.

Sabrina told Jonathan she had asked Meyer about the autopsy report. "He was all like: 'I don't have it.' "

Jonathan said, "So I tried to look that up online. I didn't see anything online."

"He's all: You don't want to go there," said Sabrina. "He's all: It's not good for you to dwell on that."

"That's the stuff that bothers me."

"He's all: I'm really sorry you're having a hard time."

"It's tough," said Jonathan. "I'm looking at it from a prosecutorial standpoint. Of course, you and I have an affair. And it's like, of course, they're going to look into that."

"I can't even imagine," said Sabrina.

"That's the reality of it."

"I understand."

"Of course, we're going to come up," said Jonathan. "What a disaster."

"What a disaster, what a disaster," Sabrina said. "I can't even think of that."

"That's the reality," he said. "I feel like: Okay, he's got phone records that just came through. So I feel like he probably has that, so then he's making up other stuff to try to pressure you into saying it was more, obviously, or I arranged it or hired somebody. "

Jonathan tried to put himself in Meyer's shoes. "Now he's schmoozing her, and he's being nicer to her than he had been before. He's never been this nice, ever, ever. And then he wants you to come to his location. These are all cookie-cutter, quintessential techniques. If you go to the book for interview and interrogation, especially for females, it's going to be your time, your schedule, your location."

"Should I ask him: could we meet somewhere?"

"Honestly, I would just say: 'I am a busy lady.' Not to be rude, because he's doing his job. He has a job to do. They're obviously not having the warrant of arrest. They need a lot of information. They have big holes to fill. They're trying to figure out who did it. And they're thinking you—"

The conversation got interrupted again by Sabrina's daughter asking for something. "Leanna, this is the third time," Sabrina snapped. Then to Jonathan: "I have to go. Thank you for all your support."

"God is good," said Jonathan.

"He is good," said Sabrina, but there was little feeling in her voice.

It was an exhausted Jonathan Hearn who called her back at 8:19 p.m. that same day. He had just come off a grueling 24-hour shift at the Redlands Fire Department.

"I'm real tired today," he said. "I haven't really gotten to sleep all day. I know you're right there with me, so I don't want to complain. I am ready for some rest, and I think God wants us to recharge and rest our minds. I really do feel more skeptical and more trippy and more this and more that and all my emotions are amplified by a lack of sleep. I don't think that's good. I want to be humble and recharged."

"I have the Bible," said Sabrina. "I'll never get this. It's so crazy, the timing, we talked about this. ... It seems shady.
"

"There is a lot I want to talk to you about," said Jonathan. "I've written a couple of things down. I do feel like one of things is to wait until tomorrow. I do want to talk to you in person. I do want to have a clear mind and not have me falling asleep. I do want to have a clear mind and be recharged for God and just be humble. Sabrina, I can't tell you how truly

I am aligned and agree with your passion and your hope and your desire, which is just to have the Bible there and find our purpose and just read the Bible and find that we have been given a purpose to live for God, to raise a family for God."

Sabrina asked if he could come to her house. She said both her children had been asking about him.

"You don't think you should go with me?" she asked about the follow-up interview with Meyer.

"We'll talk about that later," Jonathan said. "I'm sorry. I don't mean to postpone everything. I'm just kind of leery. I almost feel like they're listening in on everything, just the way they started treating you. "

Sabrina asked how difficult it would be to tap a cell phone.

"I know how it is with a house phone," said Jonathan, who then yawned. "I really shouldn't be talking. My whole body is shaking, I'm so sleepy."

Sabrina urged him to get some sleep.

"Thank you so much, I really do appreciate that," he said. "The thing is I want you to know, Sabrina, we serve a big God. He's in the business of bringing down miracles. I don't know what the miracle is we're asking for here, just that to guide this investigation."

"I agree," said Sabrina.

"I know that and I love you so much, Sabrina. I can't wait to talk to you. I do think it'll be helpful to be off on Wednesday and just spend the day together and just talk over some things. You're the one who's been so helpful. You deserve to be treated politely and well through this thing. You're the one who lost your husband."

"I'm just going to read the Bible," Sabrina said.

"That is good rest for the soul."

"Any recommendations?"

"Yes, Psalm 38 and Psalm 51."

"Okay, I'm going to read that."

"Help us stay focused."

The Bible selection spoke volumes. In these passages, King David wrestles with his conscience. He had lusted after the beautiful Bathsheba when he saw her bathing naked on a rooftop. To have her for himself, he sent her husband, Uriah, off to the frontlines of the war to die. A guilt-wracked David tells God:

For I know my transgressions,
and my sin is always before me.
Against you, you only, have I sinned
and done what is evil in your sight.

10.

The prayers and a good night's sleep did wonders for Jonathan. At 7:17 the next morning, Tuesday, Nov. 11, he awoke refreshed. He called Sabrina to say he only had to work half of his 24-hour shift that day and would be heading "back up the hill" from Redlands to Silver Lakes around 8 p.m.

"God is in control," said Jonathan. "He knows, He knows, He knows. I know our hearts are so heavy. It's tough thinking of the truth of our affair coming out. It's insult to injury. It's pain on top of pain. It would be devastating not for us as much as for everyone else. I know there's this burden, this fear of us being in the spotlight. God is on the throne, God is sovereign and God wants us to reflect his light and radiate him."

Jonathan ended the call with a prayer: "Please lift the burden off our heart," he said. "We have cheated, we have lied. God, please help our story be one of redemption and not of failure."

In another call 90 minutes later, Jonathan called Sabrina "such a blessing from God. You are such a strong girl. I just admire your strength and fortitude."

"Seriously," she said. "I don't want to be admired. I don't."

"I thank God for you, then."

"Thank you. I thank God for you, too," said Sabrina. "I do have to be strong. Those kids, I just look at their faces and they need me to be strong, that's what they need."

She spoke about how her life has changed since Robert's

death. "It's not about me," she said. "God is giving me the strength to see things that I need to see. God is giving me the strength to not just be out there partying. To have known that, that is not what I want. We were wrong for being so distracted by so many so un-Godly things."

She ruminated over whether Robert's death was part of a larger plan by God. "Robert's not here," she said. "Why? Why? It doesn't feel real." Then she said that instead of asking God "why," she should be asking Him to "use me, use me."

"I want to be used," Jonathan said.

"Whatever God wants for me."

"I just need to focus on God. Get rid of the distractions. This will be his Testament."

"God does have purpose. I know it. It's so crazy to me," said Sabrina.

She wondered what would have happened if Robert had survived the shooting.

"He wouldn't want to be in a wheelchair, just breathing through—or not being able to get up. He would not. I just think about that all the time. I think I would have taken care of him. I would have."

"I know you would have," said Jonathan.

"I would have as his wife," she said. "As his wife, there are certain honors I owe him, just as the title of being his wife."

She recalled something Robert told her shortly before his murder: "Sabrina, if I died tomorrow, I would die happy."

Sabrina said, "The timing is crazy. That's where I have peace. It's so creepy to me. The timing, it's so creepy. It's unreal. It doesn't feel real. It feels like the purpose that he left was part of God's plan."

She said she felt that "God has placed Robert here to make everyone's eyes open," to inspire other people to follow Robert's "love and kind deeds that he did for everyone."

She talked of their full life and her wonderful memories.

"People have never, ever experienced things that I've gotten to," she said. "We did a lot in our time. We have a lot of memories my kids will always have. And for that, I am so grateful."

Later that day, she called Meyer.

"Hi, Detective Meyer," she said in a sunshine voice.

"Hey, Sabrina, how's it going?"

"Oooooh, pretty good, how are you?"

"What's up?'

"Okay, well, I apologize for bothering you. Would Thursday work out with you instead of tomorrow? My kids have tutoring. I just want to make sure that I'm here. And also Robbie has soccer stuff tomorrow. I just want to make sure I have arrangements for somebody to be here."

"Same time Thursday?"

"Does that work okay?"

"I am free. That is perfect."

Sabrina said she would see him then. "I wish you a great day."

The follow-up interview now rescheduled as Sabrina and Jonathan had discussed, Sabrina called him.

He answered with his usual, "Hey, baby."

"Hold on," she said. She shouted to her son how to microwave French fries. Then she told Jonathan about her conversation with Meyer. "He said it's pretty much the same interview."

"They have more questions to ask or something?"

"He didn't say that, but yeah."

Jonathan said, "I'm just saying that's what it is."

"My sister thought it was weird, too. She's all: 'Why does he want you to come there?' "

"Right, well, okay, we'll talk tonight. It's obviously one of those things like they don't have a lot of people to bring in. I'd be interested to hear, do you have, like, Cory's number and stuff like that?"

"I do, yeah."

Sabrina had heard that Robert's coworker, Cory Hamilton, had also done a follow-up police interview.

"It would be interesting to hear," said Jonathan. "Normally, that's what they do, a preliminary interview, when they're starting to work on the case and put it all down and make it formal, then they'll bring each person in."

Sabrina expressed irritation about another interview.

"Really, it's like, my personal business is my personal business, and, you know what, my husband was murdered. So, of course they're going to look into my life. I get it. I get it," Sabrina said. "I'm already finding the purpose in my pain. I want them to find the killer, not focus on our personal life. I'm feeling my sins in the sickness of my stomach. I'm feeling the sins for a reason. But that's not due to Detective Meyer. That's due to God. God wants me to feel that way. And I did it. I feel that way. I feel like God is just: you're going to carry your sins because the sins that Robert and I have committed have led us to where we are today. I need to feel that. That's never going to go away. It's never going to go away. It's not like: 'Okay, now I'm going to live happily ever after with Jonathan.' Now it's just like ironic, like: 'Wow, this really worked out for us,' like, 'Now you get to be my husband.' No! I need to feel that pain every single day."

"And also remember that Jesus saved us," said Jonathan. "It does go away. He separates our sins from us as far as the East is from the West. The sin that we do, we didn't have to carry it all of our lives. We are forgiven by a God who saved us."

"That's the beauty of feeling good again, the joy."

"That is the beauty."

"I was talking about the same thing with my mom, and Mom was, like, tell me more," said Sabrina. "God gave us another chance, and it does take work. Now we are supposed to feel a little different way. … We have to follow God's words, but it does take work because of our sinful nature. I just know that Jesus, he's coming back. He's like: 'Hey, guys, you want to keep being rude, you want to keep stealing, murdering, being pornographic, getting drunk? Keep going, I'll be back, and it's not going to be good for you.' "

"Yeah, wow, what a good point."

Sabrina said, "Detective Meyer: I do pray for the detective." She told Jonathan that she had been reading Psalms as he suggested.

"The Psalms are so good," said Jonathan. "David is a lot like you and I, Sabrina. He is a regular guy, but he loves God, and so many of Psalms are written by David."

"I saw that."

"He was someone who made a lot of big mistakes. He was someone who committed adultery, who had an affair, who even went on to kill the guy, like sent him into battle and pretty much had him killed off. He went way out of his way to cover his sins. It wasn't about anything more than that. It was just about: 'I messed up.' "

"He lost his son later," Sabrina noted.

"But even still, after that, it says in the Bible that David was a man after God's own heart. God really liked him. He was one of God's favorite people. Even David really understands that God doesn't want us going around being prideful. He wants a relationship with us. He wants an intimate relationship with Sabrina, he wants an intimate relationship with Jonathan. Yet he tried to cover up his sins in the slaying of Uriah."

Sabrina interrupted him. Another domestic issue arose.

"Oh, my gosh!" she blurted. "Yes, darling. No, Robbie, no marshmallows!"

The kids started screaming again.

"Okay, I'm going to go," she said, exasperated. "I'm sorry."

Sin, killing, redemption: Their conversations had gotten deeper. It so happened that among those monitoring the call was Jay Both, a special agent for the Drug Enforcement

Agency and a graduate of Brigham Young University, where he studied the Old and New Testaments of the Bible and taught Bible classes. Both explained to Meyer the significance of the story of David and Bathsheba and its relevance to the murder investigation. David had slept with Bathsheba while her husband, Uriah, was still alive and gotten her pregnant. Hoping to cover up the pregnancy, David brought Uriah home from the war in the hopes that he would sleep with her. But Uriah, a man of strong character, refused to do so while other men were risking their lives in battle. That's when an angry David sent Uriah off to the front to be killed. Afterwards, Bathsheba went into a period of mourning. When that ended, David brought her to his house and she bore him a son.

It was Agent Both's opinion that by citing this story, Jonathan was admitting to the murder of Robert Limon to cover up the affair with Sabrina.

Sabrina and Jonathan never explicitly said anything about plotting to kill Robert. It was only in the context of a biblical story. Meyer wondered if that wasn't on purpose. Several times, Sabrina and Jonathan expressed suspicions they were being wiretapped. When they approached sensitive subjects, they agreed to meet and talk about it later in person. When they did discuss their worries about police, it was always about their affair and how badly it would look in light of Robert's murder.

Meyer began to suspect that "affair" was a code word for "murder."

"We felt that we were getting good information," he said later. "Just because they're not saying, 'We killed a person,' there's still going to be a lot of circumstantial stuff. We knew we probably weren't going to get the smoking gun that you would want, but we're going to get a lot of good stuff."

It would get better. Later that Tuesday afternoon, Sabrina called Cory Hamilton.

"Hi, Cory, this is Sabrina Limon."

"Hi, Sabrina, how's it going?" asked Cory Hamilton.

"Good, good. Am I bothering you?"

A child could be heard in the background.

"No, not at all. We're just hanging out playing with fuzzy balls, pipe cleaners and a colander."

"That sounds like fun. That's the good stuff in life right there."

"Yes, it is."

"Well," Sabrina said, "I was just wondering if you heard anything."

"I have not heard anything."

"No?"

"Last I heard is they were following somebody and we didn't have anything to worry about. And that's all we've been told. And that's all they will tell us."

"Have you been to the sheriff's office or anything?"

"Three weeks ago when we had to do a DNA sample. But other than that, we haven't had to do anything. Have they talked to you at all?"

"He wants me to come in, too. I was wondering why he was having me come in, you know?"

"Right after everything happened," Cory said, "they took our fingerprints. They took ours and our wives' fingerprints, anyone who had been in the shop to rule our fingerprints out. And then they had just the five of us come back just for DNA samples. They did that like, three weeks ago or four weeks ago."

"Did they take a statement, or no?"

"They did a statement that same night. Other than that, I haven't heard anything from them. I've called the detectives twice and I haven't heard back from them."

"Did you talk to Detective Meyer?"

"He wasn't there when they did the DNA sample. He was there when they did the fingerprinting, and he interviewed me that night. Other than that, all the information I've gotten is from our police."

"So nothing in Tehachapi?" she asked.

"They even released a statement to the Tehachapi newspaper that they had no new leads—or they can't release anything at this time. All the information I've gotten is from our police directly when they were working with us, recently in the last couple of weeks. He was like: 'You have nothing to worry about, trust me.' That's all he would say."

"Huh," said Sabrina. "What do you get from that?"

"Exactly, you don't get much from that? Definitely," Cory said, laughing. "They know something and they're trying to piece it together is what he explained it to me. So haven't they told you anything?"

"No, he's just kind of shady, you know," said Sabrina. "I don't know, just little bits and pieces, that's all."

"I know the feeling."

"So, anyway, that was it. I was just wondering, you know."

"Yeah, if I hear anything, I'll definitely give you a call. I was actually going to call you anyway because I got the cards."

Sabrina had sent Cory a thank-you card after Robert's funeral. "Oh, good, well, I'm so glad."

"We want to get Christmas gifts for your kids," he said. "And we want to know what they would be into or what they would like."

"Ahhh, you know, that's so nice. I don't even know. I've been trying to, like, since it's so different, I want to kind of like focus, try to focus them on like: We're so lucky. I've tried to refocus their energy on themselves."

As for gifts, all she could offer was: "Robbie is a boy and Leanna is a girl. The boy is all boy and the girl is all girl."

"Okay, all boy and all girl. I can work with that."

He asked for their ages, and Sabrina mentioned that her daughter was 8 going on 13 and was now into jewelry.

Sabrina returned to the murder investigation. "Detective

Meyer did say they were going to re-release the video."

"Oh, they are, trying to get more out of it? Interesting," said Cory. "They said they wanted you to come in?"

"Uh-huh."

"Interesting," he said.

"Gosh, I don't really know what to think of any of it. It's so random."

"Exactly," said Cory.

"I don't get it, I really don't," said Sabrina. "But I just found purpose in all this life and the love and it has really opened my eyes to a lot of things of what my focus and purpose needs to be. That's where I'm at. My strength is just God's strength, which is carrying me."

"Yeah."

"I do feel peace in a life, the moral that Robert left, you know. Anyways, it felt weird, I don't know."

"That is kind of weird," said Cory.

"I appreciate the thoughts and everybody's heart. Thank you so much. I wish you guys a great night."

Cory Hamilton would later say he was flabbergasted. Cory barely knew Robert and he had met Sabrina only once, at Robert's funeral. Now she's calling him at home pressing him on his experiences with the police and talking about God's purpose. "I found it extremely weird," he said.

Cory called Det. Meyer to tell him that Sabrina Limon had called him out of the blue sounding "confused or worried." Sabrina struck him as "very weirded out by the fact that she needed to go in and give another statement." Cory was unaware that Meyer heard every word.

Two and a half hours later, Jonathan called Sabrina from the fire station where he was wrapping up another 24-hour shift. Exhaustion in his voice, he rambled about "a lot things" going through his mind. "We are dirty rotten sinners," he said darkly. "We are spiders dangling from a thread. All it takes is a little snap of the finger and we're destroyed. I don't want that."

Sabrina countered that this was all part of plan. She inferred that Robert may have been better off dead.

"This was God's time for him," she said. "People are coming out of the woodwork saying Rob's life left a positive impact on them. For me to be part of that, I felt so blessed. The memories that my kids have—they're off playing right now. But God has a plan for us. Daddy is our guardian angel."

The alternative, she said, could have been worse. "If Rob and I did separate, maybe God didn't want that for him or for the kids," she said. "I just feel bad being my chipper self," she said. "I'm known for my sunshine. That's what everybody knows me for. I felt horrible about who I am."

She told Jonathan about her talk with Cory Hamilton, how he and his wife had provided fingerprints and DNA a few weeks earlier, but hadn't heard anything definitive since, except from a BNSF officer who told him he had nothing to worry about.

With his shift up at 8 p.m., Jonathan said he could get to her house by 9:30 p.m. "I want to talk to you about some other things," he said.

There it was again, an in-person meeting setup.

Sabrina said that worked out well because the children had school in the morning and she would be in bed by then. "It's hard to take it in and continue to juggle kids and everything," Sabrina said. "And so that's why. I do appreciate your support."

From the flat San Bernardino Valley floor to the high desert, it's a steep 2,000-foot climb up the Cajon Pass along Interstate 15, the artery between Los Angeles and Las Vegas. Trucks groan up the grade in slow gear while the smaller cars whisk by. As Jonathan approached Sabrina's home in Silver Lakes, after more than an hour on the road, his nerves were frayed. He called Sabrina from the road. She sensed his anxiety.

"What's going on?" asked Sabrina.

"There's a truck that's definitely keeping eyes on you."

"Really?"

"I'll call you back in a little bit."

Four minutes later, he called to tell her that a red Nissan Titan pickup was parked two houses down with a guy standing outside.

"As I creeped back around, I approached him straight on," he said. "Now I've got my headlights on them, and now it's a guy and a girl, and they don't look like they're dressed to be standing outside, but they are. The girl looks cold. She looks like she doesn't normally wear the kinds of clothes she's wearing. She looks like a cop."

"Are they Mexican?" asked Sabrina.

"No, they're white, and they both look like typical cops trying to pretend not to be cops. It's like they're standing to have eyes on everybody. They're both staring straight at me even though my headlights are blinding them so that they can't see me."

Jonathan said he went back to Helendale Boulevard, the main drag through town, and the truck pulled away. He followed the truck as it went through an intersection that dead-ended into a church. From a gas station, Jonathan watched as they turned around and headed back toward Strawberry Lane.

"They're obviously on the lookout or whatever," he said. "I don't know what it's for. I think they've figured out we know each other."

"You think we're paranoid?" asked Sabrina.

"I think I might be just a little bit," he said. "What's going on here? This whole thing is weird."

Sabrina said there had been a "lot of activity" at a neighbor's house recently. "I don't know if we're being paranoid," she said. "As far as our bad feelings, we haven't committed a crime. You have not committed a crime coming over here."

"I know," Jonathan said. "I'm just like why, why, why? You're completely right. I'm just skeptical. I just humble myself. It's in God's hands."

"Our sins are between us and God," said Sabrina. "It's not a crime."

Then she said something that would jolt Meyer. "I don't know if the detective's ever been unloyal to his wife."

"I seriously doubt he's been unloyal to his wife," said Jonathan. "He's a pretty mechanical thinker, and his wife makes custom furry blankets. They're like the perfect little Bakersfield couple."

"You think so?"

"I know so."

Jonathan spoke with an edge he'd never revealed before.

"You know what," Jonathan said in another call a couple of minutes later, "I'm stressed about that whole thing. Think we can meet up tomorrow? I'm thinking of heading home and meet up tomorrow?"

The call, like many, was breaking up from bad cell service. Then at 10:16 p.m., Sabrina got a call on her burner phone from a number she didn't recognize. It had a 661 area code, Bakersfield.

The only person who ever called her from Bakersfield was Det. Randall Meyer.

She answered. It was Jonathan. "Almost gave me a heart attack," she said.

Apologizing, he explained that out of caution, he was now calling her through a Skype app on his phone.

He had to cut the call short. His truck started sputtering; the gas gauge showed empty. The truck ran on diesel and a gas station would be hard to find at this hour. As he drove around Helendale, he began to pray for gas when a station appeared.

"It just shows me God is a big God," he told Sabrina, "but he listens to the littlest of prayers."

"Can I ask you a big favor?"

"Yeah."

"Let's keep your truck filled up. I'll give you cash."

For the first time, irritation had crept into her voice.

"Okay," he said, "I have some things to talk to you about. I'll be there in 15 or 20 minutes."

Jonathan spent the night at Sabrina's house and they were together the following day, Wednesday. Jonathan drove home and called Sabrina at 7 p.m. to discuss again what may come up during Sabrina's meeting the next morning in Bakersfield with Det. Meyer.

"I don't like bad news," Sabrina told him.

"Bad news," Jonathan said, "is just proof of our need of faith."

Meyer wasn't in the wire room at the time of these calls.

"I was at home," Meyer later recalled. The deputy monitoring the calls briefed him. "He said, 'I just want you to know Jonathan's mentioned that he was researching you. It looks like on Facebook. He also said you and your wife are the perfect Bakersfield couple and she makes fuzzy blankets.' And I go, 'Huh,' because she doesn't make fuzzy blankets. I went back to her Facebook to make sure there weren't any fuzzy blankets. I didn't see any. It was weird, a very strange feeling. It was very odd and kind of cold, this guy is really looking into me."

The good news was Jonathan's paranoia about the red truck showed that the wire tickling was working. Jonathan's instincts that he was being followed were correct. Meyer placed a roving team of deputies on surveillance detail. The investigators surreptitiously attached GPS tracking devices to Sabrina's Honda and to Jonathan's truck. Three days earlier, they had followed Jonathan driving his truck to a remote riverbed in Victorville where he parked and walked around. It was night and dark and the deputies couldn't see what he was doing. The riverbed was full of trees and bushes. They returned the next morning to find homeless people in tents, but located no evidence. If Jonathan had dumped something there amid the rocks and vegetation, they may never find it.

But Meyer had no surveillance assigned to Strawberry

Lane that night. That wasn't the sheriff's truck.

It appeared that Jonathan was reaching a breaking point. Meyer decided to push harder.

11.

Sabrina got up early on Thursday, Nov. 13. While her children still slept, she showered and made their lunches for school. At 7:33 a.m., Jonathan called her burner phone. Their time together the day before had done them both well.

"I slept so super amazing," she said.

"Oh, thank you, God," said Jonathan. "How are you feeling?"

"I feel good," she said. "I really have a peace throughout me. I feel good and I'm rested."

The call ended with a child's voice saying, "Hi."

"Hi," said Jonathan, "is this Robbie?"

"Yeah."

"Hey, buddy, good morning. How are you?"

Robbie said he was good.

Sabrina sent the children off to school and, with her sister Julie Cordova, headed for the Kern County sheriff's headquarters. She arrived at about 11:30 a.m. and was led into a small interview room. She sat in a folding chair in the corner squeezed between a table and the walls.

Det. Meyer walked in, sat at the table in a comfortable reclining office chair with padded armrests and said hello to Sabrina. Then a man Sabrina had never met came in.

"I just want to introduce myself. I'm Randall's supervisor," he said, shaking her hand. "I want to tell you he's working really hard. I was just looking at some stats and we followed close to 100 leads."

After he left, Meyer began the interview. "If at some point you don't want to talk anymore, you are welcome to leave."

The statement was as much for the benefit of a judge as it was for Sabrina. Meyer wanted to make it clear that he wasn't keeping Sabrina in custody; therefore, he didn't need to read her her rights. As a non-custodial interview subject, everything she said could be used against her in a court of law.

"First, I want to talk to you about my meeting with the crime lab this morning," said Meyer. "I met with them this morning. You're probably going to be excited like I am about this DNA stuff. What I'm going to do is draw you like a little diagram."

Sketching on a piece of paper, he said, "Basically, there's a new company that's developing some software, and it's called Cybergenetics."

The company analyzes DNA with super-sensitive precision, separating cross-contaminated DNA samples, magnifying tiny and broken samples. Kern County was the first county in the United States to use the software. He said the technology has been upheld in Superior Court, and it can match DNA from crimes against a database of felons. And that's what they were using in the investigation of her husband's murder.

"We located what we believe to be two sweat drops that crossed over each other," he said. "What they did is they took a sample, they take a couple of samples, and I've sent those to the crime lab to be tested along with a bunch of other DNA."

He said results should arrive in about a month.

"They're still testing Robert's DNA and all the other employees there. We're thinking that one of them is going to be Robert, but we don't know. That will leave us with the other one that's out there."

Meyer talked more about "lines and patterns" of DNA analysis as Sabrina listened with a glazed look.

"Wow, it's pretty high tech," she said.

"It's huge, and this company, it's named Cybergenetics," he said.

"That's awesome."

"I was so excited when I found this out. I was so pumped. It changes the playing field for the kind of DNA I can test. "

"It's amazing."

"It's simply amazing," he agreed.

"It's beyond my mind. I need everything explained for this simple mind because I get mixed up," she said. "So this lab will send it out and, like you said, it will ping in the system if there was already someone—"

"Arrested," said Meyer.

"Arrested," she said, "or has any kind of, someone that's been in the system?"

"It has to be someone who's been arrested for a felony. So it can't be a traffic citation or misdemeanor stuff. It's got to be a felony suspect. Now, if for some reason we don't get a hit off this DNA, and if we suspect someone in the future, we can pluck their DNA."

That discussed, Meyer changed the subject. He told her this would "probably be our last interview" and he wanted to go over one last time the topics they covered in her previous two interviews. She spoke in more detail about her life with Robert, starting from the first day she saw him.

"I was with Robert for 17 years, and I met him in Prescott, Arizona, and we were very young. I feel like my mom gave birth and Robert caught me," she said, smiling.

"Wow," said Meyer.

"Yeah, that's what it feels like," she said. She began to cry when she spoke of moving to California after Robert got a job with the railroad.

"Let me get a tissue for you," said Meyer.

"I'm okay," she said, then spoke of her wedding, buying the home in Silver Lakes and having two children. She said Robert was killed two days shy of their 14th wedding anniversary. The next few days, she said, were a blur.

"You at least have some friends who are helping you through this and stuff?" Meyers asked.

"Oh, my gosh, I have so many friends that have been helping me a lot," she said. "I'm so grateful. I do feel like I want to figure things out. I felt numb, unreal and now it's starting to—I really feel the strength. I feel God lifting me and carrying me. It is amazing. We did, like, we had fun friends. We liked to drink and carry on for a little bit. And I haven't had one drink."

"None?" asked Meyer.

"None," she said.

"Wow, that's powerful."

"It's powerful," she agreed. "I don't want to go into a dark place. I feel Robert's purpose. I do feel a purpose, and I feel a focus. The lives that he touched, I can't even tell you what's been happening. A lot of stuff has been happening."

Meyer excused himself. He said he wanted to get some water bottles for them. In fact, this was a point when he needed to confer with the other detectives who were monitoring the interview, which was being captured on a wall-mounted video camera. At times, Meyer's phone would get messages from the other detectives suggesting questions.

In the quick private meeting, the detectives decided that Meyer should not push Sabrina on all that "stuff" that had been happening since the murder.

"So let's talk about your guys' marriage," Meyer said when he returned to the interview room with the bottled water. "Some of this stuff may be a bit personal. But it's some stuff I need to know. The process is: I need to look into everything. Some of the questions I need to ask you may be very personal. What type of marriage did you guys have?

"We had a good marriage," Sabrina said.

"Did you ever fight?"

"Not a lot."

"A couple fights a month or a couple fights a year?"

"Rob didn't like anything to be fights at all."

"So during the course of your guys' marriage, have there been any separations?"

"No."

"How about: Have you ever suspected Rob of having an extramarital affair or having a girlfriend?"

"No."

"Nothing at all?"

"No."

"How about you: While you guys were married, did you ever have an extramarital affair or a boyfriend or anything?"

"No."

"Okay, so you guys got along good then?"

"Yes."

"You guys were just basically living your life there in Helendale. You said you guys liked to party a lot. Did you party there or travel?"

"We just liked to have fun. It wasn't anything. We did a lot of stuff. We traveled. We liked to go to the river."

"Which river?"

"Like the Colorado River, Lake Mojave, Havasu a couple of times. All adult trips."

She said that before Robert's murder they had another trip planned to the Colorado River with three other couples.

"You guys obviously didn't make the trip," said Meyer.

"No," Sabrina said.

"Did you guys have an open relationship?"

"No," she said, the question seeming to catch her off-guard.

"I just heard some rumors out there," Meyer explained. "That little town, it's kind of crazy sometimes."

"Yeah, no, I know how rumors go," said Sabrina. "I know that's how we were probably viewed by maybe some: Oh, here they come, oh, boy."

"I think they typically call it swinging."

"Oh, no," said Sabrina. "I would say: Let's give them something to talk about. My attitude has changed a lot since losing Robert. I really feel that this is my purpose and a responsibility of taking care of my kids. I cannot be distracted by anything else besides Robbie and Leanna and how am I gonna raise them. They're doing well." She and the children were seeing counselors.

Meyers excused himself again to confer with the other investigators. This left Sabrina alone in the room for several minutes as the camera continued to roll. She sat quietly with her hands in her lap barely moving.

When he returned, he gave her a card for free counseling for crime victims and their families. She thanked him and said she had made a lot of progress in the weeks since Robert's murder: "I feel like I'm a new mom again."

Meyers asked her if there was anything she could think of to tell him.

"I have nothing at all," she said. "Every time I talk to you, I just don't get it. It feels just unreal, like how could that have happened? I had no idea how that could happen to Rob. He was quick on his feet."

"We may never really know why it happened," said the detective.

"Is there anything you can tell me?" she asked. "I thank you so much with all my heart, everything that you have helped me with so far. I want to stay focused, and I feel like I'm—I just want to keep my focus. And if I fall into any dark areas—"

She cut herself off and asked, "I've heard you guys caught somebody."

Meyer said, "We've been looking at a bunch of people and every person we've looked at has turned out to be not involved. We actually seized the gun we thought was involved, sent it to the lab, had it tested. It came back negative."

Sabrina asked nothing more about that. She said she has survived through her faith. "I've given everything to God," she said. "Robbie prays for God to forgive whoever took his dad."

"Wow," said Meyers, "that's amazing."

After lavishing the detective with thanks, Sabrina walked out of the sheriff's headquarters and made the drive back to Helendale with her sister. As Sabrina got up the grade, past the Tehachapi Loop and near the complex where Robert was killed, her phone rang. It was Jonathan.

"I was just calling to let you know that there are a bunch of people praying for you," he said. "You're in my thoughts and wanted to see how your day is going."

"Thank you so much, it's good," said Sabrina. "My sister and I are on the way home."

"Tell her that we love her so much," said Jonathan.

"Ah, love you, too," said Sabrina. "We're actually just coming through Tehachapi right now. Everything's good."

"Everything went okay with your visit?"

"Yeah, yeah," said Sabrina. She seemed to be watching her words as her sister sat next to her. "I'll talk to you this evening. Will you be around?"

"I will be," Jonathan said.

"Tehachapi is a creepy town," said Sabrina. "It's all foggy and the clouds are low."

"Tehachapi?"

"Yeah, are you familiar with it?"

"I have been through there once or twice, but I'm not real familiar with the area. We have friends that live up there. I remember the low-hanging clouds. Kind of a bad feeling to it."

"Bad going through here," said Sabrina. "The detective is all, 'It's a nice little town and there's a lot of tweakers.'"

Meyers had said nothing of the sort.

Jonathan asked: "Were they saying anything from the DNA?"

"No," said Sabrina. "I don't know if we're going to break up because we're going through where the windmills are."

Jonathan stayed on the line.

"He was just saying they don't have anybody," Sabrina continued. "They took everybody from work to eliminate. He's just like: 'They got a sweat drop.'"

"Oh, okay."

"It's like this new system called Cybergenetics. It's like this new, like, really high-tech technology that they have. He was even drawing it out for me. Even if the DNA is just like a little bit or poor DNA, they can separate. It's just such advanced technology."

"You wonder whose sweat drop. Just hope that it's the right person's sweat drop. We'll just pray for that."

Twice during the interview, Meyer had made a point to mention Cybergenetics. This was by design to see what she and Jonathan would do next.

There is, in fact, a company by that name. It's based in Pittsburgh and does, in fact, test DNA for law enforcement agencies. Its motto: "Justice through better science."

Jonathan's computer browser records would later show that within 10 minutes of speaking to Sabrina, he was looking at the homepage of Cybergenetics.

The site had a press release showing that Kern Regional Crime Lab had become the first lab in the nation to use the company's automated TrueAllele software for analyzing mixed DNA samples. "The Kern County District Attorney's Office is a world leader in DNA analysis," Dr. Mark Perlin, chief scientific and executive officer of Cybergenetics, said in the press release. "They understand how using better technology can better protect the public from crime."

Of course, it wasn't doing that in the investigation into Robert Limon's murder, the sweat drops coming from Det. Meyer's imagination. And while it wasn't known whether Jonathan ever read that press release, he was certainly in a good mood when Sabrina called him after she returned home that night.

"Hello, my beautiful," he said.

"Hey, were you sleeping," she asked in a sexy voice.

She told him she only had a few minutes to talk before her daughter's math tutor arrived. Speaking in a quiet voice, she filled him in on more of the interview with Meyer, telling him about the DNA testing and recounting how she denied having any marital problems.

They giggled and talked about their love for one another and arranged to meet later that evening at the Round House Pizza in Apple Valley, their regular dinner spot located halfway between her home in Silver Lakes and his in Hesperia.

Sabrina brought her children.

When she returned home after dinner, her son got on the phone to talk to Jonathan.

"Hiiiiiii," he chirped.

"Hi," said Jonathan. "It's been 20 seconds and I miss you already."

Sabrina took the phone back as the kids, amped up from their night at the pizza place, screeched in the background. "It's like Chutes and Ladders," she said of her hectic household.

Their confidence was misplaced. Sitting two tables away from them at the pizza place were four undercover investigators. They weren't close enough to hear Jonathan and Sabrina, but could see them whispering.

Det. Meyer would amp up the pressure. He would tickle the wire like never before.

12.

Sabrina's cell phone sputtered. The interrupted words added to the surreal nature of what Det. Meyer was saying. "Secret Witness" … "Subject is named Jon" … "Possibly knew Rob."

"Okay," was all Sabrina said.

"Any direction we should be going on with this?"

"No!" she answered firmly, then the call dropped all together.

"Are you there?" asked Meyer. "I'm going to call your home phone."

Four days after her delightful dinner with Jonathan and the kids, Meyer had sent Sabrina into a panic. On Nov. 17, at 6:34 p.m., he left this voicemail message on her home phone:

"I've been going through some witness tips and stuff and was reviewing some video from the area around the time the murder occurred. About that time, we could see a motorcycle leaving the area and it appeared to be kind of a white male, skinny, leaving the area around whenever it occurred. Also went through these Secret Witness tips. And I got a tip today that said that we that should be looking at a subject named Jon, like J-O-N, and he possibly knew Rob."

She called him back on her regular cell phone, not the burner, but the call cut in and out. When Meyer reached her again on the landline, domestic mayhem roared in the background. Her son was yelling something.

"I'll be right there!" Sabrina shouted. "Robbie, could you please give me a minute!"

Then to Meyer, "I'm so sorry."

Repeating what he was saying earlier, Meyer told her they had received an anonymous tip directing them to a man named Jon. He asked her if she knew of anybody they should investigate.

The first name she mentioned was a former coworker of Robert's, a John spelled with an "h" who had retired to Tehachapi.

"Do you know if he owns a motorcycle?"

"Yes, I believe that he did," said Sabrina.

"Do you know if he and Rob had any beef or anything, any problems?"

"No, never."

"Have you met him before?"

"I have. He's a bigger guy. And he's not that tall."

"So he was a fat guy?"

"He's like medium build, like a little bit of a belly."

"How long ago did you meet him?"

She first met him years ago, when this John worked as a fulltime responder in Tehachapi. One weekend that Robert had pulled a fill-in shift Sabrina and the kids visited the shop and she saw him then. The next time she saw him was at Robert's funeral. She described him as white, about 55.

"Do you remember if he lives in Tehachapi?"

"He lives in Tehachapi," she said. "And there's John Justus, who Robert worked with in Barstow Yard."

"Okay," said Meyer, "We're trying to figure this out. Like I said, we got a Secret Witness tip that came in and we are trying to get a hold of that person to try to get more details. The only thing we have is that person was named Jon and possibly knew Rob. And after reviewing the video, there's somebody on a motorcycle leaving the area."

Meyer asked if John Justus was white.

"He is white," said Sabrina. "He is a tall guy and probably weighs about 230 pounds, probably. His hair is like a brownish reddish."

"How old is John?"

"Probably about 37."

"He works out of Barstow?"

"He's a responder with Robert as well."

Sabrina finished talking to Meyer and dialed Jonathan Hearn's cell phone. It was now about 7:30 p.m. and he was at work in Redlands.

"Hey," she said, urgency in her voice, "could you call me from the station phone on this line?"

"Sure thing," he said.

When he called her back two minutes later, she couldn't get the words out fast enough.

"Hey, I'm not sure what's going on, but Detective Meyer called me and he's going to call me back and he said he got a Secret Witness tip that a tall, white male was leaving on a motorcycle around the time of Robert's murder and that there's someone who called in and someone who knows Rob by the name of Jon."

Jonathan greeted the news with nothing but silence.

Several seconds passed as he said nothing.

Sabrina said, "So, I'm oh like, what? And he just, he called me a little bit ago, and he called me on my landline, which he never does that. Then he said he had a meeting and he said he would call me back, and he just called me back. It was a tall, thin white male. Jon—J-O-N—and he said it was a Secret Witness tip and that he knew Robert."

After more silence, Jonathan could be heard mumbling something in the background. It sounded like he was praying.

He then started trying to figure out who the tipster was. Then it hit him.

Kelly Bernatene.

"She's the only one I can think of," said Jonathan.

"No, no, seriously, she wouldn't do that to me," Sabrina protested. "Secret tip."

Sabrina considered what Jonathan said. "Gosh, it's true, I never thought of that."

"Sabrina, I can't think of anybody who would think that except her."

She then thought she heard something.

"There's that clicking on the phone, so you hear it?"

"Just so you know, the station phone sometimes does that," Jonathan said. "I feel like Kelly and Jason would do that just to put it out there just because they don't like me, you know?"

"That they would mess up my chances?" asked Sabrina.

"Maybe. He said it was from a secret tip. He can say anything he wants to me. I don't think that's even true, really. Should I call Kelly right now?"

Jonathan's reply was garbled. He could be heard talking about "God's purpose," then said, "I think it's somebody trying to frame me because of this affair. I don't know how, why this person—as soon as you said it, I thought immediately Kelly. How would she have known that I drive a motorcycle?"

"Is there a new video?" Sabrina wondered. "How did this all of a sudden just come up? It doesn't make sense."

In the background, her kids were screaming. "Robbie!" she shouted. "You've got 15 minutes. That's it!"

It was nearing 8 p.m., the children's bedtime.

Sabrina told Jonathan, "He wanted to know how tall the Johns were."

"That does seem like him making up something," said Jonathan, "and probably just record our conversation and see what we will say."

"That's what I was thinking, too."

They kept talking.

"God, please help us," Jonathan said, praying again. "God, we don't want this to get out. We don't want this story of our affair to get out, God."

"Amen," said Sabrina. "If he is telling me the truth about the Secret Witness— I don't think there is any Secret Witness. Would he do that to me?"

"I do," said Jonathan.

"How are they just putting that all together?"

"A tall, skinny white guy driving away on a motorcycle," said Jonathan, thinking aloud.

"Jon who knew Rob," said Sabrina.

"That just sounds like Detective Meyer trying to make something up," said Jonathan. "Then again, why would he tell you that other than to record a conversation? I honestly feel like: 'How would they know that? How would Kelly know I had a motorcycle?' "

"She doesn't, she doesn't," insisted Sabrina.

"Do we have to rule her out?"

"I would say absolutely rule her out."

Around and around they went, before Jonathan asked: "What is your gut feeling?

Sabrina's answer: "I'm just so upset."

After listening to this exchange, Meyer ratcheted up the pressure. He sent Sabrina a text message:

Hey Sabrina I just found out that there's video from a pilot gas station at 58 and 395. I'm heading out there in a few. Looks like the subject may have filled up.

She called him back and he told her: "I found out some more information. And I believe the subject may have filled up gas in his motorcycle at a gas station that's located on the corner of Highway 58 and 395. It looks like the same motorcycle."

"A new video?" asked Sabrina.

Meyer said police already had the video of the motorcycle, but that he had only recently seen it, another falsehood he was feeding her. He'd had that video for weeks.

"It looks like the same motorcycle and the same person," Meyer told Sabrina.

"Oh, gosh, that's good," she said.

"That's good," Meyer agreed.

"And so how does this tie in—like the Secret—what is it?"

"They call in anonymously. I went through those. I noticed that one of them was about a Jon that we should look into that possibly had known Rob."

He said he was now going to take a closer look at the gas station video and call her back.

"Please call me back, absolutely," Sabrina said. "Thank you so much, Detective."

She hung up on Meyer on the landline and called Jonathan on the burner.

"So that was Detective Meyer and he said they have a video out on Highway 58 out at that gas station," she said. "I'll read you the text."

After reciting the message, she said, "There's a gas station, like, out there, like at Four Corners maybe, and he said they have a video and they're going to get it right now. I have no idea what's going on."

"That's strange. I wonder why he's telling you this stuff."

Sabrina said, "I feel like they're going to show up here."

As the cell reception again fizzled, Sabrina said, "I can't hear you. The phone is crackling so bad."

"I'm just praying to God," Jonathan said. "Help us to be strong, put our trust in Him."

"Amen," said Sabrina. "Hopefully, it's the same guy in the video. You think it is?"

"I'm trying to think," said Jonathan. "I'm sure a lot of motorcycles go through there. I don't know why he'd be way over in Four Corners. They have a lot to prove. They're trying to put a story together. I just, like, at this point, I'm not sure if they'll take me in for questioning. I feel like they're just pushing on you because they're orbiting on us. It's getting to the point they're trying to frame us up and stuff. I trust in God."

"I do, too," Sabrina said. "It sure is weird."

"Here's the whole thing," said Jonathan. "If I had done something to Robert and didn't tell you, Meyer probably wants to see what your knowledge of it is, what your involvement in it is: Do we make one inquiry just that he had an affair with her? Or do we try to get her to admit that, like, I told you."

"Right."

"Clearly, they have nothing," said Jonathan. "I didn't do it and you didn't know anything."

"It's like they're not telling the truth."

"I had this, like, really yucky gut feeling that they're going to air our affair so they can say: 'Does anybody know about this,' to get more people to talk."

"Yeah, now that he's saying look into 'Jon.' If there was a last name, he would have said it, right?"

"I would have thought," said Jonathan, "but then again, if he's just yanking your chain, you probably would have said like 'Jon Hearn.' They want to say Jon so that we talk."

"I can't believe this."

In subsequent calls that night that faded in and out on the wiretap— Jonathan got terrible reception from the fire station—they spoke at length in low, somber tones about what Meyer might have on them. They wondered if police had been watching Sabrina's house and if they had gone over their phone records. Jonathan talked again about the story of Bathsheba and how he had to rely on his faith more than ever.

"I put my trust in God," he said. "I don't want to put my trust in a lawyer."

Sabrina worried about what might happen to her family and children. And she wondered why all this was happening on Nov. 17—exactly three months to the day after Robert's murder.

"It's almost, like, staged," she said, "like they are specifically looking for me."

As one conversation became overcome with cell phone

static, Sabrina told Jonathan, "I love you, I do. I love you so much. Never forget that." Then she asked Jonathan: "I don't think they're going to come tonight, do you?"

With what sounded like a heavy weariness in his voice, he said, "I think it's a possibility. I don't know, Sabrina, I have not a clue. Anything is possible."

Suddenly she said, "Hold on."

"What was that?" asked Jonathan.

It was Det. Meyer texting her. He sent her a photo from the security camera of the motorcyclist inside the gas station opening the cooler to get a drink. Meyer included the message: "Let me know what you think. It's a picture of a picture. Sabrina, we think this is our guy. Do you recognize this person on the motorcycle? Let me know what you think."

Sabrina relayed the information to Jonathan, who asked: "What's he wearing?"

"Shorts, it looks like," she said. "Tan shorts and a tank top, a black tank top. And mask, it looks like. Black mask." She was referring to the tinted faceguard on the motorcycle helmet. "It looks like the whole face is covered. Should I call Detective Meyer right now?"

"That's pretty trippy. You can't really make it out?"

"Let me call you back," said Sabrina. "Let me call him."

Jonathan kept her on the line. He warned her: "Hey, if they're just using a picture of me that they randomly found, if it's me, don't feel like, oh, no, because they could just be checking to see."

"It looks like the face is covered," she said, then reread the text, " 'Looks like we have our guy.' I don't understand."

Jonathan's words became scrambled in the bad reception, but one sentence came through: "He might just have a random picture."

"Okay, I'm calling," Sabrina said.

At Jonathan's request, she called on the landline while keeping the burner phone line open so he could hear her end of the conversation with Meyer.

"Hi, Detective Meyer, I got the picture," she said. "The helmet—I can't see."

She asked him where the photo was taken and he said it was from a gas station at Four Corners. He asked her to look at the photo and think hard if she recognized the suspect. "Okay, okay, I'll do my best. Thank you." She got back on the burner phone with Jonathan.

"It was just so weird," she said.

"Is it at the streets or at the pumps?" asked Jonathan.

"Driving behind a car. It's so weird."

She said the man appeared to be wearing long red socks and had a black backpack. He also wore a single black glove.

"If he went inside, they should be able to have the inside footage, too," Jonathan said. "They should have a license plate, right?"

"It's from the side," said Sabrina. "It's so weird."

She read Meyer's text again out loud.

Jonathan remained puzzled over why Meyer thought this motorcyclist was the same one seen leaving the crime scene. "I wonder what leads him to believe this is him."

"That's what I'm wondering," said Sabrina.

"I'm pretty sure he knows a whole lot of other stuff," said Jonathan. "He's just trying to bait you a little bit at a time to see what happens."

"Gosh, this is just a nightmare, all the way around."

"One thing on top of the next."

"Yeah, right. I feel sick," she said.

Much of Jonathan's words were scrambled and then he said, "Clearly, I see they want to look into me. Clearly, they want to look into us."

As Jonathan began praying, "Please, God, please God, help us, help me to be strong," Sabrina said, "I hate this."

"I don't like it, either," he said. He then spoke of how no matter what happened, they could still spend eternity together. "This short life will dissipate."

"Yeah," she said.

"Our story is out there, within a week, our story is going to be out there," he said. "Rob and lifestyle, the whole thing."

"Yeah, it's just so creepy."

In discussing their next moves with Det. Meyer, Jonathan said, "I almost feel like it would best to say, 'Hey, could I schedule a time to talk to you.' "

"Me?" asked Sabrina. "You think I should?"

"What do you think?"

"I don't know," she said. "If I'm going to go there—and say what?"

He suggested she say: "Hey, Detective Meyer, this whole thing is kind of tripping me out."

"No, I think that sounds suspicious," said Sabrina.

Jonathan then speculated that Meyer was calling her at night, after the children went to bed, to catch her at a vulnerable time, to keep her up late with worry that would cost her sleep and make her lose her wits.

"I just think he should know not to bother you tonight," said Jonathan.

"I just won't respond to him."

"Just say it's stressful for you," said Jonathan. "I want you to be able to have sleep."

"I'm tired," she said, "and you need to get some rest as well."

"I will," he said. "Sleep, pray, sleep, pray. I would say: Don't respond to Detective Meyer no matter what."

"Gosh, I just think about the kids, you know."

They again said they loved each other and Jonathan prayed his most desperate prayer to date: "Oh, God, we are on our faces. We have nothing left but you. God, we want to think of all these ways that our story works and think of all the ways our reputation can be saved. God, please help us to trust in you, not to fear the detective, not fear our parents." He ended by pleading, "Help us to not be destroyed."

Sabrina greeted the next morning, Tuesday, Nov. 18,

with a 6 a.m. wakeup call from Jonathan.

"Good morning," she said, but there was nothing good about it. "I hate all this." She did not call or text back Meyer overnight and he had not yet reached out to her again. "I'll call him this morning," she said. "That would be weird if I didn't."

"I suppose," said Jonathan. "Just try to feel him out."

"There's no feeling him out," said Sabrina.

"He has something on his mind."

"It's obvious. I don't know why he's doing that video. It's weird. It's random."

Their pressing question: How had Meyer linked the man in the gas station an hour away from Tehachapi with the anonymous tip of a tall, skinny white male. The tip said nothing of the man driving a motorcycle. All they could conclude was that somebody was trying to frame them.

"I've watched the investigator shows," said Sabrina. "I think that people go to jail that didn't do it."

"If I did go to jail for a series of unfortunate circumstances and events, that happens all that time," said Jonathan. "It makes me sick to think of the whole thing and in custody and sitting in court and having our relationship—but if that's what it takes for God to spank us and become humble servants of him."

"It doesn't add up."

Jonathan snuck in a quick prayer. "Do something unbelievable for us," he asked God. "Do a miracle for us."

"Amen," said Sabrina.

Jonathan asked her what time she was thinking of calling Meyer.

"I was going to say the earlier, the better," she said.

"I think they're trying to say it's me and try to get information from you and jerk you around."

"When I talk to the detective, I'll ask: 'Who's your guy?' "

"They should know by now."

Later that morning, Jonathan called Sabrina from the firehouse.

"They're down here," he said. "I just happened to notice: a car out of place."

"How do you know?"

"It was obvious there was a cop posted at a corner. He perked up when he saw me the whole time."

He spoke in rapid, clipped tones, fear and a touch of defeatism in his voice.

"It's not even a question for me," Jonathan said. "I just want to be realistic. It'll probably be sooner rather than later, so that you know, I would appreciate your prayers, and I'm going to keep praying. That's all we can do."

"Oh, my gosh, this feels so unreal. It feels so unreal. Oh, Jonathan, I'll pray."

She told him that she'd called Meyer, but he had not called her back.

"I'm sure he's got his attention more on me right now," said Jonathan, his voice taking on a sarcastic tone. "It's okay. It's part of the process. I'm going to just probably—for me, I already see what's going on—I talked to some lawyers this morning."

"You did?"

"No, I will," he said, and then told her he had to hang up and would call her back.

While waiting to hear from Jonathan, Sabrina got a text from Meyer:

"Good morning, Sabrina, sorry I was up late last night. I took this video from the video I recovered last night. It's a lot better in person. Does this person look familiar to you? This is our suspect."

Attached was a short video clip of a man on a motorcycle getting gas.

Meyer texted: "OK does this look like one of the Jon's

you were telling me about last night? We are going to release to our and your media market and see if we get any more tips."

Jonathan called her back. He was in a frenzy. "They" have been everywhere, he told her, watching their every move, listening to their every word. "They hung us up, apparently," he said.

"I can't imagine the phone line being tapped," Sabrina said.

"I'm betting it is. I'm pretty sure, if they're surveilling us, I'm sure they're listening in and all that, too."

"Oh, gosh, no wonder they think that."

"Yeah."

Jonathan now reminded Sabrina that he wasn't the only one facing big trouble; she, too, was at risk.

"Oh, my gosh," she said.

"Are you okay? I don't want you to be stressed."

"I feel God, I feel God with me," she said. "I still feel His purpose. I'm not understanding why I need the punishment."

"Sometimes punishment is hard to understand," said Jonathan. "It's justified, though. I feel it is."

"Yeah."

"I deserve a good spanking," he said.

"I do, too," Sabrina said. Then she sighed. "My kids."

They strategized. Jonathan coached her on what to tell Meyer if he identifies Jonathan Hearn as the suspect and asks if she knows who he is.

Jonathan said, "I do want you to be honest and tell him and say, 'Yes, I absolutely know who that is, and I know him well, and I guarantee he's not the one. I guarantee it.' "

"Okay," said Sabrina.

"If they went any further: 'So how do you know him? A friend, or whatever?' I don't know at that point."

Jonathan said he was planning to talk to a lawyer.

"Are you saying I'd better?" asked Sabrina.

"I have always felt, even right now, I feel weird looking for a lawyer," he said. "It's the weirdest thing. I've always assumed that only guilty people get lawyers, and now I'm suddenly realizing that the system, the well-funded government system, is against you and me right now."

"Yeah."

"And they are sitting down there watching me. They're listening to this conversation. They're trying to put together a case, go through all this work, just to tell a story and paint us in a bad light and put us in jail. That's all they want."

"They want the wife," said Sabrina. "That's so crazy. I can't even believe it. I've only watched it on TV."

"I'll be honest, because I'm kind of bummed because I bought that property."

"Money isn't—"

"—I'm just a little worried because I want to give you the best protection possible and I want someone who is good advocate who understands what they're doing—"

"Oh, my gosh, yeah."

"—and describe that for a jury—"

Sabrina asked: "Where are you right now?

"Sitting outside the fire station."

"Your job," she gasped. "Oh, my gosh."

"Sabrina, you remember right after probation I was talking about quitting. In a heartbeat, I would start from scratch or become a contractor or a developer or a missionary or whatever God needs me to be. I don't want only to do what I wanted to do all along. I would really rather be simple and poor and come home to you every night and be missionaries for Him."

"We can't be convicted for having an affair?" she asked.

"No, a lot of people have affairs all the time, and this is another one, this is one where apparently God has other plans for us. It sucks. It sucks. It's in God's hands."

The more Jonathan talked, the more intense his voice became. He blasted the justice system as the "injustice system" and prayed that God would find him a good lawyer. Jonathan said he would text the information to Sabrina.

"I want us to be on the same page," he said.

"Yeah, absolutely, thank you."

"I may have to move some money around. I might not have a whole lot of liquid funds," said Jonathan. "I hate to do this. I hate to ask this: If you think there's a couple of thousand, if I can have a little of yours."

"Absolutely, of course."

"I don't know how much you have, or if you have much."

"I have life insurance."

She had recently deposited a check for more than $300,000, the payout on Robert's life insurance.

"I appreciate that," said Jonathan. "That's a big relief for me. There's a lot of sleazy lawyers out there. We do have a story and I want it to be well represented. I love you so much."

"I love you, too," she said. "I have to go. Be safe."

They had one more phone conversation that morning. It ended the way so many others had.

"I love you, Sabrina."

"I love you, too, Jonathan."

13.

Late in the morning of Tuesday, Nov. 18, 2014, Jonathan Hearn was arrested at the Redlands Fire Department station. Offering no resistance, he was handcuffed and placed in a patrol car and driven 85 miles to a town on the western edge of the Mojave Desert. The substation in Boron, Calif., home to the world's largest open-pit mine for the cleaning supply ingredient Borax, is the closest Kern County sheriff's facility to Redlands.

The arrest came at the peak of Jonathan's paranoia, but any déjà vu he may have experienced was not a figment of his imagination. The burly crew-cut deputy who snapped the cuffs on him was Sean Mountjoy, part of the rotating surveillance detail on Jonathan and Sabrina. Days earlier, Mountjoy sat at the next table at Round Table Pizza watching the pair cuddle and kiss.

At the same time, deputies David Hubbard and Darin Grantham went to another address in Hesperia, where they spoke with Jonathan's sister, Emily. She didn't appear surprised to see them. Jonathan had called her that morning, saying he might be arrested for Robert Limon's murder. Jonathan said he was being looked at as a suspect and that detectives may have photographed him. He gave her the name of an attorney and asked her to contact him if anything happened.

The police report makes no reference of Emily calling that lawyer when the deputies arrived. They asked if she were willing to answer questions. She said she was, painting a portrait of her brother at odds with the horrible crime police believe he committed.

The second eldest of six children, Jonathan grew up in a devoutly Christian household in Hesperia. The children—Jonathan had an older sister; Emily was 3½ years younger—were homeschooled by their mother, Carol, through the Arrow Christian Academy. The administrator for the faith-based school was their father, Mike, who also operated a construction company. The family had a number of pets including a crow named Napoleon, another bird named Scooby, a mutt named Buffy and a rescue dog named Sadie.

Jonathan excelled at school; he finished his high school studies by his mother while simultaneously attending a regular junior college, taking classes in construction technology and firefighting. After the young Explorers program, he became a part-time paramedic, then full-time firefighter.

Smart and friendly, Jonathan was no ladies' man, but he wasn't the naive, sheltered young man Jason Bernatene had made him out to be. "I wouldn't say specifically he had any kind of long-term girlfriends," Emily would later testify in court, repeating and expanding upon what she told police, "but there were definitely women he hung out with for extended periods of time. He did dating things with them, but did not call any of them girlfriends."

The deputies asked if Emily were aware of a relationship between her brother and Sabrina Limon. She said it was her understanding that Jonathan met Sabrina about two or three years earlier at a party also attended by Sabrina's friends Jason and Kelly. Jonathan and Sabrina also saw each other at Costco while he was shopping there for the fire station. Emily said she didn't know when they exchanged phone numbers, but that they eventually did, and at some point, Jonathan and Sabrina met away from Costco. Everything she knew about this came from Jonathan.

"Usually, it was just light conversation in passing about how he knew Sabrina," Emily would say in court. "He would just reference her, never in specifics. They were not spending much time together, but I knew they were close. I knew that she was married and had kids, just details of her situation a little bit, what he was hearing from her and saying to me—her home life maybe not being as grandiose as maybe people viewed it to be, that maybe there were some abuses going on."

Emily was under the impression that whatever Jonathan had going with Sabrina ended around March 2013. Sabrina's husband, Robert, had apparently found out about the relationship and locked Sabrina's phone to prevent her from getting Jonathan's calls. Jonathan apologized to him and, Emily believed, had even deleted Sabrina's number from his cell phone. The detectives asked if Emily would be surprised to hear that this didn't stop Jonathan from communicating with Sabrina; Emily said it would not.

Emily recalled that in late August, she and Jonathan went to Costco in Victorville. "I was caring for my grandmother at the time," she would say in court. The grandmother had suffered a stroke that left her paralyzed. Emily's mother came by to give Emily a break and allow her to run some errands. "And Jonathan mentioned wanting to stop by Costco.

"We went and there was a gal who was the head of the ladies who give out samples, I said, 'Where's Sabrina?' "

When the supervisor told them Sabrina was taking time off because her husband had been murdered about two weeks earlier, Jonathan began "freaking out," according to Emily. Asked by the deputies if she thought her brother's reaction seemed genuine, she said that it did. She would say he "acted very surprised and very kind of shook. He's a very levelheaded and calm person. He kind of had a tremor in his voice and was just very visibly shaking and acting very shocked."

After this, Jonathan would visit Sabrina at Costco and they resumed phone calls and texting, usually when Jonathan was at work at the fire station, according to Emily. Soon, Jonathan visited Sabrina at her home, taking Emily with him.

"I work as a florist and made her a large bouquet. We had talked after Robert had died. I took her a bouquet of flowers and spent the evening there with her family at her home." Sabrina's parents came by and Jonathan made them all dinner. At one point, Sabrina's sister, Julie, popped in to give Emily some shoes she didn't want anymore.

Thus began a friendship between Emily and Sabrina. Emily accompanied her brother on visits to Sabrina's house, where they'd have dinner, play with the children and Emily and Sabrina would talk. "One night went to probably three or four in the morning," said Emily. "We finished dinner and were talking and getting the kids to bed and stuff. We were going to a church that she had attended with her family the next day. We just spent the night on her couches."

This was the only time to Emily's knowledge that Jonathan ever overnighted with Sabrina. Emily never saw them get any more affectionate than Jonathan once sitting on the sofa with an arm around her. "But the kids were sitting there as well," she said. While Emily didn't think her brother and Sabrina had become a couple in the weeks after Robert's murder, "I knew it was transitioning towards that." It was happening fast, she knew, but not too fast. "I thought at the time he was trying to fill a void in the children's life and be there to financially and emotionally support the family, do fun things and keep their minds off of it."

The "it," of course, was Robert's murder, and Emily believed that Jonathan reacted appropriately. Robert's death came at the same time their grandmother had a stroke and ultimately died. The events seemed to mature Jonathan. "I accounted (the changes in him) to understanding the gravity of life and how it can be taken so quickly," she said. "The whole mindset of the whole family was a little more grave at that time."

Asked if Sabrina ever talked about her husband's murder, Emily said she didn't say much, but did mention how much she missed him. Sabrina had photographs of him around the house.

"I remember that night I spent at her house on the couch, we were getting ready the next morning," Emily would later recall. "I was sitting on her sink, watching her put on her makeup. She teared up a little bit. She said, 'I think the best is yet to come.' I think that she genuinely wanted to move on from what had happened. I wished the same thing for her as well. If we were going to be part of that process as a family, that would be just wonderful."

If Jonathan wasted little time with Sabrina, that was because he came to realize how precious time was, Emily believed. "At the time, I was not fazed at the speed at which it was occurring," she said. "I fell in love with the family so much as well. I think because I was in the middle of it, I didn't think it was moving incredibly rapidly." Emily admired Sabrina's warmth, openness and affection toward everybody. In quick time, they had become confidantes.

"She was talking about kind of getting wasted a little bit and how that would happen on a regular basis and that there were liberties taken with some of their friends and getting a little too loose," said Emily, who would let Sabrina talk and not push for details. "It wasn't that she didn't love him. It was maybe she didn't care for him as much as people thought she did." And so, being trapped in what Emily suspected was a "loveless marriage," for Sabrina, "it didn't seem strange to me that she would move on so quickly."

Emily considered her brother a "strong male figure" and "the kindest man that I know," attentive to Sabrina's needs and welcoming to her children. "I thought anyone would fall in love with that," she said.

And, she believed, that's what was happening with Sabrina.

Deputy Hubbard told Emily that Sabrina had been talking to Jonathan on a pay-as-you-go cell phone since March 2014, and that they had communicated the day of the murder and every day since. Hubbard asked if that would change Emily's perception of their relationship. She acknowledged it seemed weird.

Hubbard asked Emily if Jonathan owned any guns. She said he had a long gun and a couple of pistols, but she didn't know anything else about the weapons other than the guns were kept either at his home or under the front seat of his truck. The deputy also asked Emily if her brother drove a motorcycle. She said he had a black motorcycle without much chrome. He then showed still photos from the surveillance video of the motorcycle rider near the murder scene. Emily said the motorcycle in one picture looked similar to Jonathan's. So was the helmet. But she didn't think Jonathan's motorcycle had chrome exhaust pipes like the one in the picture, and the silver gas tank didn't look right, either. As for the rider, she said the photo quality was too poor to say one way or the other whether it was her brother.

Hubbard next showed her a photo from video surveillance from the Pilot station at Four Corners. Emily said that motorcycle looked similar, but that the rider appeared to be slouching. Her brother always sits upright, she said. A photo from the surveillance camera inside the mini-mart captured a man who she said had the same pointy nose as Jonathan's, but looked more muscular than her brother. "It could be him," she said. She couldn't be certain either way.

Hubbard asked if she were familiar with the biblical story of David and Bathsheba. She said she was quite familiar with it—their father had taught them the story when they were kids—but thought it would be "very weird" for Jonathan and Sabrina to be talking about it.

Asked if she thought her brother were capable of murdering Robert Limon, Emily said he was physically and mentally capable, but did not think he was "humanly" capable. Still, she acknowledged that because her brother had arson investigator training, he would know loopholes to investigations.

When Grantham and Hubbard next spoke to Jonathan's

mother, Carol Hearn, they continued to get full cooperation. Grantham began by asking her if she knew Sabrina Limon. She said about a year earlier, her son began hanging around a woman who worked at Costco. Jonathan told his mother that he felt badly about his time with her. "He was going to be speaking to a woman's husband about being too close to the wife," Carol said. "There was a husband he was going to be saying sorry to."

Jonathan didn't reveal the woman's name at the time. As he was getting up the nerve to make the call, he asked his mother to pray for him. Carol could pinpoint the exact day she talked to Jonathan; she had written it down in her prayer journal: April 9, 2013.

It was Carol's understanding that the husband told him to never call his wife again and that the husband blocked Sabrina's phone from getting calls from Hearn.

One day—Carol couldn't remember the exact date—Jonathan and his sister went to Costco and when they returned, her son had a face Carol described as "morbid." Jonathan told his mother that another employee had explained that Sabrina's husband had been murdered. Carol looked up a news story about it online, and her husband said that Jonathan's relationship with Sabrina might make him a suspect.

Still, Carol felt her son was genuinely trying to figure out who murdered Robert and speculated he might have been killed while interrupting a robbery, the same theory floated to the media by the sheriff's spokesman.

Asked by Grantham if she saw a recent change in her son's demeanor, Carol could only recall one instance when he made a disrespectful comment to her, which was out of character. She said that her son was not a vengeful person and if he committed the crime, it would be out of character.

Hubbard told her that Jonathan and Sabrina had discussed the story of David and Bathsheba. Carol was familiar with the story and agreed that it looked suspicious.

In fact, she didn't know they were talking at all. It was her understanding that after her son had apologized to Robert Limon, he had stopped all contact with Sabrina.

Grantham revealed how Jonathan and Sabrina were in constant and frequent communication via cell phone before Limon's death, the day of the death and every day afterward. The mother said she felt her son had violated her trust and that she had no idea that he was still in touch with Sabrina. Asked if she thought that was suspicious, she said, "Yeah."

Shown the same surveillance photos, Carol looked at the photo of the person on a motorcycle for a long time. Asked if there was anything about that photo that she could definitely say was or wasn't her son, she went silent and never answered. The deputies noted the person in the photo had a backpack. Carol said her son did carry a pack, but she also thought the man in the minimart photo was more muscular than her son and said that she did not recognize the shirt. She gave the detectives 10 pictures of her son riding a motorcycle.

The detectives then spoke to Jonathan's father, Mike Hearn, who learned of his son's arrest from Jonathan's boss. Mike offered the opinion that if his son were fraternizing with a married woman whose husband was found dead, then his son should logically be the number one suspect.

Still, he couldn't imagine Jonathan committing such a crime. He knew that Jonathan and other family members, including his mother and siblings, had been on an "outing" with Sabrina after Jonathan introduced them at Costco. Mike Hearn believed, however, that Jonathan was having an "emotional relationship" with Sabrina, though it seemed close enough to be classified as an affair. He also knew about Jonathan apologizing to Sabrina's husband and vowing not to see her again, and about a friend of the husband's, Jason Bernatene—though he didn't know the name—refusing to accept Jonathan's apology for getting close to Sabrina.

Mike Hearn said his son owned a .22 caliber rifle and

various handguns and drove a black Yamaha motorcycle with the word "Forgiven" stenciled on the gas tank. Jonathan wore a black matte helmet that looked like it came from a German World War II soldier. Shown surveillance photos of the suspect on a motorcycle, Mike Hearn acknowledged the rider could look like his son—the helmet and backpack also looked right—but he couldn't be sure.

"It could be him," he said, though he never really paid that much attention to the way his son rode his motorcycle.

As far as Mike Hearn knew, his son never had a long-term girlfriend. But Mike Hearn did notice a change in Jonathan lately: he'd started going to a new church and become more "evangelical." Asked if Jonathan ever mentioned the David and Bathsheba story, Mike said no but that he—Mike—had taught it to his children many times when they were growing up. If Jonathan had mentioned it recently, that would strike Mike Hearn as very curious, he said.

Taken together, these were extraordinarily candid interviews, considering the severity of Jonathan's plight. He was staring down a first-degree murder charge, possibly one carrying the death penalty. Emily later explained that their reaction stemmed from their Christian beliefs.

"I don't know if they were taken aback by our family's response," Emily later said in court. "While we were very shaken by what we were hearing, I don't think that we ever said, 'This could never be. He never could have done this.' From the very beginning, we said all humans are capable of very egregious offenses."

The detectives asked if the family had any other questions; they did not. The investigators handed out business cards and left.

After Jonathan was hauled off from Redlands, Deputy Brandon Rutledge, one of the investigators who had been monitoring Sabrina and Jonathan's phone calls, executed a search warrant at the fire station. The deputy retrieved a black Swiss Gear backpack from Jonathan's work locker. In the center console of Jonathan's truck, he seized a Glock handgun, several different kinds of .45 caliber ammunition, and $2,400 in cash.

Later that night, a small army of investigators and evidence techs converged on Jonathan's home in Hesperia to serve a search warrant. It was a converted garage behind his grandfather's house on Lime Street. Deputy Kenzo Lackey led the contingent of five deputies, two sergeants and an evidence technician. The front door opened to a living room and small kitchen. On the sofa, Lackey pulled a white envelope from a cardboard box. The envelope contained a handwritten note to Jonathan reading, "Thanks for the rent—you are paid through OCT31, 2014." Several months of receipts for previous rent payments were attached. On the kitchen counter was a black glove.

In the bedroom, a dirty clothes hamper contained a black tank top and brown shorts. As the shorts from the hamper were lifted, a handwritten note fell from the left front pocket. Next to the hamper was a black backpack. A brown Ruger 10-22 rifle leaned against the wall. Lackey found the ammunition magazine full, but the chamber was empty. He removed the bullets.

On the top shelf of the closet, Lackey found a black motorcycle helmet, inside of which were a pair of black gloves and a bandana. In a box beneath the helmet, he found a greeting card and handwritten note. The closet also had three sets of black boots on the top shelf and other shoes.

Beneath a decorative sewing table next to a dresser, Lackey found a black Glock handgun case that contained a silver and grey Taurus .45 caliber-pistol, loaded with six rounds of ammunition; again, the chamber was not loaded. Another black backpack next to the sewing table held shooting glasses, a gun lock, gun cleaning equipment and a box of 40 .45-caliber Ranger bullets. Nearby were two more boxes of eight empty .45 caliber magazines and four boxes of .45-caliber ammunition.

On a shelf on the east wall of the bedroom, next to the sewing machine, a decorative cardboard box with a yellow ribbon held more cards, letters and handwritten notes.

Deputies also found in the bedroom a Salvation Army receipt for two shirts, one pair of jeans and one pair of shoes. It was dated Aug. 6, 2014.

On a shelf sat a framed photo of Sabrina Limon's children.

The other side of the wall was the rest of the garage, left in its original state. Used for storage, it had boxes piled to the ceiling. There were appliances and tools. In a white box, deputies found syringes and medication that would turn out to be the kind of steroids used by weightlifters and athletes to bulk up muscle.

And parked in the garage was a black Yamaha motorcycle.

All the evidence was logged, photographed and seized. The letters and notes would be read later.

After four and a half hours, the search was deemed complete. Deputies left a copy of the warrant in the house and headed with bags of evidence for sheriff's headquarters in Oildale.

About the same time his home was being searched, Jonathan sat in an interview room at the Boron substation. Deputy Juan Trevino introduced himself, told him he had some questions, and then read Jonathan his Miranda rights. When asked if he understood these rights, Jonathan said, "Yes."

Asked if he knew why he was there, he said it was because police thought he killed Robert Limon. Trevino asked him what he had to say about that.

"A lot," he answered.

Then he said he wanted a lawyer. The interview ended. At 3:26 p.m., he was formally placed under arrest. Deputy

Sean Mountjoy put him in the back seat of a patrol car and turned on his digital recorder.

During the drive, Jonathan told him: "I could have guessed this was coming."

14.

After arresting Jonathan, Deputy Mountjoy headed north up the Cajon Pass to Silver Lakes. He went to an elementary school and tracked down Sabrina Limon. It was 11 a.m. and she was there for a conference with a teacher. He led her to a quiet area and secretly turned on his digital recorder. He told her she was going to be detained and asked her to make arrangements for somebody to watch her children.

"Your shirt," she said to him. Mountjoy was wearing a Los Angeles County Fire Department shirt. He told her that one of his friends worked for the department and she said she knew some firefighters there. She gave him a name and Mountjoy asked if he was an engineer.

"No, just a fireman," she said, and paused. "So is Jonathan."

They spoke for a few more minutes. "I know there's no way Jonathan could have done this. There's no way," she said. She kept repeating "no way."

Mountjoy said he couldn't discuss the case. Sabrina sighed. "Oh, I cannot believe this is happening and I just can't," she said. Then she added, "I had a feeling it was possibly coming."

Mountjoy handcuffed her and put her in a patrol car headed for the same substation in Boron as Jonathan.

More conversation followed in the patrol car, and Sabrina said, "Gosh, I just thought this was railroad related, you know. Someone took a laptop in the office. I just swore it had to be somebody with the railroad." She then mumbled something. Mountjoy asked her what she said. "They can't book me on that, can they?"

He asked her what she was referring to.

"Having an affair," she said.

Mountjoy told her that he was unaware of any legal statutes that would allow him to detain her for having an affair.

"God's spanking me right now, for sure I feel it," she said. "And I deserve it."

Shortly before they got to Boron, Sabrina said she didn't want Det. Meyer mad at her.

At the substation, Sabrina was placed in a different interview room, small and airless. The door had to be kept open for ventilation. The same Deputy Rutledge who had searched Jonathan's locker and truck came into the room with a second deputy named Juan Trevino.

It was Rutledge who would do most of the talking. He began by explaining what Sabrina's legal status was. "You are detained, but you're not under arrest. I want to make that perfectly clear."

The statement would strike almost anybody who was not a criminal defense lawyer as perfectly unclear. The only clarification Rutledge offered was that since she was being detained in a sheriff's facility, he had to read her her rights. Sabrina listened as she was told she had the right to say nothing and to have a lawyer. She said she understood those rights.

"My sergeant wants to have a quick word with you before we get started," Rutledge said.

Sgt. Avery Simpson, Rutledge's boss and the head of the robbery homicide division, entered the room. Before he said anything, Sabrina asked, "Is this your station?"

"No, I'm out of Bakersfield."

"So you're with Detective Meyer and all them?"

"Yes," he said.

End of chitchat.

"This is your one opportunity, for your kids, to tell the

truth," he warned her. "These guys are willing to be patient with you, but they're not going to put up with any more lies. You're going to tell them the complete truth. This is a capital murder case, which comes with the death penalty. Prove to us how important your kids are to you."

"Absolutely," she said. "I understand."

"Okay," Rutledge then said, "do you understand what my boss said?"

"My kids are so important to me. I love them so much," said Sabrina, her voice breaking. She told him that Robbie had to stay home the day before with a stomachache, but was able to go to school with his sister today.

"Hanging in there?" he asked.

"They're actually doing good, as good as can be."

"I am sorry for what happened to Robert. From everything we know, he was a great guy. I know Detective Meyer has told you some things. We've gotten some pretty good leads as of late. We keep hearing stuff about this guy named Jonathan. What do you know about him?"

"A lot," she said. "There is a Jonathan."

"Okay."

"And I had had a relationship with him."

"Okay."

"Like an on-and-off thing. And so as far as that goes, and Detective Meyer had sent me a video, and I don't recognize who's in this video. Where the Jon comes from, like Jon? I honestly don't know."

"Let's talk more about Jonathan. What's his last name?"

"Hearn."

"And you said you've seen him on-and-off for how long?"

"Over a year."

"Did Rob ever know about this relationship?"

"He did a little bit, and then that's when we called it off. It wasn't anything. I just talked to him."

"So you're not talking to Jonathan anymore?"

"No, he's been around now, since he found out this has happened."

"Let's go back to the very beginning. When did you start seeing Jonathan?"

"Oh, gosh, I had just talked with him a lot on the phone, seeing him after work a little bit, nothing like crazy, like a year. And then I started talking to him more."

"Did you develop feelings for him?"

"Yeah," she said. "My biggest thing was I didn't want this to come out because of our family, because of disrespecting Robert, our marriage, because we had a good marriage. It was like an open kind of relationship we experienced. It's not anything that I'm proud of. I feel a lot of it very heavy, now that he's gone. I'm just being honest with you. I feel like that's my thing here. But I know there's no way that Jonathan's the one who murdered Robert. There's just no way. I know him very well."

"I'm kind of curious, how well? You said you cut it off. Do you remember what time you guys cut it off, the relationship?"

After a pause, she said, "April."

"April of this year?"

"I seriously don't remember."

"Several months ago? Rob passed away obviously this year. Several months before that you cut it off?"

"Well," Sabrina said, "I started talking to him again."

"When did you start talking to Jonathan again?"

"I don't remember. I'll have to think about it. I saw him again at work. In June."

"You were at his work?"

"No, I was at my work at Costco."

"And you ran into him at work. You're saying that your conversation with him was just casual? You see him out and just talked?"

"We talked on the phone."

"How regularly did you talk to him?"

"I talked to him quite a bit."

"Going how far back?"

"To June."

"So June you started talking to him again. Did you see him ever?"

"I see him after working."

"How were you able to hide this from Rob?"

"He worked a lot and he was distracted by other things. We've had open—we've had other things prior years ago. We kind of let him know that I felt like he was somewhere else, you know."

"Emotionally?"

"Emotionally somewhere else. But we were still best friends. We got along. We didn't fight. We really didn't fight."

Deputy Trevino now spoke for the first time. He read off a phone number with a 760 prefix.

"That's your number, correct?" he asked.

"Correct."

Rutledge asked, "You talked to Jonathan on that line?"

"Yes."

"Going back to June, you say?" asked Rutledge.

Trevino jumped in. It was becoming apparent he was going to be the bad cop to Rutledge's good.

"Well, Sabrina," he said. "I've got my records right here. Last time you talked to him on this phone was March 8 at 2:13 in the afternoon, a call that lasted 188 seconds. So you're continuing to talk to him, how are you able to talk to him?"

"I have another phone," she said.

"So you have another phone?" asked Trevino. "What's that number?"

"I don't know that, either. It's just, like, our phone that we used to talk."

"Did you talk to anybody else on it?" asked Rutledge.

"No."

"So that phone was exclusively for Jonathan?" asked Rutledge.

"Yes."

Trevino said, "When did you get that phone? And you don't know the number? Really?"

"I promise you, I've never called."

Rutledge asked: "Where's the phone now?"

"It's at home in my drawer."

"Did Rob know you had this phone?" asked Rutledge.

"No."

"Did you see what he did just there?" said Rutledge. "Have you seen where this is going? Do you understand the gravity of it?"

Trevino said, "I think you're hoping we're kind of Mickey Mousing this around, kind of throwing you some information and hunting for something."

"I—"

"Let me say something," Trevino interrupted. "We are not here to play games. Your husband was killed."

"I know that."

"Cold-blooded."

"I understand that."

"And you have been less than honest with us," Trevino said. "And I have a hard time believing that you haven't cooperated with us to conceal an affair. Call me silly. You were asked if you had an extramarital affair on two separate occasions and you said no. We asked about Jonathan, and *now* you're telling us about Jonathan Hearn?"

"I wanted to be honest with you," Sabrina said. "Here's the deal. I realize what happened to Robert. I can't believe that Robert was murdered. I can't wrap my mind around it. I know: There's no way it was tied into our personal life. My personal life."

"Your personal life with Jonathan?" asked Trevino. "Your affair has nothing to do with this?"

"Yes, that's how I felt," said Sabrina. "I could not

believe it, could not believe how random this was, you know. I still cannot believe that this has happened to Rob. I still cannot wrap my mind around the fact that Robert was murdered. And it has nothing to do with our personal life and our marriage. I didn't not want to tell Detective Meyer about relationships."

Rutledge asked: "Did you think Detective Meyer would find out?"

"I figured that it was a discussion I would have with him if he asked me about it, but I wasn't going to put forth information."

Trevino said: "He did ask about it when you came to our office last week."

"This is a personal, private matter that has nothing to do with—"

"And you don't think an affair, as a cop looking into it, as a motive." Trevino said it as a statement, not a question.

"I can see where a cop would look into it."

Rutledge said, "You've been lying to us since Rob passed away and we get a secret tip this man Jonathan is involved, then find out you've been in a relationship with Jonathan Hearn since about a year."

"But I know that Jonathan—I have talked to him about this."

"What does he say?" asked Rutledge.

"He can't believe it, either. We just felt like—I know this is going to sound so horrible—but I felt like there's a purpose, the way Robert and I have been living, a little bit wild, you know. I have to be a mom now without Robert. And I have to get right.

"I agree with you," said Rutledge.

"And I love my kids and I love Robert so much. I understand you've been hearing myself saying all of these things. It is what it is. Obviously, you guys already knew something. You brought me in here. So I might as well be honest with you about my personal life."

"I think you should start being a little more honest with us, I agree," said Rutledge.

"That's the truth right there. I can understand a detective's point. I get that. But there is no way. I figured this was tied in with the railroad."

Trevino said: "I don't like dealing in absolutes, like you're sitting here trying to convince me there's absolutely no way Jonathan had anything to do with this. How do you know that?"

"Well, I know him well."

"How well do you know him?" asked Trevino.

"I know him well. That's why I've just been so sick. I feel like there's no way."

"What's the status of your relationship right now?"

"He's come around."

"What does that mean?" asked Trevino.

"He's come around quite a bit, you know."

"Are you in a relationship right now?"

"Not dating."

"Is he stronger than a friend? Do you love him?"

"I care about him very, very much."

"Do you tell him you love him?"

"Yeah."

"So you do love him? Why are you lying to us right now?"

"Because it's a personal thing. I feel like I have to live with this the rest of my life that I was in a relationship when Robert got murdered, that's why, and I cannot believe that Rob got murdered. I can't believe he's gone. I can't believe the father of my children is gone. I can't believe that the man that so many people loved—"

"That's what we hear," said Trevino. "He was loved. It's tragic."

"I can't believe that he was gone."

Rutledge reminded her that Sgt. Simpson had told her it was time to start thinking about her children's best interests.

"Look at all the pages in there," Rutledge said, pointing to the binder. "You think those are blank sheets of paper? Because they are not. We're not going to sit here and give you a piece of evidence. We're not going to play any games. This is not good cop/bad cop. We're not going to try to do a ruse on you. There's nothing secret. What we're offering you is an opportunity, an opportunity for you to do the right thing for yourself and for your family. Only one Sabrina has a future here. You understand that. You need to choose right now. This is it. My sergeant said this is your one and only chance to come clean. You're not being honest with us. I know this. You're not being honest with us. It's time for you, Sabrina, to make a decision of what road do you want to go down."

Rutledge was now nearly whispering: "Don't say anything right now. Take a moment."

"I just felt like God's plan," she said. "I can't believe this happened to him."

"I realize you're in disbelief," said Rutledge. "It was tragic. It's very sad for such a good person to die. You're saying it was God's plan for Robert to die?"

"I felt like God had a plan and a purpose. I felt like through this pain, I felt just like... just I'm down on my knees."

"Are you and Jonathan going to be together?"

"No."

"Was it God's purpose for Robert to die? Is that what you're saying?"

"We all die. Whatever plan God has for us. I just felt like I'm living the time I have to live left, raise my children."

"You think Rob wanted to die? You think God planned to have Robbie and Leanna's dad die?"

"No, I feel like it was an act of evil."

"I agree with you there," said Rutledge. "You keep saying it's God's plan. Why?"

"I'm trying to figure that out. I have no idea how he

could be gone. So I have to put my faith in God. That's where I've been."

"Let's go back to that day that Rob died," said Rutledge. "Did you know whether or not he was working alone?"

"I knew."

"What about Jonathan: Did you talk to Jonathan that day?"

"Yes."

"All day?"

"Yes."

"What did you talk to him about?"

"How his day was at work, just kind of the same stuff we always talked about."

She said Jonathan was feeling ill.

"He was ill the day that Robert was killed?" asked Rutledge.

"He was worn out from work."

"At any time did you miss any of his calls?"

"I don't remember. Missed his calls?"

"Did you text him at all that day?"

"Probably, I'm not sure."

"Did you talk to him?"

"I talked to him."

"When you found out about Rob passing, how long after that did you call Jonathan?"

"I don't remember."

"Hours? Days?"

"Days. I was in shock. I can't feel anything."

"How often would you talk to him?"

"Every day. Every other day."

"Several times a day?"

"Not always."

"While Rob was at work?"

"Probably."

"If you didn't contact Jonathan for a few days, did he try to get in touch with you at all?"

"Yeah, I believe so, that whole time."

"How did he take it?"

"He was shocked."

"Those days after, did you keep in touch with him?"

"Not much."

Trevino jumped back in: "Not much? What does that mean?"

She mumbled a response.

"You brought up an issue I need to stay away from, and it's about God," said Trevino. "If you found God, great, but you can't give off that image and sit here and lie to us, look at us right in the face and lie. Since you brought up religion: Thou shalt not lie. I've heard it somewhere before. You're looking at me and you're looking at my partner, and you're lying. If you're saying that days went by and you didn't communicate with him, I can prove without a doubt that you communicated with him. See, you want to give us partial truths."

"There were days I didn't communicate."

"Really?

"That's what it felt like."

Trevino barked: "I can give you the amount of text messages and phone calls that were made prior to, during and after Robert was killed. I do this for a living. I'm not playing games with you."

"I understand."

"Prior, during and after: I can tell you how many times you talked to Jonathan."

The two cops fired off questions.

Rutledge: "How many voice mails did you leave him?"

Trevino: "On *your* burner phone?"

Rutledge: "Isn't that what you call it?

Trevino: "So if you want to keep giving me partial truths, that entryway for you, it's shutting pretty quick. Because I'm trying to catch a killer."

"I want you guys to," Sabrina said.

"No, I don't think you do," said Trevino. "Because you're impeding this investigation. You want to take it one step further? The person I'm going after is the guy you're saying, 'I love you' to every day. So keep giving me partial truths."

"He could not have done that to Robert. There's no way."

Sabrina started to quietly pray.

"Think hard," Rutledge said.

She kept praying.

"Stay with me," said Rutledge. "How did Jonathan Hearn act when you told him Detective Meyer wanted you to go to headquarters?"

"Um—"

" 'Oh, God, please help us.' Remember that?"

"Yeah."

" 'Oh, God, oh, God, please help us.' What was he so worried about? Think, Sabrina, what was he so worried about?"

"He didn't want the affair to go out."

Trevino said, "You want to go to that extent to conceal an affair?"

"I didn't want to tell you guys what was going on."

"You lived a certain lifestyle with Robert," said Trevino. "Okay, I would imagine there are several people out there that know about the lifestyle. And Robert is murdered in cold blood by Jonathan."

"There's no way."

"Fair enough. And now you are afraid, embarrassed, ashamed, whatever, about a lifestyle you lived, when there were two consenting adults that made the choice, and you're trying to convince yourself that that man you said, 'I love you, too,' every single day didn't kill him in cold blood? You can do everything you can to convince yourself, that's your prerogative."

A third man now came into the hot room as Sgt. Simpson

returned. "We know Jonathan Hearn killed Robert Limon," he said. "We know that. We have evidence that will prove that Jonathan Hearn murdered Robert Limon."

"Are you serious?" Sabrina said, starting to cry.

"He is going to prison for the rest of his life. If I wasn't clear to you in the beginning, this is your one chance not to join him. You understand that!"

Simpson was now shouting.

"I understand that," she said. "I can't wrap my brain—"

"We don't believe you!" Simpson yelled. "We know everything. It is your turn to tell the truth. It's time to start from the beginning and tell the truth. We know everything. We're not going to play this case in front of you. It's your turn to tell the truth!"

Sabrina then asked for a lawyer before talking more. The grilling ended.

Deputies drove Sabrina to the jail in Bakersfield. This time it was clear: She was under arrest. She was led into the basement, where she was to be booked—fingerprinted and photographed for a mug shot—when she asked to speak with Det. Meyer.

He was alerted, met Sabrina at the jail and asked if she wanted to talk to him. She said she did. She was taken across town to the sheriff's headquarters. By now, it was the afternoon of Wednesday, Nov. 19. She found herself pressed into the same corner of a same-looking interview room. She was still wearing the designer jeans and white jacket from when she was arrested at her children's school.

Meyer brought her a water bottle and box of tissues. She sipped water as he read her constitutional rights and informed her that he had obtained a search warrant to get a DNA sample, which a technician would take by swabbing the inside her cheek.

"To put me in the system?" Sabrina asked.

"It's just going to be used to eliminate you from the scene," Meyer assured her.

He adopted the same congenial tone from the earlier interview, a stark contrast to the verbal pounding she got in Boron. But he delivered the same serious message.

"So we've had multiple conversations up to this date," he said. "I know that through this investigation, there's been several times that you haven't been honest with me, and we need to get honest right now."

"I'm sorry," Sabrina said.

"I understand," he said. "You were probably upset and scared and didn't know what to say. So. I know a lot of information, and I can't give this information out, obviously, because of the investigation and because I do not want that to be revealed. I know tons of stuff and I want you to tell me the truth. I need the truth. So let's talk about when you started working at Costco."

Costco, Meyer now knew from the Bernatenes and Jonathan's family, is where it all began.

She said she had been working there since November 2012.

"What did you do there?"

"I was a demo girl. With samples."

Meyer said: "I always feel guilty when I grab a sample."

"You have no idea. People come there and eat lunch every day."

"I understand you met Jonathan there. Talk about when you first met."

"He was wearing a firefighter shirt," she said, "and I know other firemen and so, I'm a people person. We start talking, and then he came in there all the time."

"So you guys ended up becoming friendly. When did you meet him?

"I want to say I met him in December of 2012," she said, then added: "I want to be honest. I'm bad with dates, I can't think exactly when I had met him. I had been working there a little while. Maybe in the next year."

"What kind of conversations did you guys have?"

"Just fire department stuff. Like I say, I'm a people person. I would talk to people for hours. Some people come in there just for the demo girls to talk. Just fire department stuff. What's your best call, that kind of thing. Then we just kind of kept talking."

"What other stuff did you guys talk about?"

"Life," she said. She explained how she came to tell him about Jason Bernatene, the party at Beef 'O' Brady's and how Jonathan asked for her phone number.

"I had never gave out my number to a stranger before," she said. "Prior to that, I had mentioned Robert. I always do. That's my protection, especially with other men. I always brought up Robert right away."

This time, she didn't. And she gave Jonathan her number.

"So I had never done that before. I felt bad. And then he called and messaged me. I was like: 'What have I got myself into?'"

That's when she revealed she was married. She hadn't worn her wedding ring at Costco. The store didn't allow it around food.

"He apologized, said, 'I'm so sorry.' I said no problem."

"Do you feel guilty about that?"

"He was sincerely sorry. I felt bad, too. I said: 'No worries, it's all good.' I didn't feel that bad. I talk to a lot of people. Rob and I were open; he was pretty casual with me in our relationship with others."

"How often did he come into the Costco?"

"Quite a bit."

"Once a week? Twice a week?"

"Three times a week," she said.

"He was there obviously to see you, to talk to you. How much did you talk after that?"

"It wasn't a lot in the beginning. Then we started talking a lot more, a lot more, a lot more. We had a relationship."

"How many meetings after work?'

"I would see him just for a short time. A lot of times, he

would come in later and he would end up walking out with me."

"At what point did it become a sexual relationship?"

"A year later?" she said. "I am honestly super bad with time and dates. About eight months later or six months, something like that. It wasn't right away or anything like that."

After an interruption for an evidence tech to swab Sabrina's cheek and take her fingerprints, Meyer asked: "Did you guys have a relationship at your house or a hotel?"

"It was at our house and sometimes wherever."

"And how often would you guys meet up?"

"A couple times a week. Sometimes like once a week."

"Did Rob ever suspect anything?"

"Robert had found my phone," she said. She explained that she and Robert had been out late partying. "And I kind of had too much to drink and I wasn't paying attention to my phone." She paused and sighed. "I hate talking about this. Rob and I just had sex."

That's when he found the phone with Jonathan's messages professing his love for Sabrina.

"He was like: 'Who is this dude?' And he had seen him out once before, met him once"—at the Beef 'O' Brady's party—"so he was just like: 'What's up? How did this go down?' And I just kind of told him, like, I don't know, it just happened."

She apologized to Robert and said Jonathan apologized to Robert.

"I felt bad. And Rob and I just kind of kept going, and Jonathan and I stopped talking." She said she and Robert didn't talk about it afterward. "He didn't like problems."

"When he asked you these questions, did you tell him the truth, or just a little bit?"

"A little bit, not detailed," she said. "Seriously, I don't know how it happened. We were distracted with so many things, friends and partying, and we have had open relationships. So I, like, threw that at him. This was prior—parties and just kind of like a lifestyle. The kids weren't exposed to that firsthand. I was probably drinking too much."

"You talked about your open relationship before, and you told me you didn't have one."

"I didn't want any of this to come out, you know. I was tripping," she said, breaking into tears. "It's shameful. It's terrible. I'm feeling it."

"Did you guys have open relationships and meet people at parties and have sexual encounters?"

"Years ago, there was this couple, and we had never done anything like that. We were new to Silver Lakes. Robbie was in kindergarten. We met with this kooky couple—the chick for sure, the woman. But I am a people person, so is Robert. It was just a crazy experience with her and her husband."

"What are their names?" he asked, and she told them.

"That's when the door opened," she said. "Robert was—I hate to talk about him. I don't want to dishonor him. I feel like this is such a dishonor to him. He was all about it. He was into it. Whatever we had to do. This went on. Oh, my gosh, I never had such troubles. I told Robert: 'We should not get in too deep with these two.' They're divorced now. It was just one of those things. Rob said: 'It's just sexual, Sabrina.'"

"Did he have any other relationship outside the marriage?"

"She was the one. She was the only one that I knew. That's why I was wondering, too," Sabrina said, referring to Meyer's questions in to her in the days after Robert's murder.

"I was honest with you," Meyer said. "I don't know of any other relationships. Did you think it would be okay with Rob that you were seeing Jonathan because you guys had that other relationship?"

"That's how I justified it," she said. "By the end, I just talked to him: We just have to refocus some things. He wasn't all about ending it."

Three months after she and Jonathan stopped talking, she saw him again in Costco and they resumed their relationship.

"What did you learn about Jonathan while you guys were dating?"

"A lot," she said. "I fell in love with him. I learned about lots. He was like someone I never met before, really different from the social group, a smart guy, really Christian. He grew up really religious in a family of six. He was home schooled."

"I'm just finding out the depth," said Meyer. "That's a whole 'nother lifestyle.

Being home schooled, you don't get a lot of exposure. Did you ever think about getting divorced from Rob? Or did Jonathan ever talk to you about the divorce?"

"We had talked about divorce. I would say within the past, let's say, four or five months."

"Did you and Robert ever discuss divorce before?"

"Yes, it was like partying too much, drinking kind of thing, and then Rob, he'd be all good the next day."

"You said Rob didn't drink a whole lot?"

"Not as much as I did. He liked to party, but he would definitely be the one with at least some wits about him."

"What was Jonathan's take on divorce? I know he's very religious. Did he feel it was okay?"

"No, he would say it was not what God wants, but people do it every day kind of thing. I think we kind of played with the thought. He was going to have a house built. He had these plans that were, like, future plans," she said, then revealed: "We had gotten a burner phone to talk on."

"I know," said Meyer.

"I know you guys ripped me up. What do I do?" she said, crying again. "I have to live with that. It freaks me out."

In tears, she explained that Jonathan got the phone and paid for the minutes. She hid the phone in the back of a drawer.

"I knew it was terrible," she said, crying.

"Once this burner phone comes into play, did you feel guilty about having it? Shameful? Anything?"

"There were moments of feeling bad."

She said she had tried to talk to Rob at night about stopping the wild lifestyle. "I was distracted," she said. "But he was distracted, too."

"What was he distracted with?"

"He was distracted with everything. I know he did like to go to websites." She'd later say he looked at lots of online porn. "He was distracted with his phone a lot. People. He worked a lot."

"And you were distracted with Jonathan?"

"I was just living in it. It was just kind of jelling."

"Who introduced the idea of Jonathan meeting up with Rob?"

"Jonathan wanted to meet him. He did tell me and he was going to just apologize to him. And he sincerely felt bad, like he felt bad."

She pulled out a tissue and blew her nose. "I'm sorry," she said.

"I brought those for you," said Meyer. "You can use the whole package if you want. So you said that they never met, right?"

"We had gone out one time. It was just like a huge group of people."

"March Madness," said Meyer, and Sabrina looked at him with shock.

Meyer said: "I know all about it. I know everything about it."

"So you know me?"

"I've lived your life for the last three months."

"Oh, gosh."

"That's why you can't lie to me because I know all the stuff. So it's better to be honest with me."

"You say it so cute," she told him. "The other guys were a little rougher."

"I have a different personality than most. I feel like I know you intimately. I know so much about your life and Rob's life. March Madness at the bar. I actually have a picture of everybody in it, and Jonathan's in the picture. How old is he?"

"Twenty-five." He was actually 24. Sabrina was 35. "What kind of a girl can I really say that I honestly am? A mess. But I'm not one of those, those girls taking a 20-year-old."

"I'm not judging."

"It was different. He's like an old soul."

"I'm not judging you for dating a 25-year-old."

"I wasn't after anything. I didn't even know it was actually possible, just because Rob and I had a good marriage. Really, we did. There were some things that we allowed in that I feel damaged us. And I would tell him that and he didn't want to hear of it."

"How did you and Jonathan talk about his death?"

"We didn't talk about his death."

"You guys didn't talk about it at all?"

Sabrina was quiet for a moment.

"We talked about divorce and, I mean, if anything was to happen to Robert," said, then added, "not gunshots."

"How did Jonathan know that Rob was going to be working in Tehachapi?"

"He wasn't supposed to be working in Tehachapi," she said. "I did tell him. I would tell him his schedule. I would tell him dates and stuff like that because his schedule was crazy, too. I kept him posted pretty much."

"Let's talk about the 17th. Rob left for work in the morning. I noticed you had an 80-minute conversation with Jonathan. What did you talk about?"

"We talked about church. And he had worked and he was pretty thrashed from work. What he was going to do that day. We even talked about seeing each other, but I was getting the kids ready for school and it was just not going to work out. I did tell him, we were possibly going to get together, but he was doing other stuff. I think he had been to work for three days prior."

"He was a fireman," Meyer said. "They don't really work: mow the lawn, they shine the truck, cook dinner." Police officers and firefighters have a notorious rivalry. "Did he tell you he was going to talk to Rob?"

"Nothing at all."

"No indication he was going to see Rob?"

"No."

"You texted Jonathan seven different times with no response back. What were you thinking?"

"He was sleeping."

She said that Jonathan finally responded with a text message. They then spoke by phone. Meyer asked what they talked about.

"He said he was sorry."

"For what?"

"That he had been sleeping and missed my calls, and we just talked about—I don't even remember what we talked about. I said Rob's not home yet. I was getting the kids together. So it was just kind of like typical, you know."

"Did he seem to act normal?"

"He said he was really sorry for not being around and for not answering my calls."

"Did he give any indication that he saw Robert or talked to Robert?"

"No," she said, shaking her head.

Meyer said: "He did go see Rob, and I think now you probably know that."

"It's so hard for me. That's unbelievable to me. I seriously would feel like there's no way. There's no way that he would be capable of that."

She said that even seeing the surveillance video from the Pilot gas station didn't convince her. "The bike was hard to tell," she said. "Even the liquor store, it looks like a teenager to me. I can't really make it out."

"The video is a lot better in person. I know it's Jonathan. He was there. You want me to tell you what he did. He drives to Tehachapi. He checks to see if Rob's there, and Rob's not there. He comes back. And he waits for Rob to drive into the property."

"You're sure?"

"I'm positive. One hundred percent."

"How do you know for sure?"

"I have lots of evidence. He goes into the shop. They get into an altercation. He shoots Rob, twice. He gets on his bike, his motorcycle. Leaves. He changes his clothes, goes to the gas station, gets some water, gets some gas, drives home. Gets home. Sees your text messages. Calls you, texts you."

She protested several more times until he asked her: "At what point did you realize Jonathan did this?"

"He's never told me that he's done this."

"He's never told you that?"

"In words. I didn't want to hear that, you know. I don't want to hear that. He never told me in words."

"So how has he told you then, if not in words?"

"He hasn't. His behavior," she said. "In the moment, it made sense, but even like riding over, I thought: in the moment, it was just like protective, like, oh, okay, this situation sucks, it doesn't look good. But I just watched it over and over and over and over again, and still my brain wouldn't let me see him."

Meyer returned to the question of how Jonathan knew Rob would be working that day alone.

"I told him where Rob worked. I told him it was in Tehachapi. We discussed the town and the shop. We talked about the town of Tehachapi and that I'd been up there before and how the building was."

"Did he ask you questions about the building, like what color is it?"

"No."

"Did you give him the address?"

"I didn't give him the address," she said. "So I take it Jonathan's arrested? Oh, my gosh."

"How did he know the shop was there?"

"I didn't know the address. I just kind of explained how it is. He inquired before. We talked a lot: Yeah, Rob's in Tehachapi. Kind of like what he did."

"You talked to him in the morning and you told him that Rob was going to work. Why did you tell him Rob was going to work?"

"Just so we could talk. Possibly see one another and talk."

She said she told him that Rob's shift in Tehachapi was a longer day, a 12-hour shift.

"So you told him this so you could have the opportunity to see Jonathan?"

"If he was available, if it worked out, to just to, like, talk, to be able to know that there was not a time limit. It's a longer time limit. I hate this."

"I have to believe there was more going on than that."

"We talked about church. He wasn't like: I'm going up to Tehachapi to take care of Robert."

"You guys didn't talk about that?"

"No, no, I promise you that."

"You've lied to me before."

"I understand, but no, I could say no. That's the truth."

Meyer said, "He had actually been there before."

"He had?"

"He had been out there in June, scoping it out."

"In June?"

"He drove up there, checked it and put his plan together." (Meyer actually had the date wrong; according to phone records, Jonathan was in Tehachapi in late May).

"This is bad," said Sabrina. "Rob was so strong. This is so crazy."

"Jonathan is a pretty strong now," Meyer told her.

"Why?"

"Because he's taking steroids. I can tell from the crime scene photos and stuff there was a struggle." Meyer pulled his chair closer to Sabrina, leaning forward, crowding her into the corner. "So Rob's fighting for his life, and this fucking douchebag is killing him because he wants you and the kids. He wants to be Rob. He wants to be Rob."

"I don't want to believe that," she said, crying. "I can't believe that."

"It's terrible. It's sad to take these kids' father away from them. Took their father away from them because he wanted to be Rob. Terrible."

"So what do I do now?"

"You tell me everything you know because, I'll be honest with you: What I get out of this interview is going to make a huge decision on whether you touch or see your kids again, ever, in your entire life. Right now, I feel like you have more information that you're not giving me. Now is the time to tell me the truth about everything."

"I feel like I'm completely out of my mind."

"I have to let you know you have to be totally honest with me. This is so frickin' serious. I can't tell you how serious this is."

He told her how much he knew about her relationship with Jonathan. He knew about the burner phone. He knew about the thousands of text messages and conversations. He told her he knew what they had talked about, how Jonathan had plans for their future.

"At what point did Jonathan say he could possibly take care of it for you?"

"He never said he could take care of it," she said. "He said we could be together and live for God."

"What did you think of that?"

"I just kind of live. I would think about it, but it was like I was living two lives, you know."

"So a life with Robert and a life with Jonathan?"

"In a way, yeah."

"Did you know that he had planned to murder your husband?"

"No, no, no," she said, sounding stunned.

"You did not know that?"

"I didn't know that he planned murdering Robert."

"Because he did."

"I can't—I just can't. It has to be a lie. There's just no way."

"After the murder, has he talked to you about it and told you why he did it?"

"He never said: 'I killed Robert.' "

"Do you know that he has two firearms that are the same caliber that killed Robert?"

"Same caliber? What's that?"

"Same size bullet."

"What kind of gun?"

"Semi-automatic handgun."

Rubbing her forehead, Sabrina whispered, "I knew that he had a gun. I knew that Jonathan had a gun."

"Tell me about that."

"I just knew that he was an investigator for the fire service."

"What kind of investigation did he do?"

"Fire investigation. But he did carry a gun."

"He's been telling you all about my investigation, how my investigation goes, what I'm doing, totally feeding you a lot of bullshit about the way things go."

"And for some reason, that made me feel better. I don't know why he made me feel better. He made me feel better just talking to him. I just felt like the whole thing was about an affair in my head."

"An affair?" Meyer asked incredulously.

"An affair, yeah."

"You don't know anybody who's had an affair?"

"Their spouse wasn't murdered. Oh, my gosh, this is like such horrible timing. We have discussed it a lot, kind of like what to go over and say."

"Why would you discuss that if it was just an affair?"

She stumbled over her words: "To take off—not—um, not for the affair but— we had a great marriage, perfect, everything's perfect. We have talked about just the lifestyle that I led, but just so—"

Meyer said, "I can tell you that this wasn't about the affair. All these conversations that Jonathan's had about you about not talking to me, that was to conceal him committing the murder. It wasn't the affair."

"I felt like it was about the affair. I felt like it's so amplified because Rob was murdered."

"It wasn't about the affair. He's trying to tell you all this information and feed you all this bullshit, not because he didn't want it to be revealed that he was having an affair with you, but because he knows we're going to look for him and talk to him."

Meyer excused himself and left her alone in the interview room, the camera trained on her. He told her he was going to the restroom. In fact, he was conferring with other detectives monitoring the interview. When he returned, Sabrina started talking immediately.

"I was just thinking about so many things," she began, but he stopped her.

"Let's talk about last week when we met. You leave here, you talked to him on the phone. Then after you and I spoke, you called him and said, 'Hey, we're good.' "

"I just felt like, I was just worried about phone records. I seriously thought we were getting arrested for an affair. And I know that sounds retarded. I just felt guilty for the affair and Rob being gone. But then hearing it out loud."

"Sounded retarded, right? Also you had a conversation about me, too."

The perfect Bakersfield couple. Wife who makes furry

blankets.

"I never had said your first name. And he looked and checked you out."

"How did he do that?"

"I guess the computer, I don't know. I don't do any of that stuff a whole lot. So I just kind of felt he was doing homework for us."

Meyer showed her photos of the motorcyclist driving to and from the crime scene. He told her that Jonathan bought those shoes, pants, jacket and shirt from Goodwill nine days before the murder. They knew that, he said, because they found the receipt at Jonathan's house.

"It's hard for me to imagine that honestly you didn't know this was going on, with all talk on the burner phone," Meyer said, an edge creeping into his so-far friendly voice. "It's hard for me to know you don't have knowledge."

"I understand that it would be, now that I'm looking at the outside of it."

"What do you think is going to happen to you right now?"

"I don't know. Going to jail?"

"With all this information, you think you're going to be able to see your kids again?"

"I hope so," she said. "It's a nightmare."

"How do you think Robert felt? What was going through his mind? Was his heart racing? Scared? Thinking about his kids and his wife? Jonathan was trying to murder him for what? So he could have his life. This guy wanted Robert's life. This guy murdered him in cold blood. How do you think Robert felt? He had to be fucking scared?"

"I didn't even wanna—I just wanted to know if he suffered. And he said he didn't suffer. I didn't know details."

Meyer continued, "One second everything is cool. Next second, you're fighting for your life. They were fighting over the gun. Then—pow!—the gun goes off. Then what are you thinking? You start thinking about your life."

Meyer now was pleading with her. "Give me something that's good. I need to know. I need some information."

"You have all the information right here," she said, pointing to the papers and photos on the table.

"This looks horrible," Meyer said.

"I know it does."

"This guy murders him because he wants this life."

"And I gave him the address."

"You did. You told him where your husband worked at, where the shop was, what days he worked."

At this point, another detective entered the room. Kevin Brewer was louder and meaner. His voice dripping with disgust, he told her: "Let me tell you what a jury is going to think. The same thing I am right now and the same thing you are. We have some problems. You need to tell me why you're not an accomplice to this murder."

"Why am I not?"

"Yeah," he said.

"Because I didn't want Robert dead. I would never want him dead, ever."

"Yes you did," Brewer said. "You've been talking for weeks and weeks about how this is God's will, that you guys get together and marry."

Brewer blew his top, yelling, "At what point did he tell you he shot Rob?"

"He never said that he shot Rob."

He demanded to know if "six or seven little ladies sitting on that jury" would believe that, or anybody else for that matter.

"What will your kids think when they find out and the whole world will find out in the next three days because this paperwork will go public? You want people hearing some of that stuff without explaining some of that stuff to us? Tell me when he told you he killed your husband. If he didn't tell you, then you knew it already."

"I didn't know," she insisted.

Then a third detective came into the room to take another crack at her. It was Juan Trevino, who had confronted Sabrina hours earlier in Boron.

Standing over her, he said, "I think a decision needs to be made right now. You requested this. You wanted to talk to Randall. We're four hours into this and you haven't said anything different to him than you told me. If you have something you need to say, now is the time because I'm ready to cut this off."

"It's clear and it's my fault for telling Jonathan where Robert was that day."

"Most certainly it is. It is your fault."

"I know."

"He's a scumbag," Trevino said. "Why you're telling a man you're sharing a bed with where your husband works is beyond me. If you don't have anything for us, I think we need to get you into jail."

"Okay," was all she said.

"I'll take that as: 'Yes, I don't have anything to tell you.'"

"I said everything."

"You told him the same thing you told me, only I wasn't patient for four hours. I was trying to move it along after about an hour of listening to you tell me nothing. He's a lot nicer than me, a lot more patient. So what I need you to do, I need you to stand up and turn around."

She did. He snapped handcuffs on her. "Obviously, since you were already brought down here once before, you were told what you were under arrest for, correct?"

"Yes," she said, but he was going to tell her again.

"For conspiracy to commit murder and accessory to murder."

She had turned and now faced him. She had a pained expression and nodded.

"Have a seat," he said.

She sat in the folding chair, this time with her hands

behind her in manacles.

Det. Meyer looked at his phone and sighed. "Four hours and 40 minutes."

Trevino said, "So *five* hours you managed to tell us nothing," and walked out.

Meyer scooped up his papers and walked out without saying anything to Sabrina.

Sabrina sat there in the corner, hands cuffed behind her, the water bottle and tissue box Meyer so courteously brought her, out of reach on the table. She sat for two entire minutes without moving, frozen in the chair, staring into space. She then leaned over as far as she could in the handcuffs and dropped her head.

Trevino came back in and asked if she was right- or left-handed. She said right. He uncuffed her right hand so she could sign the card on which she had put her fingerprints and palm prints.

She mumbled something

"What was your question?" he snapped.

"I just don't understand," Sabrina said softly. "If you guys have all of the evidence, it's not like he was going to confess it to me that he did that. He's not going to say those words to me. I didn't know he was going to Tehachapi that day."

"He did."

"I don't believe it."

Trevino lowered his voice. He spoke for the first time in a soft, almost caring way.

"I guess people react different to stuff," he said. "This whole time you find yourself not being able to believe it. But not once have you showed any anger or disgust. That bothers me. And through all of this, your children really haven't been a concern to you. It's unfortunate, because they definitely deserve better than what you're giving them. I hope they get it. I hope they do."

He shrugged and said, "I'm staying out of this. Let's get

you to jail."

The next day at the jail, Sabrina had a visitor to her cell. She was being held on suicide watch on C Deck at the Central Receiving Facility.

"Do you remember me?" It was Det. Brandon Rutledge, who had interrogated her in Boron. "Did you get some sleep? Not much else to do, huh?"

She said she did. It was 10:30 a.m. on Thursday, Nov. 20, 2014. A jailer escorted them to a small meeting room. He was running his recorder. The din of the jail could be heard: banging, loud announcements, people yelling.

"You have court today at 3 o'clock," he said. "Your cellmate said you were thinking about me. What were you thinking?"

"That I want to talk to you guys."

Sabrina sounded exhausted.

"Are you ready now? I want to hear everything. Okay, Jonathan killed Rob, didn't he?"

"Yeah."

"How did you help him?"

"I let him know where Robert worked. I didn't know he was going to Tehachapi that day to do that."

Rutledge said, "You remember those rights I read to you a dozen times, just formality stuff."

"I understand," she said. "I just love my kids."

"I talked to Julie, just briefly, of course," he said. "They're not happy, but they're doing fine."

"I have a good family. Of course, Julie is taking care of them. They love me so much. They loved Robert. I loved Robert."

"There's no doubt about it. But you loved Jonathan, too?"

"It's so crazy, loving two guys."

"I'm listening. I am listening." Rutledge then played portions of the wiretapped conversations. She listened as

Jonathan prayed that Sabrina would find the "right words."

"I'm playing these for you just to make it clear to you: Sabrina, how soon after Rob's death did you know Jonathan did it?"

She was silent for a long time and then said, "Not that long."

"Day or two? Week?"

"Pretty quick."

15.

Lydia Marrero received a call from her sister who had just spoken to a Det. Randall Meyer of the Kern County Sheriff's Office.

"Did you hear?" Chris said.

"Hear what?" Lydia said

"They arrested a man and a woman, and you know who the woman was? Sabrina."

"What!"

"Sabrina and this guy named Jonathan were having an affair."

A thousand thoughts raced through Lydia's head.

Robert's death devastated a family that had already been reeling. Lydia's mother had died earlier in the year. A week after Robert was murdered, his father, who long had been ailing, died. Robert's mother never recovered. The following June, she also died.

That Sabrina might have had a hand in causing this suffering seemed inconceivable.

Since Robert and Sabrina had moved to California 14 years earlier, Lydia and her husband visited them and the kids six or seven times a year, for Christmas, Easter, Thanksgiving, birthdays. They'd gather in the house or at a nearby park. Robert would often take them out on his boat. They played with the kids and exchanged gifts and cards. Sabrina also made sure the kids sent thank-you notes for presents. There were absolutely no signs of stress between Robert and Sabrina.

At the funeral, Sabrina hugged Lydia. A few weeks

later, Lydia went to church with Sabrina and the children, and then afterwards, they met for lunch at a pizza parlor, where Sabrina's father gave Lydia a cross that contained some of Robert's ashes.

Lydia had held hope that an arrest would be made, but said, "I never thought it would have been that close to home."

On Nov. 20, 2014, the Sheriff's Office presented its case to the Kern County District Attorney. After reviewing the evidence, the DA decided to charge Jonathan with first-degree murder and conspiracy with the special circumstances of lying in wait and using a firearm. These enhancements would make him eligible for the death penalty.

At his first appearance in a Bakersfield courtroom, Jonathan stood and pleaded not guilty to all charges. He wore the paper clothing typically given to prisoners on suicide watch. News about Jonathan and Sabrina had reached the media, and reporters were on hand for the court hearing. Outside, a sheriff's official answered questions. "Jonathan Hearn had become involved in a romantic relationship with Sabrina Limon in the months leading up to Robert Limon's murder," sheriff's spokesman Ray Pruitt told reporters.

Jonathan had retained the services of Bakersfield lawyer Clayton Campbell, who began the media spin immediately. "This is the United States of America," he told reporters. "Just because you're accused, it doesn't mean you're guilty."

The judge sent Jonathan back into custody at the Central Receiving Facility in Bakersfield to await his next court date. Because of the severity of the charges, Jonathan was not eligible for bail.

Sabrina Limon never made it to that court day. After reviewing the evidence against her, the Kern County District Attorney's office declined to seek charges. Nobody would say why. "I can't comment on that because I cannot comment (on the) facts of the case," a prosecutor told the *Victor Valley*

Daily Press. "I have no comment as the case is pending."

That was three "no comments" in one statement.

Pruitt from the sheriff's office would only say the case was "in their hands"—the DA—and he made no secret of the sheriff's disappointment in the lack of charges. "We believe we developed probable cause to believe that Sabrina Limon was responsible for her husband's death and she had conspired with Hearn in the murder," Pruitt told the *Daily Press.* "That's what led to her arrest two days ago."

The sheriff's position was underscored by the release of the detectives' probable cause declaration. First reported by the *Bakersfield Californian*, the declaration revealed Sabrina and Jonathan exchanged thousands of text messages before Robert's murder. It also revealed Sabrina had told Jonathan where her husband was working on the day of the murder— though it left out her explanation that she did it so they would know how much time they would have to talk and possibly meet.

The declaration said investigators found video surveillance of Jonathan fleeing the murder scene, which was an overstatement. There was no positive identification of him as the person on the motorcycle. (The sheriff's office even admitted it couldn't make out Jonathan for the man walking across the industrial complex. "We have not been able to positively identify that person, so we have not identified if that was, in fact, Jonathan Hearn," Pruitt said. "We released the footage in August and recently re-released the footage because we are actively trying to identify and question that person.")

Southern California news organizations jumped on the story. The visuals proved irresistible. A few small pictures showed Jonathan beaming in his fire helmet, but it was social media that proved to be a bonanza. Sabrina and Kelly Bernatene's Facebook photos documented the parties and fun-in-the-sun of the Silver Lakes crowd. Sabrina and Robert were pictured snuggling at parties and on boats or posing with their children for holiday portraits, the perfect young family. The biggest find was that Beef 'O' Brady's picture that Kelly had taken of Sabrina wrapping her arms around Jonathan.

Los Angeles TV crews loaded up the satellite trucks and hit the freeway for the high desert seeking out interviews. "Mom and Dad are a very loveable, Christian family. There's no way that he would have done anything like that," one of Jonathan's neighbors told KCBS-TV. "He was not one of those kids that would go party or go get into trouble. Very quiet."

The Redlands Fire Department confirmed Jonathan's employment, but said nothing else, though old news stories from his local newspaper, the *Daily Press*, revealed he had graduated from the Victor Valley College Firefighter I Academy and came from a prominent local family. The *Daily Press* reported that Jonathan's grandfather, William Alves, was the first honorary mayor of Hesperia and worked in real estate with his late wife, Aileen, who was involved in everything from the Hesperia Kiwanis to the Hesperia Property Owners and Lamplighters group. A biography on Jonathan's firefighter blog said he "places great emphasis on interpersonal development and ethics being the foundation of service" and that "his greatest moments are those spent with his family or friends."

In Silver Lakes, reporters went door knocking on Strawberry Lane and found stunned neighbors. "We always seen them around the neighborhood with his wife. They looked like a good couple," one of them, Obehi Aisuan, told KCBS-TV. He added that he had once seen Jonathan at her house after the murder. "The time they were mourning the husband and stuff, he was one of the people that was over there."

Soon, the national press picked up the story. "California Firefighter Accused of Killing His Alleged Lover's Husband," headlined an article on *People* magazine's website, which likened the case to "the plot to a trashy romance novel gone wrong." The *New York Daily News* offered a typically pithy lead: "A love triangle burned up in a Southern California firefighter's face." *Slate* gave it a long write-up with links to the *Bakersfield Californian* and other outlets.

Neither Jonathan nor Sabrina granted interviews. "Right now, our family is not talking to the media," his sister, Emily, told the *Daily Press*. "Any comment will come through our attorney, Clayton Campbell." When approached by a TV reporter, Sabrina's father was more blunt. "It's none of your business."

After this initial burst of activity, things slowed down, the justice system taking its sweet time. It would be eight months before Jonathan appeared before a Bakersfield judge for a preliminary hearing. The proceedings were to determine if prosecutors had enough evidence to try him for murder. With a low legal bar, the prosecution needed only to present a barebones case.

Among the evidence, revealed publicly for the first time, was a portion of the letter to Jason Bernatene in which Jonathan wrote, "I showed such pride in not seeing my mistakes as having such horrible and dangerous consequences." One of the wiretaps also was played for the first time publicly. "In the next 100 years, you and I will be in eternity together and all this will seem like nothing," Jonathan could be heard telling Sabrina. "And, hopefully, in two or three years, all of this will be done and over with."

The two days of evidence also included surveillance video and photographs, and on July 24, 2015, Judge Charles Brehmer announced that he was convinced. He bound Jonathan over for trial for murder. "Almost all the evidence is circumstantial, but there was a lot," Brehmer said, according to the *Daily Press*.

After the hearing, Campbell went back into spin mode. He told reporters the prosecution would have a "very hard time" proving Jonathan's guilt beyond a reasonable doubt.

He genuinely felt good about his chances. And there was at least some good news out of the hearing: the DA announced it wouldn't go for the death penalty. It was now life without parole.

Criminal defense lawyers take their victories where they can find them.

Robert's sisters, Lydia Marrero and Chris Wilson, sat through the hearing. As they looked at Jonathan Hearn, the man who allegedly murdered their brother, they could shake their heads. They had never heard of him before. The first time they saw him was in court. "He was a young kid," said Lydia. "What did she see in this guy?"

Answers to this or any other of the family's burning questions would not be forthcoming from Sabrina.

About a month earlier, Lydia had called Sabrina to tell her of the death of Robert's mother. Lydia could hear Sabrina tell the kids in the background that grandma had died. A heart-shaped wreath arrived by delivery.

Sabrina had stopped talking to Robert's family and was staying far away from Jonathan's court dates.

According to Sabrina's sister, Julie, life had become unbearable for Sabrina and her children. After release from jail, Sabrina came home to a maelstrom. Her longtime friends abandoned her, led by Kelly and Jason Bernatene. Classmates taunted her children, calling their mother a murderer. People started following her in their cars. "They would sit outside her home and, like, stalk her," her sister, Julie, later said in court. At least once, Julie said, somebody tried to ram Sabrina's car on the road. The media continued to pester her and hit up her friends for quotes. Comments on social media got so vicious that Sabrina shut down her Facebook page.

Every day, she lived in fear that she would be arrested again. Authorities almost seemed to be taunting her by suggesting they may drag her into court for Jonathan's trial.

"She is not charged in the case and right now, she's free to do whatever she wants," Deputy District Attorney David McKillop told the *Victor Valley Daily Press*. "If we end up finding out she needs to be subpoenaed, we will subpoena her. If we don't, we won't."

About the only one from Sabrina's circle of friends who would see her was Dale Smith. The former swinging partner had long since gotten divorced and moved on from that lifestyle. He would later say in court that he stopped by Sabrina's house as a friend. "I believe that if the tables were reversed, Rob would have done the same thing for me," he said.

Otherwise, it was angry stares and worse, and finally Sabrina gave up on Silver Lakes. She pulled her children out of school and her sister Julie began home-schooling them. She sold their house for a modest $17,000 profit, which went to pay off her car and other expenses, and moved to Camarillo, a quiet upper-middle-class suburb not far from the beach, between Los Angeles and Ventura. She rented a three-story condominium in a complex that had a pool, soccer field, park and neighbors who had no idea who she was. The children began to adjust to their new life. Sabrina's family visited regularly.

Life was beginning to have some semblance of normalcy. Then one day, the cars arrived.

Julie was at the condo and saw them through the living room window. It was Jan. 6, 2017, just over two years after Sabrina was arrested and released. There was a knock at the front door and Sabrina opened it to see Det. Randall Meyer and other investigators, along with a deputy district attorney she'd later learn was named Eric Smith.

They asked her step outside. She was barefoot, so her sister went to find shoes. By the time Julie returned, Sabrina was getting handcuffed. Julie dialed the phone and managed to reach Sabrina's new lawyer, Bakersfield criminal defense attorney Richard Terry. He issued hasty legal advice, which

Julie repeated by yelling, "Don't say anything!"

Sabrina couldn't hear her. By now, she was in the sheriff's car. It drove off toward Bakersfield, toward that same noisy jail where she had a sleepless night back in November 2014.

It all lasted seconds. Sabrina's parents were there and witnessed it all. The children were spared. Leanna was playing with a neighbor; Julie texted them to bring her inside and keep her there for now. Robbie was at a friend's house.

Sabrina's family couldn't figure out what had happened. They had heard nothing officially from law enforcement on Sabrina's status in the investigation since her release. Jonathan had made a court appearance, but what little evidence that came out was nothing new. It looked like all the same information police had at the time the DA opted against charges for Sabrina.

Something big had changed, and for now, nobody was telling them what it was.

16.

From the moment of his arrest, Jonathan was eager to talk. He almost did at the Boron substation. Months of mounting anxiety and spiritual turmoil had ground him down. When Det. Juan Trevino asked him how he was doing, Jonathan said he had come off an ordeal that was overwhelming and embarrassing.

Then he told Trevino he had better wait to talk to a lawyer, ending the interview on the spot. Like Sabrina, Jonathan had 90 long minutes to think in the squad car on the way to the jail in Bakersfield. Like Sabrina, he asked to speak personally with Det. Meyer.

Unlike Sabrina, he changed his mind. He invoked his right to counsel and remained silent.

While his family was open in their conversations with detectives, they still protected him. His family got in touch with a close friend, who happened to be a prosecutor in Ventura County, seeking a recommendation for an attorney. The friend connected them with one of his longtime friends, Clayton Campbell, a leading private criminal defense lawyer with offices in an historic brick building in downtown Bakersfield, blocks from the courthouse.

Within hours of being retained, Campbell went to the Central Receiving Facility, which is attached to the courthouse. A deputy led Campbell into a small secure room.

"When I first get on a case, I want to meet the client," Campbell later said in an interview. "I want to see what kind of person they are. The better you can relate to the client, the easier it is to see things from their perspective and prepare their defense. I had met his family and got a good idea of what kind of people they are. Interestingly, his background is similar to mine."

Campbell, too, was home schooled with a faith-based curriculum. Both are Christians. "I could immediately relate to him," he said.

In their brief initial meeting, Campbell explained the next steps: Jonathan would be appearing before a judge the afternoon of Thursday, Nov. 20, then return to jail without bail. This was the court date in which Jonathan wore the paper jail uniform, though Campbell saw no evidence Jonathan was suicidal. The attorney warned Jonathan and his family to brace for the media onslaught and to let him do all the talking.

"They're very honest people," Campbell said. "When the detectives came to talk to them, they shared whatever information they had. They're not criminals. They don't have any private experience with having a relative in trouble. As far as talking to police, it was just natural to them."

But Jonathan's family was the least of his concerns.

"When I met with him the second time," Campbell said, "he told me that basically, he was guilty. He wanted to come clean. He wanted to admit guilt."

It was Jonathan's faith that was driving him. "Christians are people that acknowledge that they do something wrong and they need grace. That's really where he was coming from," said Campbell. "His conscience had been bothering him. He said he was getting close at the end to where he was almost just ready to go and confess."

There was a difference between coming clean with God and coming clean with the Kern County District Attorney. Campbell had seen none of the evidence. Thousands of pages of police reports and hundreds of hours of wiretap recordings had yet to be handed over to the defense. And while Det. Meyer had invented the sweat stain evidence, DNA tests were being conducted from samples lifted at the scene, as well as from the mouths of Jonathan, Sabrina and the BNSF workers. A backlog at the lab meant months before the results arrived.

What's more, as far as a plea was concerned, there was no wiggle room for negotiation for the defense. Jonathan was charged with first-degree murder with special circumstances and theoretically faced the death penalty, pending a final decision by the DA. The defense had nothing with which to bargain. "He wants to plead guilty," said Campbell, "but the DA doesn't go around giving deals for first-degree murder with special circumstances. It would be totally irresponsible to allow that."

Campbell prayed for Jonathan—and advised him to keep his mouth shut.

"As a Christian, I understand what he wants to do, and how maintaining a not-guilty plea, when you know you're guilty of what they're accusing, is a problem. You're basically lying about your guilt," said Campbell. "But as a criminal defense attorney, I have to tell him there's a process we have to follow to prove you're guilty. It's more of a procedural thing to enter a not-guilty plea at the outset."

As the evidence began to arrive, it became clear that the prosecution had a strong case. Jonathan was the secret lover of a woman whose husband wound up murdered. That was incontrovertible. Sabrina admitted it, on videotape, to police. Phone records confirmed they were in constant contact before the murder and on the day of the murder. Jonathan drove a motorcycle similar to the one on the surveillance video. He had guns like the one in the murder. He had no alibi. And all those wiretaps sounded bad—very bad.

But all was not lost. The deeper Campbell got into the evidence, the more opportunities he found for a defense. With no eyewitnesses or forensic evidence tying Jonathan to the crime scene, the prosecution would have to construct a circumstantial case. Campbell could mount a traditional reasonable doubt defense by chipping away at the foundations of that case.

The security footage was too blurry to identify Jonathan. It didn't even look like his motorcycle. The suspect's bike had chrome pipes and gas tank; on Jonathan's, those were black. The police, the defense could argue, developed tunnel vision. Once they suspected Jonathan, they dismissed other promising leads, like the man with the limp who was interviewed at headquarters and then released. "There were all kinds of things we could use," said Campbell. "We were running down a lot of leads that I thought quite frankly were not explored by the sheriff."

As for those wiretaps, they contained no admissions of murder—only constant anxiety over the affair. "If you're having an affair and your spouse is suddenly killed, you're going to feel extremely guilty about the affair, just for betraying the spouse," Campbell said. "On top of that, you know the social stigma from the affair is going to be magnified by 10 now that the offended spouse is dead." The argument would go that it would be strange if they didn't lie about the affair.

Reasonable doubt, though, would only take Campbell so far. "We needed alternative theories," said Campbell. "We needed to show somebody else could have done it."

In circumstantial cases, jurors are instructed by the judge that if there are two reasonable interpretations of what happened—one that points to guilt and the other that points to innocence—they must go with innocence. "The rule doesn't say you have to choose the one that's most reasonable," said Campbell. "You can have one that's more reasonable than another. But as long as they're both reasonable, you have to go with the one that points to innocence, even if it's less likely."

This strategy hinges on jurors who can understand nuances of the law and apply them, no matter what common sense tells them. "It's the hardest thing for a jury to accept," Campbell said. "We normally make decisions based on the most likely accurate story. It's the preponderance standard and we apply it almost everything else in life."

Under the circumstances, Campbell felt this was the best and only way to proceed. "That was our strategy," he said. "We had to show that other people could have had the same motive. You have to give the jury something to point to and say that could have happened."

What better place to look than the secret steamy side of Silver Lakes. "The swinger thing, this lifestyle, to me, created a whole bunch of alternative theories," said Campbell. "Police were certain that a jealous jilted lover could do this. Then we can go to all these other people who are potential candidates. We had this big swingers group. And we had information that Robert had relationships with other people that were not necessarily involved in the swinger thing. It looked like something was going on."

So the behind-the-scenes work of criminal defense continued, Campbell and his investigator searching for evidence to bolster alternative theories. "We had a lot of investigation going on, interviewing people, taking pictures, going through the phone records, listening to all of the recordings," he said.

Of course, with a client who still insisted he was guilty, that search could lead to dark places the defense would not want to go, like the cluttered garage next to Jonathan's rental unit behind his grandfather's house. The unit had remained vacant and untouched since police searched it the night of Jonathan's arrest. One day, Campbell and his investigator checked it out.

"He just doesn't throw stuff away," said Campbell. "He has boxes and boxes of old irrelevant paperwork, including receipts for any time he went to a restaurant or the drive-through on the way home from work. He has a very meticulous personality. He would write notes to himself, notes on everything. That was his way of remembering things."

While the sheriff spent more than four hours there, uncovering such important evidence as the receipt for the Goodwill clothes, they didn't look everywhere. The garage was so messy, it would have taken them weeks. But Campbell knew where to look for certain things because Jonathan told him—the conversation kept secret under the cloak of attorney-privilege.

"The sheriff didn't know there was a flash drive missing," the lawyer said. "It wasn't even hidden where Jonathan thought he had it. I can't even believe we found it." But there it was, stashed amid the junk. Campbell popped the drive into his laptop and up came photo after photo of Sabrina, a collection of mostly selfies; in at least 20 pictures, she was topless.

This was not unexpected in light of their romance. What was unexpected was what Campbell found when he ran the flash drive through a utility that searches for deleted files, the same utility that police use with electronic evidence. Another set of pictures emerged. Campbell's heart dropped.

The photos had been taken in May of 2014 in Tehachapi. Police would glean from triangulating cell phone calls to the nearby towers that Jonathan had called Sabrina from Tehachapi that day. What they didn't know was that Jonathan had taken a bunch of pictures of the industrial complex where Robert was later killed.

And that wasn't all. Amid piles of papers, Campbell and his investigator found a Walmart receipt. Jonathan hadn't told them about it; they uncovered it by chance. The receipt documented a purchase on Aug. 17, 2014, the day of the murder. For a brief moment, Campbell held hope the receipt could prove an alibi by placing Jonathan far from Tehachapi at the time of the murder. But the purchase was made that morning at a store between Redlands and Hesperia as Jonathan was driving home from work. He had paid cash. The receipt listed the purchase as "ammo."

"I thought, 'Oh, crap,'" said Campbell.

If Campbell took the items off the premises and didn't tell police, he could face accessory-after-the-fact charges. But as Jonathan's lawyer, he had certain protections against incriminating his own client. He did not have to tell police about the items, as long as he left the evidence where he found it. Detectives could then theoretically get the stuff any time with a search warrant.

Campbell carefully slipped the flash drive and the receipt back into their original hiding places.

The discovery of the flash drive photos and the receipt "was like a gut punch," said Campbell, who feared police would conduct at least one more search before trial. "If they come out here and find this stuff, then we're totally cooked."

These would not be the only secrets Campbell would keep. Jonathan told him about other incriminating items. Buried deep in a dirty, stinky chicken coop, Jonathan said, were a silencer and a gun barrel that would match the bullets that killed Robert. Campbell didn't even bother looking for them. He had enough bad news already.

The defense strategy that had once seemed so promising now faced potentially serious problems. Jonathan was running out of what few options he had. Then help came from an unexpected place.

The family of Robert Limon.

17.

Clayton Campbell was in the courthouse one day when he happened to run into a sheriff's deputy working on the Limon murder.

"We had a passing conversation about the preferences of Robert's family, how they wanted to see her convicted because they grew convinced she was involved," Campbell recalled.

In fact, Robert's sister, Christine Wilson, and her husband had corresponded with Jonathan, according to Lydia Marrero.

"They wrote to Jonathan in jail," said Lydia, "and asked him: 'If Sabrina was involved, why do you want to take the fall yourself? She's just as much responsible. Why do you want go to prison for the rest of your life and Sabrina's out walking around?'"

The letter also happened to mention that while Jonathan was locked up, Dale Smith had been spotted at Sabrina's home.

"Maybe they did this to poke the bear, I don't know," said Lydia. "Jonathan wrote back. His letter was more on the religious side, again talking about God and things about how the truth will come out."

While the District Attorney's office doesn't specifically represent victims and their relatives—its clients are all the people of California—prosecutors tend to be sensitive to their desires. An elected DA would be foolish not to—particularly in a high-profile case in which these family members are regularly quoted in the media.

Campbell didn't know if detectives had passed on to the DA the family's feelings about Sabrina or if the relatives had expressed this to the office directly. It was entirely possible that investigators, still stung by Sabrina's release from jail, were using Campbell to nudge the DA's office.

Either way, "We decided we had an opening," said Campbell. He now had potential leverage for a plea deal. Jonathan could provide information that would nail Sabrina and satisfy Robert's family. In exchange, he could make a conscience-easing confession and get a sentence better than life in prison without the possibility of parole.

It was ultimately up to Jonathan: try to work out a deal that at best would still carry a long prison term, or roll the dice at trial.

"I felt that with everything we had to work with, we had a good shot—or at least a reasonable chance of winning the case," Campbell said. "That's a lot to gamble with for the rest of Jonathan's life: a reasonable chance of winning. So it's easy for me to say, 'I'd love to try this case.' It's another thing for me to tell Jonathan, 'I really think you ought to risk your life.' "

To make any sort of deal appealing to the DA, Jonathan would have to tell all about Sabrina. "He can't go in there and tell part of the truth," said Campbell. "Otherwise, the DA wouldn't have any use for him. Why would the DA cut him any slack just for being honest? So he needs to tell the whole truth."

Which was difficult for Jonathan. "His desire to confess was really because he wanted to come clean on what he did," the lawyer said. "He's not the excuse-making type who says this is all Sabrina's fault. Jonathan was saying, 'I'm responsible for what I did; she's responsible for what she did.' And so that was kind of a difficulty: How much of his testimony would necessarily implicate her and not just him."

In the end, Jonathan concluded that Sabrina "needed to admit what she did herself," said Campbell, "because that was the right thing to do." She obviously had no intention of coming forward. So Jonathan gave his lawyer the green light to approach the DA.

As always, this was a delicate dance for a defense attorney. He had to maintain the client's total and complete innocence while suggesting there may be room for an admission of guilt in exchange for leniency. To walk that fine line, Campbell would present a proffer, a detailed explanation of what Jonathan would theoretically say, if given a deal.

Smith was receptive. A framework for a deal took shape. The DA would get Jonathan's full and complete confession and all the dirt on Sabrina in exchange for a prison sentence that left room for parole one day. The DA also would grant him immunity from additional prosecution, agreeing not to use against him anything he would say or police might find in the Limon investigation.

"Once we had this kind of an agreement for ground rules for the proffer, I had a meeting with the DA, just in case they weren't satisfied," said Campbell. "I wanted to give them everything we found so it wouldn't be used against him. So we tell them everything that's on the flash drive, the password to Jonathan's phone. We give them the silencer, the ammo receipt, everything that could possibly hurt us, we put on the table."

The DA accepted, tentatively. After Jonathan coughed up the proffer, the DA checked it for accuracy, comparing his account against the known evidence: phone records, letters, photos and security video and the wiretaps.

Satisfied that Jonathan was telling the truth, the deal was sealed. Jonathan would plead guilty to voluntary manslaughter and other lesser charges for a sentence of 25 years and four months. With credit for time served and good behavior, he could be out in time to celebrate his 50th birthday.

All he had to do was testify against Sabrina.

On Jan. 3, 2017, Det. Meyer sat down with Jonathan

for the first in a series of interviews in an interview room at sheriff's headquarters in Oildale. By Jonathan's side sat his attorney, Clayton Campbell. Also attending were Det. Grantham, Deputy District Attorney Eric Smith and evidence technician Kevin Thompson. The session was videotaped. "I wrote 150 questions, stuff I wanted to know," Meyer said later. "I just let him talk. And he talked a lot." Meyer had conducted many interviews with people who had committed heinous crimes.

None with somebody so forthcoming. "Most people are like: I'm taking this to the grave," he said. "It's very rare."

Jonathan spoke for hours. Meyer's report ran to more than 100 pages. Jonathan told them everything — and a whole lot more. After months of work on the Robert Limon murder case, Meyer finally got what he considered a complete and unvarnished account from Jonathan Hearn, with all his questions answered. "It was," Meyer reflected, "a very good feeling."

For years, authorities had been unable to unlock Jonathan's cell phone. Not even the FBI could penetrate it. In one breath, Jonathan gave them the code and out came photo after photo of Sabrina, dressed and undressed, and outpourings of love, all sent after Robert's murder:

"I adore you Jonathan Hearn you sexy guy," she wrote 19 days after the murder.

"I want to kiss you right now and not stop. I love you so much baby, miss you so much tonight. And I feel God's purpose and strength working in my life and our relationship," she wrote 21 days after.

"You are so good to me. We can only get better with God. That is so exciting. There is no greater peace to find. I feel super blessed," she wrote 25 days after.

"Baby, I love you soooooooooooo much," she wrote 26 days after.

And on Oct. 5, a month and half after, she wrote, "Baby, you are my partner in this life to live for God. I am so ready to live my life. I AM READY FOR US. I am in love with you deeply. A love that I have never felt before."

The phone also yielded her worries about the Bernatenes, including the message about running into Jason at the Silver Lakes Market, the note she ended with a frown face emoticon.

Jonathan also pointed the deputies to a wealth of evidence they had missed in the initial search. They found the Walmart receipt for the ammo where Clayton had left it. They also found the flash drive.

Buried deep in a stinky old chicken coop next to the garage, they found his homemade silencer. Inside were the remnants of a bullet from a test fire. They also found a black backpack with a bullet hole in it.

And in a five-gallon bucket, inside a decaying bag, deputies found a medicine bottle. The shooting was not the first attempt on Robert's life. And Jonathan said Sabrina knew all about it. The white label read "Arsenic Trioxide."

Three days later, a caravan of law enforcement personnel went to Camarillo.

18.

Nine o'clock in the morning in Bakersfield, and the temperature already had hit nearly 100. The National Weather Service issued severe heat advisories for the San Joaquin Valley. Bakersfield schools canceled sports practices and other outdoor activities.

Dozens of people summoned to jury duty sweated outside the Superior Court building on Truxton Avenue downtown. Two blocks away, the long freight trains of BNSF crept along tracks, blocking passage between the courthouse and the parking lot.

In this stifling morning, the jury prospects lined up for last-minute instructions from sheriff's deputies before they were led through glass front doors and metal detectors and into the blissful air-conditioning.

Jury selection for Sabrina Limon's trial began on Aug. 28, 2017, three years and 11 days after her husband's murder. Over the next week and a half, 209 prospects would go up the escalator to Judge John R. Brownlee's second-floor courtroom to determine their suitability and availability for what was expected to be a month-long trial.

It had been an occasionally eventful eight months since Sabrina's arrest and this moment. There were shocking revelations and a flash of courthouse violence that had kept the case in the news.

Back in January, the sheriff's department wasted little time announcing Sabrina's second arrest, issuing a press release shortly after she was picked up in Camarillo. The release said that after 2½ years of "exhaustive investigation," the department obtained an arrest warrant charging her with murder, attempted murder, accessory, conspiracy, soliciting a crime and poisoning. She was being held on $3 million bail.

The allegations of attempted murder and poisoning came as a surprise. Neither the sheriff's office nor the DA offered an explanation; they had only previously said that Sabrina was accused of conspiring with Jonathan to murder her husband. Had there been more?

Then the following Monday, Jan. 9, there was another twist in the case. This was the day that Jonathan was scheduled to go on trial on charges of murdering Robert Limon. As far as the public knew, the case was all set for jury selection. Instead, the trial was off.

Jonathan donned a dark suit, blue shirt and tie, stood before Judge Charles R. Brehmer at 2 p.m. and pleaded guilty to voluntary manslaughter, attempted murder and poisoning in the death of Robert Limon. The judge announced that Jonathan had reached a deal in which he agreed to testify against Sabrina. Jonathan also would formally apologize to Robert's family.

Answering questions from the judge, Jonathan confirmed he understood and signed the deal. He said no more.

The next day, Sabrina, wearing a gray jail uniform with her hands shackled, also appeared in court. She pleaded not guilty to the charges contained in the arrest warrant. Again, there was no explanation about the alleged poisoning. In a press conference, Robert's sister, Chris Wilson, said just be patient, everything had been revealed.

"This is a win for Robert today," she said, Lydia Marrero by her side and supporters in "Justice for Rob" shirts behind them. "We have asked for the truth to be told since August (2014), and it has been told. I don't care by who it has been told, but it's told. Sabrina's behind bars, maybe for the rest of her life, who knows. But she's going to have to sit there and think about what she has done."

In light of Jonathan's plea deal, it seemed she was talking about him, and tellingly, neither sister mentioned him by name.

They saved their anger for Sabrina.

"We have answers to the questions we were asking two-and-a-half years ago that Sabrina and nobody else would give us," said Lydia. "It's a shame that it breaks both sides of our family like this. I don't know how she can bring that kind of grief, disappointment and embarrassment to her family, to our family, to all the friends that gathered, that tried to sympathize with her in the past, the stories she told. It just wasn't right."

It would have been a routine arraignment—Sabrina standing next to her attorney, Richard Terry, to answer to the charges and have a preliminary hearing set—but for a commotion outside the courtroom.

"You're going to hell!" a woman said as she plowed into another woman in the hallway.

Court documents later revealed that Karen Lynn Hudgins, identified as a friend of Sabrina's, was arrested after she used her shoulder to slam the woman into the wall. Randall Meyer and another detective dragged Hudgins downstairs through doors leading to the jail.

The target of her rage: Kelly Bernatene.

The poisoning allegation finally was explained in the criminal complaint against Sabrina. It said that in March 2014, Jonathan plotted with her to mix poison in the food, drink or medication intended for Robert. Court documents filed the following week filled in the details. Jonathan had put arsenic trioxide in a batch of Robert's favorite dessert, banana pudding with Nilla wafers. Sabrina was to give the pudding to her husband. But the plan was abandoned at the last minute out of fear they would get caught if the poison were found in Robert's system.

The documents added this shocker: Researching the effectiveness of the poison, Jonathan laced a piece of salmon with arsenic and gave it to an annoyingly barking neighborhood dog. Jonathan never saw the dog again.

A murderous love triangle with poisoned pudding was too much for the news to resist. The case got blanket coverage on Bakersfield television. Sabrina's lawyer, Richard Terry, got edgy about the publicity—none of it good for his client. He asked the judge to move the trial because of the threat of a tainted jury pool.

Judge Brownlee said no for now. He wanted to hear what the potential jurors had to say.

From Aug. 28 to Sept. 8, as part of the jury selection process, those prospects who came in from the heat were screened for media bias.

Jury selection is normally open to the public, but the judge barred the media from the courtroom as this was going on. In the end, the judge gave hardship releases to 86 people. Of the remaining 104 prospects, 44 people weren't exposed to any news reports on the case at all. Another 31 saw some coverage, but weren't influenced a bit. Only 16 said their opinions would be swayed by news stories.

The pool deemed free of pollution, on Friday, Sept. 8, Brownlee announced that the defense motion for a change of venue was denied and the trial would proceed in Bakersfield.

What's more, after conferring with attorneys, Brownlee rejected defense attorney Richard Terry's objections to cameras in the courtroom and allowed a single television camera, operated by NBC's *Dateline*, to capture nearly every moment of the trial. The proceedings would be live-streamed online and preserved on YouTube.

With that, from an original pool of more than 200 people, a jury was selected, consisting of nine women and three men. Trial would begin the following Monday. The internet would be watching.

19.

Trial began on a day of death and terror, Sept. 11, 2017, the 16th anniversary of the Twin Towers and Pentagon terrorist attacks. In remembrance, Judge Brownlee asked everybody to stand and recite the Pledge of Allegiance.

Then it was on to the business of murder.

Deputy District Attorney Smith began his opening statement with a mini-geography lesson. "What this case—where it occurs—is here in Kern County," he told the jury, showing them a Google map on a big screen, "but a lot of it occurred in San Bernardino County, which is our neighbor to the east." He explained to jurors where Tehachapi was in relation to Helendale. He then laid out the evidence, piece by piece, that he said would support the circumstantial case that Sabrina Limon conspired to murder her husband, Robert. What the presentation lacked, soaring rhetoric, it made up for in clarity, logic and precision. Since Smith would provide no eyewitnesses to the murder and no physical evidence tying Sabrina to a murder plot, these would be vital ingredients for a case that would call on jurors to make inferences and connect dots.

It was also in keeping with Smith's courtroom style. A nothing-but-business prosecutor, Smith was the workhorse of the DA's office. He was named California's Outstanding Prosecutor of the Year for larger counties in 2014, a testament to his monster caseload and impressive track record. The year before, he had tried eight cases—seven of them murder cases—to verdict, spending 236 days in trial, more than any other attorney in the office. The murder cases ended in six guilty verdicts and one hung jury.

"We will show," Smith said, "that Robert Limon was killed to replace him as the father to Leanna and Robbie. You will hear that Robert Limon was removed as a husband, as the leader of the house, by both Sabrina and Jonathan. This was their plan. This was their purpose."

As he spoke, Sabrina sat at the defense table, occasionally taking notes. Before the jury was seated, she had been led into the courtroom in shackles, which were then removed. By agreement with her attorney, the TV camera would not show any of this. There would be no footage of a manacled Sabrina. When her hands were freed, she would open a compact and in the little mirror freshen her makeup. Gone were the baggy jail uniforms.

Sabrina wore a smart black blazer over a purple blouse and dark slacks. The dazzling smile of so many pictures would not be seen in court. At most, Sabrina would crack a grin. Mostly, she looked away to the right, head down, her face in profile to the jury.

"She was vulnerable, she felt loved, she felt she needed someone to lean on." This was her attorney, Richard Terry, now telling the jury why the woman who would sit to his right throughout the trial fell into the arms of a firefighter 10 years her junior, and why she continued with the relationship before, during and after her husband's murder.

His opening statement varied greatly in style and substance.

Stocky, bald, with a big bushy mustache, Terry looked like a favorite eccentric uncle, loud and loveable. A longtime public defender before going into private practice—he has offices in the same brick building as Jonathan's lawyer, Clayton Campbell—Terry had an amiable demeanor that collided with the nasty nature of cases he's taken: a Mexican national charged in a plot to kill three Mexican drug runners and steal their crystal methamphetamine, two pot-smoking teens accused of beating and stabbing to death a sweet elderly couple in their home, a mentally impaired man prone to courtroom outbursts prosecuted for murder, and a man accused of fatally shooting his fishing buddy in the face.

Stashing his reading glasses in his jacket pocket, Terry flashed his big mustachioed smile for the jury and then laid out the defense. This was a case of a simple outgoing woman, a high school dropout unhappy in her marriage, who fell under the spell of a "highly intelligent" killer who used romance and religion to suck her into a murder cover-up without her ever knowing it.

Terry unveiled a defense that straddled a fine and precarious line: Sabrina was unhappy enough with her husband, Robert, to have an affair, but not so miserable she'd want to kill him, much less participate in the plot and its aftermath with her lover, Jonathan.

"People are fully capable of loving two people at the same time in different ways," Terry said. "We all are. We have that capability as human beings. Jonathan made her feel different. He was smart and intelligent, and spoke in a way she'd never heard before. She loved the feeling and he played on that, and used that, and manipulated her. And he killed her husband."

It was an affair, not a murder that Sabrina covered up for so long in her misplaced love and affection for Jonathan and protectiveness of her husband's legacy. "The only evidence they have that Sabrina is involved is Jonathan."

With the burden of proof, the prosecution—as always—would go first. Smith began, as prosecutors usually do, with the crime scene.

Calling several deputies to give an overview of the garage and the nuts-and-bolts of evidence collection, Smith next had Sean Ware recall finding Robert slumped dead against the truck.

It created an indelible first image of violence and loss, and showed how murder leaves more than one victim, as when Smith asked Ware why he requested a transfer from Tehachapi to Kansas City immediately after Robert's murder.

"I didn't want to go back to work in that place anymore," Ware said.

"Did you ever go back to work in that shop?" Smith asked.

"No," he said.

The case moved at a brisk pace, Smith calling more BNSF workers before summoning Sabrina—actually, her voice—to the courtroom. Through Det. Meyer, Smith played recordings of her initial two interviews with him, the first one just hours after finding out Robert was dead, the other days later. Jurors listened as Sabrina denied having marital problems or having a boyfriend.

This was the first hint at trouble behind the Silver Lakes facade. On the second day of trial, all illusions were shattered with the testimony of Jason Bernatene, who spoke of Jonathan's phone conversation with Robert and his later strange voicemail and letter that sent Jason to police.

Sabrina kept her head turned away from Jason as Terry began a cross-examination that zeroed in on sex in Silver Lakes.

"You became aware that they had an open marriage, correct?" asked Terry.

"I would not call it that," said Jason.

"You know they were involved in a swingers group, right?"

"I would say no."

"Did you ever participate in that group?"

"There wasn't a swingers group, sir."

"According to you."

"According to me."

"Was your wife involved in the swingers group?"

"There was no swingers group."

"Did your wife often take her clothes off and send

pictures of herself to other people?"

"I would say my wife did not do that."

"Ever?"

"I would say not that I'm aware of."

"On these trips that you took as adults, was there a lot of partying?"

"Yes, we would drink."

"Did you and your friends engage in wife swapping?"

"Nope."

"Were you ever aware that your wife was actually having an affair with Robert?"

"No."

"So you weren't aware that your wife at any time had sex with Robert Limon?"

"My wife never had sex with Robert Limon."

"That you knew of?"

"That's the only thing that I would testify to, is what I know."

Terry sought to clarify, if the Bernatenes weren't technically swingers, what actually did go on between them and the Limons.

"So my wife and I and Robert and Sabrina would engage in sexual activities, but it was not wife swapping, it was more girls," he said. "I never had sex with Sabrina."

"As far as you know?"

"As far as I knew," he said, and added: "There was no club."

"I didn't say club; I said group."

"There was no group."

But there were photos. Showing Jason a picture of a topless woman, Terry asked, "Do you recognize the person depicted in that photo?"

"Kelly."

After his testimony, Jason walked out of the courtroom, averting his eyes from Sabrina, who continued to keep her head down.

The same happened with the next witness, Kelly Bernatene. She took the stand without so much as a glance at Sabrina. Kelly then explained her transition from best friend to police informant.

"Why did you speak with Detective Meyer?" asked Smith.

Fighting tears, she said, "Because someone killed my friend and they needed to pay for it."

In what would be a testy cross-examination, Kelly revealed that she and Jason were no longer married.

"A couple weeks ago, you had a divorce party?" asked Terry.

"I've never had a divorce party," she said. "But divorce is great."

"I'm happy for you."

"Thank you."

It was a sarcastic exchange but one that revealed the divergent fates of two Silver Lakes women. One marriage ended in divorce, the other in murder.

Terry also asked Kelly about her deteriorating friendship with Sabrina.

"You said Sabrina was your best friend, too sweet to be true?"

"That's what I thought."

"Now you've change your mind, is that right?"

"Definitely."

As he did with Jason, Terry brought the questioning quickly to the bedroom.

"Did you and Ms. Limon and her husband and your husband engage in sexual activity together?"

"Yes, we did."

"When your husband, Jason, was present he basically only wanted you to engage in oral sex, is that right?"

"Yes."

"When your husband wasn't present, how often were you having sexual relations with Robert Limon?"

"I was not."

"Did you ever have sexual relations with Robert Limon where it was just the two of you?"

"No."

She denied sending naked photos to Robert. Terry showed her a photo. She flinched.

"That is me and an old friend of mine and my husband on a cruise."

"Do you normally take your top off on adult vacations on a ship?" asked Terry.

"I don't think I took my top off. I think it was just a flash."

"Especially after you've had a few?"

"Yeah."

Terry wrapped up his questioning by asking sharply, "Is there some reason in particular that you really want to get Sabrina?"

"She killed Rob."

"She didn't kill anybody, did she?"

"I believe she told Jonathan to shoot Rob."

"You're out to get her because of that belief?"

"Yes."

"You'd do anything to get her because of that belief?"

"I know she knew by her behavior."

"Or you want to believe that, right?"

"I do believe it."

"You *want* to believe it?"

"I do believe it."

"Because of that feeling, you want to get Sabrina?"

"I believe she should pay for this murder."

"And that's because you care about her husband so deeply."

"I believe I cared about him more than she did."

On redirect, it was left to Smith to show just exactly what happened during those adult getaways.

"Are these wild sex orgies going on at the river?"

"No," she said. "It was usually Sabrina and I, and then we go have sex with our husbands."

Smith asked, "Did you have anything to do with Robert's death?"

"Absolutely not."

"Did you have a boyfriend who drove to Tehachapi and killed Robert?"

"No, I did not."

Kelly walked out of the courtroom, eyes straight for the door.

The tone shifted abruptly with the next witnesses. After John Justus explained the scheduling issue that brought Robert Limon to Tehachapi, more law enforcement witnesses came in to describe the crime scene and phone records. Railroad benefits guy Daniel Flatten Jr. recounted his dealings with Sabrina and her sister.

Then it was onto Jonathan's family. After testimony that was by turns grim, titillating and boring, Emily Hearn was like a blast of fresh air. Bounding into the courtroom with a smile, she spoke lovingly of her brother and of her admiration for Sabrina.

"My brother is the kindest man that I know," she said.

"Has your opinion changed?" Smith asked.

The question brought her close to tears.

"It's shaken a little bit. But I see strains of the man that I've known all along, and I don't think it's completely ruined my image of him."

Jonathan's mother next took the stand. Appearing nervous, she recounted the period in which Jonathan skipped communion, something she saw as a sign of his moral and spiritual integrity. But under cross-examination, she acknowledged she now knows he had kept profound and awful secrets from her.

"Is it safe to say that your son, whom you bore and raised, was successful in hiding from you the fact that he killed Robert Limon?" asked Terry.

"Yes, sir."

"He deceived you the entire time. Would that be accurate?"

"Not totally accurate."

"He deceived you from the time he was arrested until he confessed to the police that he had not been involved in Robert's death?"

"That's not entirely true," she said. "He had written some letters to me that, in so much as I believed my son could not do this, there were some wording that made me have suspicions that his hands were not clean. I believe he was trying to prepare us. In a letter, he told us the truth would come out at this trial. He was going to be telling the truth."

Carol Hearn wept as she seemed to blame herself for Jonathan's troubles. Speaking quickly, she talked of how distracted she was caring for her stroke-stricken mother, dealing with her 92-year-old father and keeping the family construction business going.

Finally, Terry said, "I'm going to stop you. I've been there. I've gone through that myself. I understand that your focus was not entirely on Jonathan."

"It was not," she said.

She left the courtroom ashen-faced and shaken.

The last of Jonathan's family members, his father, Mike Hearn, was the polar opposite of his wife. Practically beaming as he walked into the courtroom, he sat in the witness box, smiled at the jury, and then said he could completely understand how his son could succumb to sin.

"He was like everybody in this courtroom, capable of doing things he shouldn't do," he told Smith.

During cross-examination, Terry brought him through the story of David and Bathsheba that Mike Hearn used to teach to Jonathan and the other children.

"All of this is David's doing, right?" asked Terry.

"Yes."

"In fact, Bathsheba never knew that David had done

this?"

"I don't know if it ever mentions it."

"There's no mention that Bathsheba ever knew," said Terry.

"Objection," said Smith. "Misstates the Bible."

Judge Brownlee said, "I don't want to get into a theological discussion." He told Terry to restate the question.

"So, based on your readings and everything, there's nothing that you saw, obviously within the scripture, that indicates Bathsheba knew what David had done?"

"That's correct."

Mike Hearn left the courtroom the same way he entered, smiling. But the grin appeared more strained.

The trial was racing along. More detectives came and went, called mainly to lay the legal foundation for the introduction of documents and the wiretaps. The coroner testified about the unusual upward angle of the two gunshots, getting a bit of a grilling by Terry, but not much. The cross-examinations were by and large brief and uneventful.

Much of this had to do with Brownlee. He had a judicial temperament that could be described as affably stern.

On the one hand, he kept the courtroom relaxed to the point of informality. While most judges enter with fanfare, having the bailiff shout, "All rise!" Brownlee would quietly take the bench with no announcement. Under his robe, he favored short-sleeve shirts and no tie. Observers knew this because before court sessions, he could be seen, robeless, chatting with his staff and bailiffs.

His Friday ritual was to give jurors Jolly Rancher candies in the afternoon. Brownlee himself wandered up to the jury box during a break, his robe flapping behind him, distributing the candies on each juror's chair.

A former star prosecutor for the Kern County District Attorney's office, Brownlee was named to the bench in 2007 by then-Gov. Arnold Schwarzenegger for a new position created because of the exploding population in Bakersfield. When appointed, Brownlee told an audience of family and colleagues, "I will be human, I will be engaged in life and I will still be approachable in the street."

That approachability reached a scary point in 2011. A neighbor threatened Brownlee outside his home, in front of the judge's 4-year-old daughter, wrongfully accusing Brownlee of speeding through the neighborhood. (The car spotted by the man was not Brownlee's.) A shaken Brownlee followed the man to his home, got his address and called police. The man was later sentenced to anger management and slapped with a restraining order.

It served as a reminder that Brownlee was not a man to be taken lightly.

Court started on time and ended on time. Lunch breaks were 90 minutes, from noon to 1:30 p.m., on the dot. In this trial, lawyers from neither side even dared test his patience. Objections would be few and far between, always ruled on quickly and with no discussion. Brownlee kept sidebars to a minimum and apologized to the jury profusely after each one. He told jurors that the trial would last no longer than the first week of October and he was determined to keep that promise.

But the fast pace of the trial also had to be attributed to the fact that, aside from Kelly Bernatene's sex life and Richard Terry's grasp of the Bible, little was in dispute for the better part of four days of testimony.

That was all about to change.

"People call Jonathan Hearn," said Smith.

20.

For a few moments, the witness stand sat empty while everybody waited. "One second, ladies and gentlemen," Judge Brownlee told the jury.

A door to the left opened and Jonathan Hearn was escorted in by a deputy. Jonathan didn't look like a prisoner. He looked like a young executive in a dark blue suit, blue shirt and print tie, his hair neatly and stylishly cut.

But for one thing.

He was shackled by the hands and legs. He rattled up to the witness stand and raised a chained-up hand as far as it would go to swear to the tell the truth, the whole truth and nothing but the truth.

"Good afternoon, Mr. Hearn."

"Good afternoon, Mr. Smith."

A bearded man in a suit took a seat behind Jonathan. That was his attorney, Clayton Campbell. He'd be listening carefully.

Jonathan had as much riding on this testimony as Sabrina. His formal sentencing had not yet taken place.

Smith began by asking, "How old are you?"

"Twenty-seven years old."

"How old were you when you were arrested Nov. 18, 2014."

"Twenty-four years old."

"How old were you met Sabrina Limon?"

"Twenty-two years old."

It was a sly beginning for Smith, setting the stage for testimony and arguments to come about who controlled whom in the relationship between Jonathan and the decade-older Sabrina.

Smith then led Jonathan through the details of the plea agreement, signed by Smith and by Jonathan's attorney, that made his testimony possible.

"Did you sign that document as well?"

"I did."

The agreement was then read in court, stating in formal legal language that Defendant Jonathan Hearn agreed to plead guilty to the listed charges in return for his full and truthful testimony in court proceedings involving Sabrina Limon. Failure to do this would void the agreement. He agreed to apologize to Robert Limon's family. He agreed to be sentenced after the proceeding against Sabrina to 25 years and four months for pleading guilty to voluntary manslaughter, a gun enhancement, attempted murder and accessory.

With that, Jonathan began his testimony in earnest—the centerpiece of the prosecution's case.

He spoke of his youth, the home schooling by his mother in a Christian-themed school, followed by his training as a firefighter and arson investigator. He became a temporary junior volunteer firefighter at age 16 with the San Bernardino County Fire Department, then got a full-time job at age 18 in 2009, working several shifts with Jason Bernatene.

"When did you first meet Sabrina Limon?" asked Smith.

"August of 2012," said Jonathan.

"Please point to her location."

With a shackled hand, he pointed to his left and below at Sabrina. "She's in the darker colored shirt," he said.

The judge said the record would reflect that he identified the defendant in court.

Sabrina kept her head down and turned to the right, making no eye contact with her former lover.

Smith asked, "What led you to meet Ms. Limon in August 2012?"

Jonathan spoke of that day in Costco when, shopping for the fire station, he saw her giving out food samples.

"We struck up a conversation," he said. "She asked what I was shopping for. I explained some of that. She explained she had a friend who was a firefighter as well, who was named Jason. I let her know that I knew Jason. We had that in common. She seemed very friendly, very nice."

As his duties that summer required him to keep the station stocked, he made regular trips to Costco. The second or third time he ran into her in the store, she said, "Hi, Jonathan."

"I couldn't remember her name and was feeling bad about that," he said, "and also kind of noting she remembered my name, which was neat. So I think it was on the third time I was in Costco that I got her number."

She had no wedding ring on her hand and she hadn't said anything about a husband; it wasn't until after they talked and texted many times that she confessed, "You know I'm married, right?"

Jonathan recalled, "We had been flirting back and forth. At that point, I recognized that she was married. We agreed to just talk as friends. However, the flirting did continue over text and phone calls."

"When you first met Ms. Limon, were you attracted to her?" Smith asked.

"I was."

"Were you seeing other women?"

"Yes."

"At that point had you had a steady girlfriend?"

"No."

"Had you been in a relationship with anyone?"

"Um, not very steady ones, no."

Sabrina was something new and different for him; he was surprised with himself that he would be attracted to an older married woman with children.

"It didn't necessarily look like the match I would be

going for," he said. "She was somebody who stood out to me immediately, who had a real magnetic personality. She's a very loving and attentive and caring kind of person."

At the time, he was working on a book of stories culled from firefighters around the nation. He posted a story he wrote on his website called "Silver Lakes" and in the fall of 2012 dedicated it, on his site, to Sabrina.

On Oct. 24, she left a comment section in all capital letters: "YOU ARE SO AMAZING AND I AM SO LUCKY TO KNOW YOU!"

They were still talking and flirting. By November, they were making out. It was going too fast for Jonathan. In late November, he expressed concern about their relationship and suggested it "wasn't the wisest thing to progress." Over coffee one morning, he told her: "I'm trying to look to the future and I don't see it leading to anything good. So let's kind of back off."

She became teary-eyed and hugged him.

"It kind of made an impression on me that perhaps I was a little more meaningful to her at that point than I had recognized," he said.

She agreed not to take it further, asking only if they could still talk as friends. They did, and the flirting quickly resumed. By December, it became "a full-blown affair," Jonathan said.

"You used the word 'affair,' " said Smith. "You were having sex with Ms. Limon?"

"Yes."

"Where did that occur?"

"At that time, at her house."

They would get together when Robert was at work and the children were in school. When they were apart, they sent each other texts and photos; in her pictures, Sabrina was sometimes topless. In one picture, she bared her naked behind.

By January, they would meet at his house in Hesperia

for sex "numerous times," he said.

He would continue to visit her at Costco. On Jan. 8, 2013, he took a picture of her in her red apron as she gave out food. On a napkin, she had written, "I love you more Jonathan."

As the days and weeks passed, Sabrina kept sending pictures, many of which Smith flashed on a screen for the jury to see: Sabrina making a sexy kissing face, another of her dramatically backlit by the sun.

Noting he had been raised in a strict Christian household, Jonathan said he felt torn by the relationship with a married woman, but every time he would think of ending it, he'd go right back, "which is to my shame."

Smith asked why.

"Just to give a sense of her personality outside of this courtroom: She's a very, very friendly person, and very encouraging, attentive," he said. "Almost all of her words are very kind toward everyone. She's very upbeat and just has a reserve of optimism no matter what's going on."

This contrasted with his "probably subpar" previous relationships, he said. "They were not people like her. I know in most affairs you would assume it's the sexual draw or something along those lines. With her, while we are engaged in that, there was a lot more than that. I just found her to be a very entrancing person."

He spoke of that night at Beef 'O' Brady's, where he got a big hug from Sabrina and met Robert for the first time. He recalled later hearing from Sabrina that Robert had found out about them, and how he called Jason Bernatene to contact Robert so he could apologize, only to have Jason put Robert on the phone.

"I talked to him for a little bit and without confessing to a full-on affair, I did acknowledge—as he had seen some of our gushing conversations in her phone— that we did have a pretty serious emotional affair," he said. "I did apologize for that."

Wracked by guilt, he wrote of the moment in his journal on April 22, 2013:

"I begged Robert's forgiveness and pray for his salvation. God has showed me grace. Shall we continue in sin that grace may abound? No way. I am blessed but torn. I cannot afford to hurt Robert again yet I love Sabrina.

"Ultimately I want this woman to know that she is amazing and loved by God and me but I cannot also disrespect, hurt or dishonor her incredible husband. Next time we will discover the beauty and balance of forgiveness. Forgiveness is a challenge."

Jonathan said that he found it even more challenging to stay away from Sabrina. Within a month, they were sleeping together again. It continued month after month, interrupted only by Jonathan's occasional pangs of conscience, which he would quickly snuff out. When not having sex once or twice a week, they talked and texted daily, usually multiple times a day.

By early 2014, these conversations drifted toward Sabrina's feelings about Robert.

"We became close enough where she began to express the negative things about him," he said. "The biggest thing was, as far as their marriage, she expressed that he perpetuated a very image-based lifestyle. They had an open relationship where he was pretty exploitative, at least she expressed to me that he was pretty exploitative, and objectifying her, and pretty much the emotional entanglement or conflict with that was. Here she was married to him, but yet he was pretty much willing to pass her off to any other guy and not leave the doors of their marriage closed."

When she tried to talk to Robert about this, he grew distant and absorbed himself in his work and hobbies. "She expressed that he rarely included the kids in his projects, but was pretty focused on his partying, his truck, his boat."

Smith asked: "How did you feel when she was telling

you these things about her family life?"

"The foundation of a number of our conversations were justifying in nature," he said. "They were to look for justification for an affair that we were carrying on and shouldn't have been and over which I felt guilt for. They were meant to alleviate."

The longer Jonathan testified, the more formal his syntax became. He was matter-of-fact to the point of emotionless. As Smith drew Jonathan into increasingly more sensitive subjects, his words and sentences got longer.

His demeanor in court clashed with the raw emotions he was describing. By late 2013, he said, he was deeply conflicted and deeply in love. He ached for Sabrina and he wanted Robert out of the picture. God, he felt, would not approve.

In December, wrote her a note full of pain.

My truest love,

I didn't know (paused to cry for a while). I didn't know that love would feel this good! I know we are doing the right thing. It just hurts so bad. It shouldn't hurt this bad because we aren't 'breaking up' with each other, only doing the <u>right</u> thing and showing the responsibility that will <u>save</u> your marriage. It's crazy to think that we really truly could have caused your divorce within a few months. I love you so much. But I never want to hurt your family. And I know you know <u>everything</u> that I'm writing in this letter. It just helps me feel better writing it to you. You are the best thing that has ever happened to me, Sabrina Limon.

Such intense feelings were alien to Jonathan. They overwhelmed him and left him despondent. It was all so new and strange that he memorialized in, of all things, a selfie he snapped in Sabrina's bedroom. Taken Dec. 27, the photo showed him crying while holding that very letter. Behind him, on the wall, hung a crucifix. He explained that he took the picture because he always wanted to remember how he felt at that moment.

Despite all this, Sabrina didn't want to end the affair. And she wasn't ready for a divorce. The Jonathan/Sabrina separation, such as it was, ended quickly. The makeup sex was incredible.

They became "definitely more passionate, way more serious than before," he said. "Her raw emotion was something that I was not wanting to cause. It really broke my heart to see her upset."

This was, he said, "probably the most pivotal time in our relationship."

Sabrina seemed to agree. On Valentine's Day, Sabrina sent him this note:

My Jonathan,
I love you!
I love you for finding the part of me that I never thought I'd find.
I love you for wanting and needing me by your side.
I love you for trusting me with your heart, your pride, your wisdom and soul.
I love you for the intimate exchanges we have.
I love you for me being the one you choose to care of.
I love you for the special meaning you have brought to my life.
I love you for hopes and faith in our future together.
I love you for giving me a new perspective on life.
I love you for wanting to live for God.
I love you for seeing more than my 'parts and pieces' and loving all of who I am.
I love you for believing in me and all that I have to offer.
I love you for so many reasons. I've only written a few but in all that years bring to us I never want you to forget that you were made for me, I was made for you.

Your first true love

Being showered with 13 "I love yous" sent Jonathan past the point of no return. They needed a more permanent solution.

Smith asked: "Was the decision made to kill Robert Limon?

"Yes, sir," Jonathan said.

21.

It began as a bad joke. They would wonder aloud how much simpler life would be for them if Robert were just gone.

But the deeper they fell in love, the darker their conversations turned. "It definitely turned from humorous into something that actually began to materialize," said Jonathan.

Divorce, Sabrina said, simply wasn't an option, for her or for Robert. "As ironic and sad as this sounds, for Rob's sake, she expressed that he would honestly rather be dead than divorced, and that losing her would essentially kill him, which was something she didn't want to cause," said Jonathan.

Sabrina asked Jonathan for ideas. He suggested a car accident or an arson fire. Those options were scotched as too complicated and risky. They settled on poisoning.

Smith asked: "What information did Sabrina provide to you?"

"A lot of things, including but not limited to, she did express that he had a little bit of a kind of a rare medical condition, the name of it escapes me, that presented with some symptoms that might be mimicked in a poisoning attempt," said Jonathan, referring to Robert's 2005 bout with Guillain-Barré syndrome. "She also mentioned that recently, he had been having some stomach issues."

The poisoning could be done in a way to show flu-like symptoms. Robert would be pronounced dead on site or in the hospital without a criminal investigation. They just needed the right poison and the right circumstances.

They opted for sneaking poison into food.

"Which food types did she suggest that Robert Limon was sure to eat?"

"She gave me two suggestions. One was some sort of sandwich or wrap that can be purchased at Costco, and then also banana pudding with Nilla wafers."

An inveterate keeper of lists, Jonathan included the poisoning plot on a to-do list that also, perversely, included his daily errands and his longer-range plans with Sabrina. Later found when deputies searched Jonathan's house, the list read:

Diet
Workout for race
Best Buy
Get hard drive
Make backup discs, install new HD
New phone
Sync old and new phone
Buy Tupperware, milk, med Pestle
Make sample batch, mix with water, neighbor dog

Mountain biking!
Engineer book!

Savings:
Ring 5k
Wedding-10k beach?
Honeymoon-10k

On March 19, 2014, Jonathan ordered a vial of arsenic trioxide from LabChem Inc. of Jackson's Pointe, PA. He purchased it through mail order using a prepaid debit card loaded through a PayPal account under an alias. He had the arsenic sent to his grandparents' commercial arts studio. The cost was $115. The arsenic arrived on April 19.

On the internet, he researched how much poison relative to Robert's weight he would need to use. "I experimented that on a neighbor dog that had caused me considerable issues in the past," he said. He laced a piece of salmon with arsenic and tossed it over the fence. He never heard the dog bark again.

For a recipe, he typed the search words "easy banana pudding with 'nill wafers" into JustAPinch.com. He then put on a mask and gloves and mixed the poison into a batch of Jell-O brand pudding.

Sabrina didn't want Robert dying at home, where the children might find him. So he and Sabrina decided it would be best if Robert ate the poisoned pudding while working during one of his long solo shifts out in Tehachapi.

That would mean hours could go by before anybody found him. And when somebody did, Jonathan felt, the paramedics and hospital care in the little desert town would not be as good.

Jonathan made two batches of pudding, a large portion without the poison intended for Sabrina's family, a second secret smaller batch laced with arsenic just for Robert.

"I drove out to see Sabrina. I believe Robert was working that day," said Jonathan." He gave her two Tupperware containers of pudding and explained "the smaller portion was the portion that had the poison in it to put in his lunch the next day."

Jonathan went home and triple-bagged the arsenic. He stowed it away where he thought nobody would find it— deep in the chicken coop behind his rental unit—with the idea he'd dispose of it permanently later.

The next day, the plan was scotched. He and Sabrina decided not to put the poisoned pudding in Robert's lunch. They feared that after Robert died, their relationship would be discovered through phone records, and it would look terrible.

"We agreed to call him, if possible, and divert him from

eating that poison-laced pudding," said Jonathan.

Sabrina phoned Robert and told him stay away from the pudding because the bananas had gone bad. He didn't eat it, and lived long enough for Jonathan and Sabrina to come up with another idea.

After that, they decided to be more careful. Around this time, Robert had somehow seen Sabrina's gmail account, which she and Jonathan had set up for heightened secrecy after Robert saw her cell phone messages. Robert again saw their love notes. Caught a second time, another argument ensued between Robert and Sabrina, followed by a second reconciliation, with Robert not wanting to talk about it anymore.

That's when Jonathan got the burner phone. He would keep his cell phone, but Sabrina would only talk to him on the phone with prepaid minutes, purchased by Jonathan with cash.

They maintained their affair, as passionate as ever, but tabled murdering Robert for another three or four months to put some distance between them and their calls shown on the pre-burner cell phone records.

"After the poison attempt, these were probably the darkest conversations we had about him," he said. "Maybe there was an exaggerated sense of her vulnerabilities and an exaggerated scrutiny of his faults. He was spoken about poorly quite a bit during this time."

Jonathan listed Robert's shortcomings on a yellow legal pad, another list found at his house.

Gave *his wife away to another man to share passionate experience that humans can share together?*
gave his wife away to other women
wants to have a threesome
views his wife as his cum(?) dumpsters (and she is amazing)
Defied _the_ LIVING GOD

please kill him God!!!

I love you: My vision has not changed
Divorce or wait for Rob to leave
God's punishment

After a few months, they returned to the murder plot, opting this time against poison. "It was just based on if I was made a suspect, I figured, with my medical background and training, poisoning might make me more of a suspect than something that was more out of character for me, like violence," Jonathan testified. "I reconsidered and I thought it might be better to approach him directly for the killing."

The best way, he decided, was with a gun.

Smith asked: "Did you tell Sabrina that you planned on confronting Robert directly?"

"I did."

"Did you tell her that you were either going to shoot him from a distance or close range?"

"I know that she knew I was going to be confronting him at close range."

"Did you tell Sabrina what you intended to do?"

"I don't recall the exact details, whether I expressed what kind of weapon I would be using or not."

"Did you express to Sabrina that you would be attacking Robert Limon with violence?"

"I guess that's inferred that we were going to be encountering each other and he would be dead afterwards."

Borrowing from the poisoning plot, Jonathan decided to kill Robert in Tehachapi while he worked alone.

"What information did Sabrina provide you?"

"She described the facility for me because I didn't have knowledge of the layout," he said. "So she expressed it was an industrial building at the end of a long road, and its proximity to some houses nearby."

She next described the interior of the BNSF workshop

and the layout of the office.

"She gave me some advice on avoiding detection. She told me the responder vehicles at the location had recently installed forward-facing cameras on the utility trucks and just obviously to avoid the front of the truck."

She also suggested he ride his motorcycle instead of his more conspicuous truck, which ran loud on diesel.

He scoped out the facility in May while returning home from a training conference in Monterey, driving through the complex and taking those photos his lawyer would later find. He noted the shop was marked only by the BNSF insignia stenciled on the concrete parking blocks.

He also noticed that Robert's truck was parked there.

Jonathan called Sabrina from the road.

"I expressed to her that I was able to find it and had seen it and I believe I mentioned that Robert was there at the time," he said.

When he returned home, he and Sabrina discussed timing. They wanted to do it sooner rather than later, but then Sabrina's mother broke her hip and had to recover in a nursing facility. "She expressed she would rather wait until her mom was home and settled from a broken leg," he said.

But Sabrina didn't want to wait too long. "They were planning a river trip and it was something that Sabrina was not interested in attending yet again, something that they used to do every year," he said.

The river trip promised to be another one of those drunken bacchanals that inevitably ended with partner swapping or other sexual activities with their friends. It was set for late August or early September, Jonathan said.

"She wanted to make the killing attempt prior to that and was kind of pushing for that," he said.

They decided to strike the next time Robert had a solo fill-in shift in Tehachapi.

"Did she keep you up to date on his schedule?"

"Yes."

On Aug. 17, he got off work in Redlands at 8:30 a.m. He had pulled his third straight 24-hour shift in a row. He headed up the Cajon Pass toward Hesperia, stopping at a Walmart to purchase ammunition. He didn't need the bullets; he already had box full at home. He purchased a different caliber of ammunition as a diversion in case police checked later. He got the receipt that his lawyer was so disappointed to find.

Jonathan said he may have spoken to Sabrina from the road, but couldn't remember for certain. After getting home, he tested a silencer he had made himself with the Maglite, gluing four or five car parts called "freeze plugs" inside to muffle the sound of the bullet as it passed through. The results pleased him.

"The firearm was extremely quiet, probably no louder than a pneumatic nail gun used for carpentry, even though it was a .45-caliber gun," he said.

One problem was the silencer reduced his semi-automatic, in which a bullet is fired every time the trigger is pressed, into a single-shot pistol. He would have to manually move a new bullet into the chamber before firing an additional round.

He dressed in the clothes he'd purchased from Goodwill and stuffed his gear—the gun, silencer, extra ammo and a mask of an old man's face—into a backpack, which itself was placed inside another backpack. He disguised his motorcycle by placing silver adhesive flashing over the rear fender, exhaust pipe and gas tank. This obscured the "Forgiven" written on the tank and gave the illusion that his all-black bike had chrome accents.

"Did you speak with Sabrina Limon?" Smith asked.

"I did."

"Did you tell her of your preparations?"

"She asked me how I was feeling. She asked me if I could be detected. I explained the clothing and the mask. I didn't think I would be recognized. She asked me about my motorcycle, if that would be noticed. It had custom lettering on it. I explained I was taking measures."

It was a lengthy conversation, he said, with Sabrina's voice coming over the speaker of his phone while he got ready. He said he was more focused on his preparations and didn't remember everything she said.

"Did she express any other concerns?"

"One thing she mentioned in that conversation was just to be careful because she told me that Robert would likely put up a fight and could fight," he said. "She also expressed that she thought I was getting a late start because I was still at home."

She told him that if he got to Tehachapi too late, he might run into the responder relieving Robert for the night shift.

Smith asked: "Did she express that same concern for Rob's safety?"

"Not with respect to his life, no."

The plan called for shooting Robert and staging a robbery scene.

"Sabrina told me about the Tehachapi Loop areas as it pertains to the railroad," he said. "Tehachapi already was sort of a hotspot for robberies."

She related stories from Robert about how trains that had to slow down as they went up the Tehachapi Loop fell prey to robbers seeking goods in the shipping containers. Robert had called it a dangerous area.

They also discussed what they would do if police started poking around in Sabrina's personal life.

"First and foremost, we were hoping to not use any alibi, that hopefully, it would be investigated as a robbery," he said. "But in the event that the investigation was pointed at her, I encouraged her not to mention our affair at all because that would obviously open up room for scrutiny."

If police did happen to come upon records of their phone calls, love letters and other evidence, "Our agreed-upon alibi was that any indication of us being sneaky about anything was more so about us having an affair, as opposed to anything more than that. In the event that it did come up, it could be simply excused as trying to hide an ongoing affair."

Jonathan got on his motorcycle and headed toward Tehachapi, leaving his cell phone behind so that his location could not be tracked by GPS. He had also taken the license plate off the bike. Along the way, he stopped at the gas station at Four Corners to top off his tank.

"What's going through your mind?" asked Smith.

"It was my initial thought or intention to use this trip out there as a sort of reconnaissance again. Because of the amount of time that had passed, I couldn't remember clearly where the facility was or which industrial building he worked in. I was going to be using this as time to reconnaissance and re-familiarize myself with that area as a dry run for a later date."

Sabrina had given him some other dates that Robert would be working overnight shifts. Jonathan preferred the cover of darkness.

Jonathan said, "I was definitely armed to kill him; however, I wasn't sure if I could do that or not."

In Tehachapi, he found the turnoff. As he drove down Goodrick toward the facility, a BNSF utility vehicle came toward him. He assumed it was Robert, so he turned around and parked on a cross street. When the truck passed, he drove toward the industrial complex and parked across street, stashing his bike in a "secluded area" behind a pile of asphalt. He walked around the perimeter of facility looking for the BNSF garage, staying far away from a security camera he had seen in May at the front of the complex. Or so he thought.

He had on a long-sleeved shirt and loose pants of the sort he had never worn before and was carrying the backpack with the gun and silencer. He found what looked like the outside of the BNSF garage and paused there for about 15 minutes next to barrels and piles of scrap metal. He went around the front of the building. The BNSF garage door was closed and he saw no entrance door.

"I decided to call it off and walked back toward my motorcycle," he said. "As I was heading north back up outside the perimeter of the facility, Robert drove back in and opened the garage door and pulled into the BNSF garage."

This was Robert returning from the call on the UPS train when he spoke on the phone to Sabrina.

Jonathan's mind was racing.

"I had some pretty conflicted thoughts, ultimately leading to the thought of not really wanting to go through all this again," he said. On the other hand, he was locked and loaded. "As I was considering coming back there at night, I considered just the simplicity of maybe confronting him right then."

He walked across the center of the facility—and in front of the security camera that captured the footage that would later be released to the public—and got close to the garage that Robert had entered. The door was still open.

Jonathan felt apprehensive. "I think I already addressed most of my guilt and excused it away as this was sort of an inevitable act that just needed to be carried out," he said. "As unappealing as it was for me, it was something I was eager to get over with."

Suddenly, a van pulled up and parked in front of the BNSF shop. He hadn't expected anybody else to be there that Sunday. He wondered if Robert had a visitor. He dashed into a breezeway and waited for 10 to 15 minutes. The van driver went somewhere else. Robert appeared to be alone.

"What were you mentally going through?" asked Smith.

Jonathan gave one of his most long-winded answers.

"Somewhere along the lines of summer of 2014, there had been an ongoing narrative of Sabrina and I seeking purpose in our lives," he said. "At that time, as I stopped in that breezeway, I specifically remember praying and sort of seeking that purpose that I had set out to find. The foundation work behind that purpose was essentially that it was inevitable that Rob needed to die for Sabrina and I to move forward with our relationship."

The prayer focused on moral conflicts inherent in seeking that purpose. "I know now this is the product of extremely twisted thinking. I apologize for that," he said. "At the time, it felt like I was approaching something that inevitably had to be done."

After praying, he entered the shop. Robert saw him.

"He had been in the office, which is in the back corner of the garage," Jonathan said. "And—"

Jonathan went silent for a moment.

"Uh, uh, we briefly spoke," he said. "I don't have distinct recollection right now."

They were 10 feet apart, Jonathan's face covered by the old man's mask.

Jonathan walked along the driver's side of the truck, mindful of the front-facing security camera on the vehicle that Sabrina told him about.

As Robert turned his back and "retrieved some things," Jonathan reached into the backpack and felt the gun.

It was stuck. The big silencer was pressed against the side of the backpack. He couldn't get the gun out.

Robert turned back around to face Jonathan.

"I fired the shot from within the bag," he said. With the bag held low, the shot traveled upward.

"After you fired the first shot what happened to Robert?" Smith asked.

"He fell, seemingly mortally wounded," said Jonathan.

"After he fell, what did you do?"

He paused again. "Um, so as to avoid the front of the truck because of the cameras, I went around the back of the vehicle and then headed up into the office to follow through with the previously discussed plan of overturning the interior of the office making it look like a robbery."

As Jonathan testified, Sabrina continued to avert her

gaze, her head down and turned to the right.

The jurors appeared glum. Some took notes. But most had their eyes locked on Jonathan.

Jonathan said he grabbed random paperwork from file drawers, tossed some on the floor and stuffed some in his backpack. He also took the laptop computer from the desk and stashed it in his pack.

Jonathan started to walk out of the garage, then stopped.

"Previously, when I had shot Rob and he fell, he exhaled in a way that made me believe he was dead," he said. "But I questioned that as I was about to leave, thinking I really didn't want to leave him if he wasn't entirely dead. I went back around the back side of the truck and quickly fired one more shot at him."

Rob was lying on his back. Jonathan fired from his feet toward his head.

He left the garage, closing the door behind him.

"Did you have any indication of whether he was alive?" asked Smith

"Other than that audible gasp," said Jonathan, "no."

He ran from the shop to his motorcycle, got back on Highway 58 and headed east.

"As you're riding away, what are you thinking?" asked Smith.

"That I would like to quickly get out of this current disguise just in case anyone had seen me. I didn't have any reason to believe there were witnesses. I wanted to get back dressed into some ordinary clothes and get home."

"Were you feeling happiness, elation, excitement?"

"Immediately after leaving, probably fear," Jonathan said. "Later on that day, it was more just a feeling of—I'm sorry, this sounds bad—but relief, that what had been in the works for so long was finally done."

22.

Pulling off the road into a remote area, Jonathan changed out of the murder clothes into shorts and a black tank top. He yanked the silver flashing off the motorcycle. He stashed clothes and adhesive into the second backpack. He put the license plate back on.

Back on the freeway, a problem arose; he feared he might run out of gas. The main tank went empty, so he switched to a backup tank. Fifty miles out of Tehachapi, he just made it into Boron, searching the main drag for a station, and finding none.

Running on fumes, he got back on the 58 and pulled into the Pilot Travel Center, where he'd stopped on the way to the murder scene. He filled up and went into the store to buy a water bottle and Gatorade. To conceal his identity, he kept his helmet on with a red bandana around his neck. He paid cash for the gas and drinks. The security cameras caught his every move.

It was now an hour after murdering Robert and "I wasn't feeling so good." He downed the water and Gatorade, tossed the bottles in the gas station trash and headed home. The only other hiccup along the way: He nearly slammed into a mattress on the road.

The man who had just murdered a romantic rival in cold blood pulled over and courteously removed the mattress to keep other drivers safe.

He reached Hesperia at dusk. Several texts and missed phone calls from Sabrina awaited him.

He called her back.

"She was worried," he said. "She expressed that she was glad to hear from me. She hadn't heard from either of us and had been trying to call both of us, referring to both me and Robert."

He told her that he still had to get rid of a few things, and she was surprised he hadn't done that already. He destroyed the laptop, which he considered the most incriminating item, and tossed most of the pieces into a Dumpster behind a nearby store. He left at his home, for reasons that would never be clear, part of the screen. The rest of the items—the murder clothes, the silencer, the backpacks—he stowed away in the chicken coop.

"What was your state of mind at the time?" asked Smith.

"Probably pretty paranoid, pretty frantic, and just burdened by the fact that I just committed a really egregious act," he said.

As an arson-investigator-in-training, he knew that if police discovered his affair with Sabrina, they would become top suspects. He felt he could take the heat if it came, and thought Sabrina could, too.

"Frankly, this was the culmination of something we had essentially planned together and so, perhaps my weakness—my trust—was pretty strong in her," he said.

"Did you discuss at length with her the need for that trust between you and her post-murder?" Smith asked.

"There were three months after the time that I killed him and the time that I was arrested," he said. "During that time, there was a progressive tightening of the stress that we were both were going through."

In the days after the murder, he took a previously planned trip to San Diego to visit family members, then returned to the high desert to resume his relationship with Sabrina, now without Robert alive. Again, they had a plan.

"Simply, I could be a friend from work, which is where I had met her," he said. "It was our intention over time to slowly introduce ourselves to one another, the more naturally we spent time together, the more it would seem an organically flourishing relationship."

That Costco visit with his sister, where Sabrina's boss told them of Robert's death, was completely staged—using his sister, Emily, as an unwitting accomplice. But he said his reaction was true. Emotions had been building and to hear the words out loud that Robert had been murdered genuinely moved him.

After that, he and Sabrina began seeing each other again, usually with Jonathan's sister in tow. They constantly sent messages and spent hours on the phone—Jonathan on his cell, Sabrina still on the burner.

Everything was working well, but for one nagging concern.

"She and I agreed that Jason and Kelly Bernatene essentially posed the only real substantial risk of discovery by law enforcement," he said. "They were the only ones we knew of that knew we had something of an affair back in 2013. It was our intention to sort of gradually distance ourselves from them."

In that spirit, Jonathan left the messages with Jason apologizing for abusing Jason's friendship and getting close to Sabrina before Robert's death. Jonathan told Sabrina in a Sept. 8 text: "I am going to pray about writing Jason's letter today, also do a bunch of homework, laundry and start drawing the house plans for the first house to sell."

It was the first of many prayers about the Bernatenes, for two weeks later Sabrina sent him this text with her frowny face emoticon: "What a day :/"

"Hey, baby!" he texted back.

"Kelly just texted me asking who's (sic) truck was here last night. She was wondering if it was Dale's :/ she said she saw unfamiliar rim's (sic)."

Three days later, Sabrina had another unsettling Bernatene encounter. "Omg ... the kid's (sic) and I just saw Jason at the market while we were getting ice cream and

Robbie brought you up :/"

Their concerns, of course, proved warranted as Jason forwarded Jonathan's messages to Det. Meyer, who from that point on, focused only on Jonathan and Sabrina.

The Bernatenes were not the only source of stress. One night, Jonathan went to Sabrina's house and saw a lurking man Jonathan worried was an undercover officer. After Jonathan left, he messaged Sabrina: "I am home now; I didn't lay down; I was feeling apprehension about that guy. The more I think of it, the less I assume he was someone of interest. ... Hopefully he was just going for a walk."

The next month, November, three undercover officers would follow Jonathan and Sabrina around—"They dined with them regularly," Meyer said in an interview—but this man wasn't one of them.

The rest of Jonathan and Sabrina's anxiety would be delivered to the jury in real time in their own words.

For much of five court days, Smith played recordings of the wiretapped conversations leading up to the day of their arrests. Jonathan's wide range of emotions—friendly, loving, spiritual, passionate, fearful, anxious, paranoid—stood in sharp contrast to his measured and mechanical testimony.

The jury had transcripts to follow along with the recordings, which often were difficult to hear because of the bad phone reception. Smith would pause the recordings to get Jonathan's explanation for what he was thinking at the time.

Over and over, Jonathan explained that throughout the calls, he and Sabrina had used the word "affair" as a code for "murder."

As the wiretaps showed, they suspected early on that they were being monitored. He said any explicit talk of killing Robert was done in person.

Jonathan wrapped up his direct testimony by recounting that phone conversation with Sabrina when he had returned home from murdering her husband.

"She was initially worried about me and asked if I was okay," Jonathan said. "I don't remember my exact words, but in essence and form, I said I had done it and that things would be changing."

23.

Richard Terry took off his glasses and rubbed his eyes. He said something got in there and apologized. But this was his normal routine before every cross-examination, as if bracing himself for what he was about to have to watch.

"Mr. Hearn," he began, dispensing with his usual good morning greeting of a witness, "part of your deal with the prosecution to provide this testimony against Ms. Limon, before your deal was consummated, you spoke to police?"

"That's correct, sir."

Jonathan confirmed that during his four police interviews he revealed the location of evidence such as the silencer and the poison. He confirmed that he had immunity from any additional charges linked to the Limon case.

"I'm a bit of a poker player," said Terry. "That's what we call a free roll. In other words, you got a free shot at this without any consequence to you, right?" Jonathan answered: "I'm not sure of the game of poker."

Terry asked: "Now there's been talk about giving truthful testimony as part of your deal. With regards to that, that's for the jury to decide if your testimony is truthful, right?'

Jonathan listened to the question, collected his thoughts, and said in a calm, clear voice: "That's my understanding."

"In other words, you can get up there and say whatever you want, as you've done in the past and gotten away with it, and it's up to the jury to decide whether you're telling the truth now, right?"

Another brief pause. "I would certainly hope so."

"The only way your deal gets undone is if the DA, Mr.

Smith, decides if you lie under oath, right?"

"That would be one aspect that could potentially undo the deal, yes."

"You would agree that up until January 3 of this year, my client was not in custody until *you* talked to the police?"

"No," Jonathan corrected him. "She was previously in custody."

Terry asked: "And released while you were still in custody."

"Yes, sir."

It was only a moment, fleeting in the larger context of the trial, but an important one for Jonathan, and by extension, the prosecution.

On direct examination, he may have come off as cold and clinical. But on cross, that pose played more as unflappable. He never raised his voice, never protested the insinuation of a question. If he didn't understand something, he said so. If he needed clarification, he asked for it. If he could answer with only a "Yes, sir," or "No, sir," he would do so.

What's more, he knew the case. He knew the evidence, the testimony, and the timeline.

Terry sought to show that his skill as a witness was no accident. He confronted Jonathan with personal notes taken at a paramedic training session in which one of the seminars touched on how to conduct oneself on the witness stand.

"You were taught to listen to the entire question?" asked Terry.

After a pause, Jonathan said, "Yes, sir."

"And then you were also taught to pause before you answer, right?"

"Yes, sir." For this one, Jonathan answered quickly.

"One of the other things you were taught was to answer the question succinctly?"

"I believe so, based on my notes."

He confirmed he was also taught how to spot trick questions and anticipate lawyer objections.

"You were taught how to testify, right?" asked Terry.

"It was a very small component of our training, yes."

Terry spent the next large chunk of cross-examination retracing Jonathan's relationship with Sabrina.

"You talked about her family, her children?"

"Yes, sir."

"Eventually, she opened up to you about her open marriage with her husband, right?"

"Eventually, she did."

"When did this occur?"

As he had on direct examination, when Jonathan was not giving short answers, he would deliver long, detailed ones, setting up the history and context before getting to the answer. He said that he first suspected Sabrina's sexual past when she mentioned the names of some of her friends who worked as firefighters. Jonathan not only knew of these men, but the buzz around the station was that they were into wife swapping.

"I asked her if she was a swinger," said Jonathan, "and she said, 'Oh, no, no, no.' She definitely denied that. But then in time, I asked the question a number of times and in different ways, trying, I guess, to develop where her emotional neglect had come from, and eventually, she did tell me that they were swingers."

She said this about a month after Robert had found out about Jonathan and Sabrina.

Terry pressed Jonathan on who exactly these firefighter swingers were. For the first time in the cross-examination, Jonathan fumbled with his words. He said he didn't know all their names. Pressed by Terry, he identified by name—in court, on live-streaming video—the name of a fire captain and his wife.

Jonathan said: "She mentioned another captain whose name I can't recall right now." She then mentioned yet another firefighter later.

Terry asked incredulously: "You're saying there were

that many firefighters you worked with who were involved with swinging?"

"Sir," Jonathan said, returning to his calm voice, "San Bernardino County Fire Department has, I want to say, 500 and something firefighters. So it accounted for a very, very small percentage."

Terry then moved from swinging to murder.

"Did you actually discuss with her that you were going to shoot him?"

"Yes, I did."

"Of course, you have evidence that these discussions actually took place other than your testimony?"

"I bring no evidence into the court."

"No text messages?"

"No, because we had discussed not leaving traces like that."

"Are there any notes she wrote?"

"I'm not sure. I've been here the last three years. I'm not sure what things are still in my old residence. I'm in custody, sir."

"Emails: those don't exist anymore either?"

"I can't speak to their existence."

Moving to a subject of which there was much evidence, Terry asked Jonathan about the wire-tapped conversations, specifically the ones in which they discussed Sabrina's meetings with Det. Meyer.

"You were telling her what to say to Detective Meyer, were you not?"

"I'm sure the jury all had a discerning ear," Jonathan said. "At times, I offered suggestions of what to say. Certainly, we were agreeing on a line of rhetoric and narrative."

"You told her what to tell Detective Meyer," Terry snapped.

"No, I offered suggestions. I didn't force her to say anything to Mr. Meyer, as she didn't force me to make the bad choices I made."

"Mr. Hearn, I know you want to go back to your script," said Terry. The rest of his question got shot down by a sustained objection from Smith.

Terry asked: "All of these efforts that you and Sabrina talked about, according to you, were with regard to trying to alleviate suspicion from you?"

"Certainly, I was taking measures to alleviate suspicion from her."

"And yourself. You disguised yourself."

"Of course."

"She wasn't there when you built the silencer?"

"No."

"She was not there when you bought the clothes you wore to murder Robert Limon?"

"No, she was not."

"She was not there when you disguised your motorcycle."

"I was on the phone with her describing that I was concealing the appearance of my motorcycle."

As for also calling her while scouting the murder scene in May, Terry said, "Again, the only evidence of the purported conversation with Sabrina is your testimony?"

"I'm not sure."

"Did you record the conversation you had with Sabrina?"

"I did not."

"So is there anyone else who was present when you supposedly had these conversations with Sabrina?"

"I guess. Sabrina could tell the truth."

Terry asked, "You planned out a way to try to give Rob Limon this poison? You did, right?"

"Alone?"

"I know what you want to say," said Terry. "Did Sabrina buy the poison?"

"No, I purchased it."

"Did Sabrina make the pudding that you say you supposedly gave to her?"

"No, I did."

"Did Sabrina poison a helpless dog and kill it like you did?"

"As I said, I never confirmed I killed the dog. But, no, she did not do that."

"There's no way that Sabrina would ever have poison in her house that her children could get at, right?

After the judge sustained Smith's objection that Jonathan was being asked to speculate what was going through Sabrina's mind, Terry reframed the question.

"During the timeframe of your relationship with Ms. Limon, you believe she was a loving, caring mother, right?"

"Generally speaking, yes, sir."

"Would you agree that she is extremely protective of her children, based on your observations and dealings?"

"I would not characterize her as extremely protective, sir."

"Because she got involved with you?"

Jonathan didn't offer an answer.

Terry asked, "You are not a very emotional person?"

"In my previous testimony, I was speaking about December 2013 and the time prior to that when I hadn't cried or showed much emotion in quite some time."

"You now are in touch with your emotions?"

"No, sir, you just embellished on what I just said."

"Are you saying now that you're able to express your emotions better than you were in December 2013?"

"I think it's pretty obvious I'm a pretty emotionally guarded person, and I certainly don't sensationalize anything I'm saying. I'm a pretty objective person."

"You described fairly clinically how you murdered her husband."

"Sir, I worked in emergency services. I've seen death and destruction. Microwaved infants. I apologize if it's disturbing that I can speak about something horrible like killing a man with a straight face."

Terry asked, "Never once in the time that you were

involved with Sabrina did it ever come to your mind to say, 'Oh, heck, I'm not doing this'? Right?"

"As I testified to having reluctance, yes, I did think that on a couple of separate occasions, but something overcame those better judgments," he said. "Someone."

"You're saying Sabrina controlled you?"

"On one level, certainly, I'm saying that. On another level, of course, I have free will. I'm an adult responsible for my own actions."

"How did Sabrina overcome your free will to get you to murder her husband?"

"Mr. Terry, I could recite our story from the beginning of 2012. That's probably not what you want. It won't provide any logical explanation. The fact that I sinned in killing her husband cannot be pathologized, cannot be made to make sense. It is illogical. It is wrong. It was a horrible act and I do live with the guilt and regret from that."

Jonathan continued: "The fact remains we had a very sordid, ongoing affair for years, and she did play a very influential role in my life. I'm not using it as a justification. Also, I want to be very clear: I'm not blaming her for doing something that I, myself, am responsible for. I'm not here to judge. I'm here to speak the truth."

"You'd have done anything for her?"

"It seems I did, sir."

24.

Dramatic surprises from the witness stand are rare. Witnesses almost never drop bombshells on direct examination and they rarely crumble on cross. That's the stuff of crime thrillers.

The reality is that by the time witnesses testify, they've faced the same questions and given the same answers countless times and, if anything, the testimony comes off as rote.

Jonathan had spoken to Meyer and Smith for 15 hours over four days. Some of what he said in the trial came out in his testimony at a preliminary hearing for Sabrina.

So testimony has to be evaluated in increments. For the prosecution, Jonathan said what he was supposed to say. His account fit Smith's theory of the case and much of it could be corroborated with the physical evidence and the wiretaps. He implicated Sabrina in the murder plot without hesitation and without expressing any malice against her. He still had feelings for her.

"If I could make this point abundantly clear, I don't have a romantic love for her anymore, but I certainly love her," Jonathan told Terry.

"Time apart, you became less enamored with her?" the lawyer asked.

"It's a much different kind of love."

Whether other feelings simmered beneath the surface, only Jonathan would know.

The prosecution wrapped up its case against Sabrina by playing the three police interrogations after her arrest in which she was first pummeled with questions in Boron, given an easier time by the more friendly Det. Meyer in Bakersfield—until detectives Brewer and Trevino took over—and finally, that last session at the jail before prosecutors declined to file charges and she was released. It was a final opportunity to hear and see Sabrina, this time as she reluctantly, under great pressure, admitted to the affair and her suspicions about Jonathan's innocence.

Cross-examining Det. Rutledge about the fierce Boron interrogation, defense attorney Terry sought to show that much of what Sabrina told police stemmed from multiple law officers calling her a bad mother and telling her she'd never see her kids again.

"Why didn't you just get a rubber hose out and beat her, sir?" Terry snapped.

The judge said, "Sustained," before Smith could even complete his objection.

"Would you agree," Terry said, "by using her children as leverage to get her to talk to you—that would be coercive?"

This time, Smith got out his entire objection, the judge told Terry to restate his question, which he did.

Rutledge said, "I did not feel at the time I was being coercive."

"But you were hoping that would get Sabrina to tell you things you wanted to hear?"

"We were attempting to get her to tell the truth."

After the jury heard the interrogation by Meyer, Terry launched the same line of questioning. Noting Meyer had made a "series of lies and misstatements" to Sabrina, the lawyer asked if he was trying to pressure her by saying she had a huge decision to make if she wanted to see her children again.

"I wasn't trying to pressure her," said Meyer. "It was a pretty relaxed interview."

He completed his testimony by unveiling the last piece of physical evidence. It was contained in a brown paper bag. On the stand, Meyer used a big pair of scissors to open the bag and remove a heavy, round object wrapped in more brown paper. Removing the paper, he held a snow globe. Inside was a silver planet Earth. Sparkly flakes fell. It was found on Jonathan Hearn's kitchen table during the January 2017 follow-up search. An inscription read, "Love, Sabrina." It was her Christmas gift to Jonathan in 2013.

On Sept. 28, 2017, after 12 days of testimony and evidence, the prosecution rested.

25.

Richard Terry, self-described poker player, faced a betting decision. Should he play it safe and hope that he'd scored enough points during the prosecution case to instill a sense of reasonable doubt? If so, he could call a few safe witnesses, family members of Sabrina's, to play to the jury's emotions, and try to win the case in summation.

Or did he think the jury would want to hear directly from Sabrina Limon?

Her voice had already been heard in the courtroom. It was her many words—on wiretaps, to police—that had been used against her. Could Terry risk that she would say more that could get her in deeper trouble? Many defense attorneys are loathe to have their clients testify for that very reason. Eric Smith would savor the opportunity to cross-examine her.

But then this was a case that could very well turn on the question of credibility. Sabrina could show a different side of herself to the jury. She didn't have to be the perfect witness. She just had to be more credible than Jonathan Hearn.

On Sept. 28, 2017, Terry announced his next move.

"At this time," he told the judge, "the defense would call Sabrina Limon to the stand."

He would go all-in.

As the prosecution had done with Jonathan Hearn, the defense called three members of Sabrina's family to set the stage. In Sabrina's case, two of them were children. Sabrina's eyes welled with tears as Leanna, now 10, and Robbie, 14, were escorted into the courtroom by Richard Terry.

Leanna climbed up to the witness stand to a warm welcome from Judge Brownlee, who smiled and told her she didn't have to be nervous. The attorneys would be kind. By arrangement, the children's testimony would play out only in the courtroom. The TV camera was turned off.

"What is your relationship to Sabrina Limon?" asked Terry.

"I love her," said Leanna, smiling at her mother at the defense table. Sabrina beamed back. Leanna said she missed her mother very much and remembered how upset she was the day her father died. It was the last day of summer before school was to start. She and her brother had already gone to bed when she heard her mother screaming. They ran out to find her mother sobbing on the floor.

Leanna was also asked about Jonathan Hearn. She said Jonathan went with them and their mother one day to the beach. When Leanna got sand in her eye, Hearn told her to "stop whining."

Robbie next took the stand, Brownlee tried to put the boy at ease by telling him he was so tall that he should play basketball.

Under gentle questioning from Terry, the teen also remembered spending time with Jonathan. They went on hikes and talked a couple of times about guns. Robbie never told his mother. He said he liked Jonathan.

"He tried to act like my dad," said the boy.

Prosecutor Eric Smith declined to cross-examine the children and they left their mother in the courtroom.

The next witness, Sabrina's sister, Julie Cordova, got considerably different treatment in court. She testified on direct examination about Sabrina's emotional collapse after she found out her husband was dead.

"She wasn't eating," she said. "I went over there every day. I took off work. And she was not doing well. She would collapse on the floor when the kids would be asleep. I would have to get her off the floor. I would dress her. She was a mess."

She acknowledged that she didn't know that Sabrina was communicating at the time with Jonathan Hearn. But Julie found it inconceivable that Sabrina would knowingly let a killer into her house.

"Julie, in your mind, would Sabrina ever do anything to intentionally place her children in danger?" asked Terry.

Smith objected that Terry was asking Julie to render an improper opinion rather than stick to facts, but Julie answered anyway. "Absolutely not."

"Was she protective of her children?"

"Very much, as I am," said Julie, who has custody of them. "She is an amazing mother. Her heart and soul is everything in those kids. I remember when she wanted to be pregnant. That's all she wanted was children. She's worked with children. She took care of my children, my two boys. She had nothing but love. Love, love, love."

"Based upon your observations, did anything indicate to you that their relationship had gotten to a point where Sabrina would take steps to harm Rob?"

"No, no. She took care of him."

But Julie was candid in saying she didn't like everything she'd seen with Sabrina.

"Were they partiers?" Terry asked.

"Yes."

"And that was even after Leanna was born?"

"Yes."

"Were you aware they had opened their relationship?"

"Yes."

"How did you go about becoming aware?"

"Well, Brina always wanted us around," said Julie, "but their friends were also there all the time, and they were always drinking. They would hang out in the backyard a lot, too. I would see Kelly take off her shirt. She would take off her shirt at night when they were drinking. They had a zip line and she would strip down naked."

Sabrina's drinking got so out of control that Julie spoke to Robert about it. He did not seem concerned, telling Julie, "Oh, sister, it's going to be fine."

But there were things that Julie didn't know about.

"Were you aware that from sometime in 2013 until Rob's death that she was involved in an extramarital affair with Jonathan Hearn?"

"No."

"Did she even mention Jonathan Hearn?"

"No."

This time, Smith did conduct a cross-examination, suggesting that Sabrina's standard of living improved.

"So after Robert Limon died, Miss Limon moved from a desert community, kind of in the middle of nowhere, to Camarillo, which is in Ventura County, not far from the beach, into a three-story townhome, is that fair?"

"No," said Julie, who insisted that the new home, while located in a comfortable complex with pool and soccer field, was no mansion, but a rental condominium.

Smith also suggested that Julie advised Sabrina to get as much money as she could out of the railroad.

"That's not what I said!" Julie shot back.

"Well, what did you say?"

"I said: 'We have to figure out what Rob's career would be, so these children are taken care of.' Robert was a worker, as my husband was, and they needed to take care of the kids."

"So if Rob worked 20 years, that's about $2 million?"

"If that's what it is," said Julie.

With this testimony over in the morning court session, it was time for Sabrina.

Any time a defendant takes the stand, it's a risk. In this case, it was perhaps more so. The jury likely would be focusing as much on how she speaks as on what she says, weighing her credibility against that of Jonathan.

Whatever strategy discussions over testifying she had

with Terry would remain their private matter. But, by law, the final decision on whether to take the stand rests with the defendant, not the lawyer. The judge needed to make that clear for the record, asking Terry to lead Sabrina through a series of questions outside the presence of the jury.

"Ms. Limon, do you understand that you have a constitutional right to remain silent?

"Yes," she whispered.

Terry asked her to speak up.

"Yes," she said more loudly.

"And you understand that if you take the stand in your own defense, that you waive that right to remain silent?"

"Yes, I do."

"You understand that no one can force you to take the stand to testify in this proceeding?"

"Yes."

"And are you still wanting to take the stand and testify in this case?"

"Yes."

"Is this of your own free will?"

"Yes."

"Do you understand you're the only one who can decide whether to take the stand and testify in your behalf?"

"Yes."

"And is it your wish to testify in your own behalf in this case?"

"Yes."

Judge Brownlee added: "Miss Limon, you understand that Mr. Terry will ask you questions, but Mr. Smith also has the opportunity to ask you questions?"

She smiled. "Yes."

"And having that in mind, do you still wish to testify?"

"Yes."

"All right, Mr. Terry," said the judge, "I'm satisfied."

As Sabrina walked around the defense table and up the steps to the witness stand, she scanned the jury and smiled.

Terry began by having Sabrina retrace her life with Robert: dating him when she was 18, marriage at 20, the move from Arizona to California for Robert's new job with the railroad, two children three years apart, a house they fixed up in Silver Lakes. It was a good life, she said.

"Over time, did your and Rob's marriage change in some way?" asked Terry.

"It did," said Sabrina. She said it happened in 2008 when Robbie was 5 and had started kindergarten and Leanna was 2.

"How did your relationship with Rob change?"

"We opened our marriage bed and it changed the dynamics of our sacred bond."

"Who was it that you initially became involved with in that sense?"

"At the time just one other couple."

"Who was that?" asked Terry, and she gave their names.

"How did this opening up of your marriage affect your relationship with Rob?"

"I don't even know how to explain it," she said. "Our sacred bond that we had was broken as soon as we made that choice together, and—I don't even know how to explain it."

"During this time did you begin drinking more heavily?"

"Yes, that's when it started."

"Were you and Rob partying a lot at that time?"

"We had just started to. That's when things changed for us. We weren't like that before. And I stayed home with the kids and we just lived quietly and together, happily. Once we opened that door, so much changed in our life."

"At some point, did you and Rob get involved with other people who were involved with open marriages?

"Yes."

"Was it only couples involved in this? Were there any single people involved with any sexual relations outside the marriage between you and Rob?"

"No, not really."

"Did you have a group of friends that you regularly partied with?"

"Yes."

"Were these the groups of friends that you went on adult-only vacations with?"

"Yes."

"Were these people part of a group that you engaged in sexual encounters with outside your marriage to Rob?"

"Yes."

"Were Jason and Kelly Bernatene one of these couples?"

"Yes."

Rob, she said, had become overly fixated with sex. When they weren't swinging, he was on the computer looking at porn.

It was against this backdrop that in 2012, she met Jonathan Hearn. He was young, smart, caring, attentive and deeply religious. She covered the same ground as she did in her last interrogation with Det. Meyer about how the relationship grew from a casual friendship to something sexual and spiritual.

"Was there something about your relationship with Jonathan that you felt you needed?" asked Terry.

"Apparently, there was," she said. "It became our sacred relationship, and I guess now looking at it, what was lacking in my life, in my marriage."

"In the time that you are involved with Jonathan, did he make you feel like he was dedicated solely to you and interested in you?"

"Absolutely, he did."

"Did that make you feel special to him?"

"Yes, I was very taken by his affection toward me."

She recounted that night at Beef 'O' Brady's and how soon after, Rob found Jonathan's love messages and poetry on her phone.

"What happened right after Rob found all this stuff from Jonathan on your phone?"

"He called him."

"Were you present when Robert talked to Jonathan?"

"Yes, I was."

"Was Robert angry?"

"He wasn't happy."

"Did he do anything with your phone after talking to Jonathan?"

"Yeah, he broke my phone."

"After he had broken your phone, what happened next?"

"He went and bought me a new phone, the next morning."

"Did you guys do anything else besides him buying you a new phone?"

"We made up."

"Did you guys argue about that?"

"Robert was upset and he wanted to know who this guy was and what was so special about him. And I told him that Jonathan had dedicated a book to me."

"Did Robert tell you never to see him again?"

"Yes."

"Did you continue to see Jonathan after Robert told you not to?"

"Yes."

"Why?"

"I wish I knew why," she said, shaking her head. "I can't say why Jonathan came back into Costco, but it wasn't just his fault. I was, in a way at that time, just addicted to his attention."

"Did you think you had an issue with substance abuse or addiction?"

"Absolutely, I do."

As the relationship resumed, Jonathan spoke of a future together.

"I definitely listened to his goals and dreams in life and fantasized with him a lot. But I was also living a fantasy on the other end of the spectrum as well with Robert."

"On the one hand, you were living with the fantasy of a perfect marriage with Rob and the fantasy of a future with Jonathan?"

"Yes, I guess so," she said. "I played into dreams and ideas and thoughts and life with this guy, but I had a life of my own as well. It's hard to explain today, that's for sure."

"In your mind the best of both words?"

"The best of both worlds, but not really. At the time, it felt like I did, I guess. I don't know."

"Did you discuss leaving Rob with Jonathan?"

"Yes, I guess I did, yes."

"Was that part of playing into the fantasy?"

"Yes."

"Were you at any time seriously considering leaving Rob?"

"No."

"Why not?"

"I couldn't imagine my life without Rob."

"Why?"

"Because I loved him."

"You said he was your best bud."

"He was my best bud."

"He was still your best friend?"

"Absolutely, he was."

"And he was your partner with your children?"

"Absolutely, he was a good dad," she said, her voice breaking. "I never said he wasn't. Ever."

"Although we all have our shortcomings—I know I do—was he a good man?"

"He was a great man."

Like Jonathan, Sabrina showed none of the range of emotions jurors heard on the wiretaps. Jail and the stress of the case had clearly been rough on her. She was at times slack-jawed and looked tired. Her morning makeup application couldn't cover deep lines on her face missing in the many pictures shown in court. Her eyes seemed more sunken. Her drawn-on, pencil-thin eyebrows drew mocking comments on YouTube. She answered the questions calmly and slowly, but she often repeated what Terry said or answered yes or no to his leading questions or said she didn't know how to explain something.

Terry then led Sabrina through more areas she spoke to the police about: the continuation of the affair with Jonathan that led her to send the gushing Valentine's Day card—she said she was in a "fantasy state of mind, I guess"—their brief breakup after Robert discovered them again and the resumption of the affair.

Although smitten with Jonathan, Sabrina said it wasn't always perfect with him. She found she had to limit how much she told him about her life with Robert.

"He was a pretty critical guy, so I did not tell him details if it was a wild weekend," she said. "I'd tell him I'm back from whatever trip we went on, or whatever we were doing, but I wouldn't go into detail of things that I knew that he was going to criticize me or Robert."

Moving to the day of Robert's death, she said it began like any other in her double love life. He went off to work in Tehachapi and she got on the phone with Jonathan. They talked about her children, Jonathan's job, love and religion.

She remembered very little about what happened after she got word Rob was dead—"such a blur," she said—and had little recall of texting and talking to Jonathan that night and the next morning.

"What did you do when you were told Robert had been killed?"

"I dropped to my knees and started crying."

"Did you and Jonathan at all that day talk about him killing Robert?"

In a rare flash of emotion, she said in a firm voice, "No."

"Were you aware at that time that Jonathan had killed Robert?"

"No."

She repeated what she had told police: that she lied about Jonathan and her issues with Robert about swinging because she was embarrassed and was trying to protect Robert's legacy.

Over the next three months, Jonathan played into those fears and ultimately paranoia about the ramifications of their affair getting exposed.

"I trusted him. I felt at the time in a way that he was protecting us, protecting me. I believed him."

"You believed in him or did you believe him?"

"I believed in him, and I did believe him because I didn't want to believe that Jonathan had anything to do with Robert's murder."

"Is that because you loved him?"

"Yes."

"Did you ever begin to have some doubts about whether or not Jonathan was involved in Robert's death?"

"There were times that it felt weird, things that he was saying, or acting, but I didn't want to believe that that could be possible."

"What do you do when there is something that you don't feel comfortable with? What is your typical response?"

"I block it out. I had a lot of responses with how I dealt with things back then. I would just not really deal with it."

She denied Jonathan's contention, in his testimony, that their conversations about Robert had taken a dark turn.

"Robert wasn't dark," she said. "Robert was happy, Robert was energetic, Robert was hardworking. Robert was fun. Robert was not dark. Those are not dark. I couldn't paint Robert to be dark even with our definite character defects."

"How would you describe yourself, your personality?"

"Robert and I got along so well because we were very much alike. We were very capable. We both were energetic. We both loved life and people and just were a lot alike, we really were."

"Why, after the short period of time after your husband's

death, did you immediately turn to Jonathan?"

"I wasn't really given a break, an opportunity," Sabrina said. "I don't know how to describe that time in my life because it was such a surreal time for me. And Jonathan ended up feeling to me to—he felt like he was going to care for me and that he was like—he felt like my rock at that moment in time. For whatever reasons, he is what I held on to, I guess."

"The snow globe that Mr. Smith put into evidence: Is that something you had given Jonathan?"

"Yes."

"Do you remember when you gave it to him?"

"I had given it to him as a Christmas gift."

"Was that Christmas of 2013?"

"Yes, I believe so."

"The inscription: 'Love, Sabrina.' Is that something that you had done and gave to him?"

"Yes."

"Did he ever give you gifts?"

"He gave me lots of gifts. He would give me gifts that were thought-out and thoughtful and very detailed, lots of writing, just very deep thoughtful gifts, from my favorite flower seed to plants in a gift basket with a watering can, just very thought-out. He gave me jewelry, wrote lots of things on cards."

"He sounds like he was very charming."

"Very charming."

"Was that part of the attraction that caused you to become enamored with him?"

"That was the attraction."

Even to the very end, when shown the security video by Det. Meyer of the man in the gas station, she convinced herself it wasn't Jonathan.

"I wouldn't allow that in fully. I hadn't even processed what had happened to Robert."

"If you knew that Jonathan killed your husband, would

you have been involved in a relationship with him after your husband was killed?"

"No."

"Would you allow someone who killed your husband to be around your children?"

"No, absolutely not."

"Why not?"

"Because I wouldn't allow that. That's horrible. That's dangerous. That would be putting Robbie and Leanna in danger."

"What do your children mean to you?"

"They mean the world to me."

So why, Terry asked, did she ultimately tell Det. Rutledge in her final interrogation at the jail that she suspected Jonathan shortly after Robert' death?

"They got mad at me for not saying what they wanted me to say, which was that I knew Jonathan had killed my husband," she said, "and that it was the only way that I was ever going to see my children again. And so they did like the good cop/bad cop thing to me. I was scared."

That, combined with the information police had been telling her the last two days about Jonathan's involvement, made her give in.

"I say things that people want to hear," she said. "That was what I did because I thought that was what I was supposed to do at that point. They told me that I was in their world now, that they were the way to go."

"Did you, in looking back at it, did you feel in some ways that Jonathan was trying to control you?" asked Terry.

"Jonathan was very controlling, yes."

"How so?"

"Jonathan knew how to play his cards right," she said. "Looking back through all this, he knows what he's doing and everything he does he has, I guess, an approach to get kind of what he wants. So Jonathan controlled me through carrying his Bible with him everywhere he went and using that to guilt me, but also make me feel safe and secure and like I was doing right, I guess, even though I knew there were definitely things I was doing wrong in my life."

Terry asked Sabrina if she ever discussed with Jonathan killing her husband.

"No, I did not."

"At any time did you discuss about wanting Robert to be gone or dead?"

"No, I never said dead or gone," she said in a halting voice. "I did not want Robert gone."

26.

Like a football coach icing the opposing kicker, Eric Smith let Sabrina sit up there on the stand in silence for two full minutes, while he shuffled papers. Then he finally said, "Good afternoon, Ms. Limon."

"Good afternoon," she said.

He began with Sabrina as he did with Jonathan, by establishing how old—or young—Jonathan was at the time they met.

"How long did it last that you didn't know his age?"

"It lasted awhile," she said. "I was already carrying on conversations with him and getting to know him. He had me look at a website for that book he was writing. I do remember it said he had been with the fire department like eight years or something like that. I thought he has to be in his late 20s. He was older than my nephews. He sent me a very long explanation of his views on age, this whole long story and let me know that he was 22 and I was 32 at the time. I was shocked that he was that young, much younger than my own nephews. But at that point, it didn't really matter to me."

"So you are 10 years older than Mr. Hearn?"

"Yes."

"You are sending a 22-year-old naked photographs of yourself?"

"Yes."

"So these are photographs that you have taken of yourself and you're sending to him?"

"I had plenty of explicit photographs of myself."

"These are actions taken by you and provided to Mr.

Hearn?"

"Yes."

"You were controlled by Jonathan, but you were sending him explicit photographs of yourself on a regular basis, is that fair?"

"Regular basis? I don't remember that. Yes, that is fair."

"How regular did this sexual affair occur?"

"Ah, it just varied."

"Where did it take place at?"

"There were different places."

"Describe some of them."

"My home, different places we would meet. His home."

"Did you invite him to your home for the sexual affair?"

"Yes, I would invite him to my home."

"Again, this is something that you are doing, directing toward Jonathan Hearn, in your relationship, bringing him to you?"

"Yes, I allowed him into my life."

"These different places you would meet: Where were these at?"

"Different places we would meet where we would hike, more secluded places, places he knew."

"How did these meetings occur? How were they set up?"

"We would talk about whenever there was an opportunity to see one another, we saw one another."

"Did he force you to go?"

"No."

"You went on your own to where Jonathan was?"

"Yes."

"When you were going to his home in 2013, where were your kids?"

"They would be in school."

Smith displayed a photo she had sent to Jonathan, a selfie making a kissy mouth.

"The reason for that?"

"I don't know."

"Are you being controlled here in this photograph by Mr. Hearn?"

"No."

"You did this on your own? You're puckering your lips and you're sending this photo to Jonathan Hearn?"

"Yes."

Smith showed another photo found on Jonathan's phone of her flashing her bare backside.

"I'd never seen that picture before," she said.

"Where are the kids?"

"They were in school, I'm sure."

He showed her the photo Jonathan snapped of her at Costco, writing, "I love you more, Jonathan," on a napkin.

"Did he force you to write that?"

"No."

"Was he controlling you at that moment?"

"No."

"You are 10 years old than Jonathan Hearn?"

"Yes."

"You are, in your words, energetic, outgoing—a people person, correct?"

"Yes."

"We've seen photographs that you sent to Jonathan Hearn."

"Yes."

"Notes that you sent to Jonathan Hearn?"

"Yes."

"You went to his house on your own?"

"Yes."

"You allowed him to come to your house for sex?"

"Yes, I did."

"And you want to testify now that he controlled you?"

"He did not physically control me. I became, I guess, mentally (controlled). He ended up having control. He liked control. He liked to be in control. And I allowed him to do that."

"Where in any of the photos that we have is there any element showing control by Jonathan Hearn?"

"You won't see that in a photo."

"How about the snow globe. Did he force you to give a snow globe to him?"

"Absolutely, not."

"How about that Valentine's letter?"

"No."

"Did he force you to write it?"

"No."

"Where is there anything whatsoever that shows any element of control by Jonathan Hearn?"

"I guess I have no evidence," she said, "any physical evidence."

Smith then showed her the photo of her embracing Jonathan at Beef 'O' Brady's.

"Did he force you to give him that hug?"

"No, he did not."

"You did that on your own?"

"I sure did."

"Where was your husband at this time?"

"He was—there."

"Did you worry that your husband would see you hugging the man you were having an affair with?"

"No."

"Why not?"

"Because we were very social. We hugged a lot of people. We talked to a lot of people. That wouldn't be anything that was really out of my character that I would do."

Showing her group photo at the bar, he asked: "Your husband on the left, your lover on the right? Have you ever contemplated how entirely disrespectful this is to invite your lover to a restaurant where your husband is going to be?"

"Yes."

"Did you not care or what?"

"I wasn't thinking."

"Oh, you had to be thinking, because you did something. What was your reasoning?"

"I guess that I don't have a good answer for that."

"Would it be fair to say that if you did something like that you don't care that much about that person's emotions or feelings if they were to find out?"

"I did care."

"You cared so much you invited your lover to a night out with your husband?"

She went silent for a moment. "I don't have an answer for that."

"What from that evening, in the photos that we've seen, shows that you cared about your husband?"

"There's nothing that shows in that photo. I'm not in that photo."

"What about the other photograph?"

"It shows that I care about Jonathan."

"When your husband found out you were having a sexual affair with a man 10 years younger, would you characterize your marriage as a good marriage?"

"Our marriage had lost what we shared that was sacred. Yes and no. It was complicated, I guess."

"At this point in your marriage, it was different than it had been?"

"Yes, it was different. When we opened our marriage, the dynamics changed."

"For you, how did the dynamics change?"

"I was no longer sacred to my husband anymore," she said. "He kind of gave me a long leash and he had one as well. But between him and I, we always were good to one another, we took care of each other, still loved each other very much. But our marriage did change."

"Did you think how he acted cheapened how you felt? Did it make you feel less in his eyes?"

"Sometimes, but Rob always gave me a lot of

compliments and didn't make me feel less, necessarily."

"So your husband was seeing other women?"

"Yes, we had opened our marriage."

"And the sexual relationships with other women, that only caused you to feel a little less, not a lot? It didn't affect you that much in your marriage?"

"Looking back, it affected me a lot. In the moment, it became who we were. It only progressed. We were partying, drinking, livin' the life and it just ended up becoming who we were not. We were just livin' it."

"Your husband is having sex with other women, you're drinking a lot of booze and you felt it was a very fun time?"

"Yes, it was a very fun time."

"What about it made it fun for you?"

"We had a good life. We were on the lake all the time. We had a boat. There was always music. There was always drinking. And we would get wild. It was fun."

"It's been kind of intimated in this case that Miss Bernatene was having an affair with your husband. Was she?"

"Yes."

"So let's add into the picture then: that your best friend at the time was having an affair with your husband, and this was still in your mind a fun time?"

"With her, it wasn't a fun time anymore," Sabrina said. "Yes, there were fun times, for sure."

"Just trying to understand what was going through your mind. You were okay with your husband having an affair with your best friend?"

"Yes."

"You never complained about that at all?"

"I would, minimally, to him."

As the cross-examination continued into the next day, Sept. 29, the prosecutor led Sabrina through more of the same ground covered by the police interrogations, and got mostly the same answers. Yes, she told Jonathan the location and layout of Robert's shop. No, she only told him that so he would know they'd have more time together. Yes, she spoke to Jonathan at length on the day of Robert's murder, sometimes while Robert was on the other line. No, they didn't talk about Robert's demise.

Near the end of the questioning, Smith brought Sabrina back to the days after Robert's murder, when she spoke twice to Det. Meyer saying her husband had no potential enemies.

"Did everybody love Robert at that point in time?"

"I felt that way in my head in my world."

"How would Jonathan not come to mind?"

"It just didn't. I didn't feel like Jonathan hated Robert at all."

These and other statements to police, she repeated, all stemmed from trying to hide her relationship with Jonathan.

Noting that she and Robert were swingers, Smith asked, "Would an affair have been a big deal?"

"It was outside of the group. So I didn't have permission to go astray from our group of friends."

"Who had to give you that permission?"

"Robert," she said. "I didn't have permission because there were no benefits for Robert. It's a lifestyle that I don't expect people to understand. At this point in time, I wished I never allowed those sorts of doors to be opened in our marriage.

The lifestyle ended up controlling us. I'm not expecting you to understand that."

"Jonathan Hearn was controlling. Now your husband was controlling. Do you make decisions on your own at any point?

"Yes, I sure do," said Sabrina. "Apparently, many bad ones."

Sabrina's testimony was interrupted to squeeze in two out-of-town defense witnesses out of order to accommodate their travel schedules. The first was Jennifer Lentz, a woman with eerie parallels to Sabrina. She was a married mother of two who met Jonathan Hearn on Facebook at the end of 2012 or beginning of 2013.

"It started out just very innocent, like commenting on one another's pictures," she said. They exchanged hundreds of text messages. "He's very well spoken, very smart, and I would tell him that often," she said, "that he was very smart and just seemed way older than he was."

It never got farther than that, she said. Her husband found out about the correspondence and they stopped communicating. But after she got divorced, she got in contact again with Jonathan in early 2014, around the time he was with Sabrina allegedly plotting Robert's murder.

The other witness was Dale Smith, who spoke of how he and his then-wife met Sabrina and Robert in 2008 when their kids were playing on the same baseball team. The friendship turned to swinging.

"We opened up our marriage, my wife and I at the time, with Rob and Sabrina," said Smith. The wife swapping ended, he said, when his wife and Sabrina had a falling out. The Smiths later divorced.

For the redirect examination, Terry presented a slide show of some 30 Limon family photos. There were pictures of Sabrina and Robert together and with the kids, enjoying outings on their boat, to the beach, to a museum. As the pictures came up on the courtroom screen, Sabrina choked up as she remembered what she called the happiest days of her life, their Silver Lakes dream.

But in a second round of cross-examination, she was confronted with phone records showing that on a day one of those photos with her husband was taken, in July 2014, she was in contact with Jonathan Hearn.

"Is it not true that you spoke to Jonathan for five hours on the phone?" asked prosecutor Smith.

"If that's what it shows here, yes."

"You had 80 text messages, incoming and outgoing, to Jonathan Hearn."

She shook her head and smiled. "I was having an affair."

As she said it she shook her head and smiled. It was a sad smile that could have related to so many things, all of them ending badly.

The defense rested.

27.

On the morning of Tuesday, Oct. 3, Eric Smith dragged the heavy wood podium to the front of the jury. It was the most noise he would make for a while.

After opening the prosecution case with a map, the deputy district attorney ended it with a list: six charges against Sabrina Limon, from attempted murder to first-degree murder to accessory after the fact.

After recapping the witnesses with thumbnails of their testimony, Smith spoke of the alleged poisoning attempt in April 2014. "They were going to get rid of Robert Limon. They were going to get married. That was the plan in this case," he told the jury.

It was the weakest part of the prosecution case and perhaps that's why it came at the beginning of what would be a day of speeches to the jury. Here, the prosecution truly had nothing more than Jonathan's word, the evidence pointing to him alone. No witnesses besides Jonathan linked Sabrina to the purchase of arsenic or the creation of the pudding.

Phone records did put Jonathan in the Helendale area on April 24, 2014, but then he was often in the Helendale area with Sabrina. Sabrina did call her husband that afternoon at work, but she often did that, too.

Smith used the pudding portion of the case to pivot to the moment Jonathan and Sabrina stopped using her regular cell and landline and started using the burner phone.

"On the day that they tried to kill her husband with poison, and they decide that law enforcement could learn of their connection with each other, that is the day these calls stopped, and that was to escape law enforcement detection down the road," said Smith.

Now the evidence pointed to both of them, some 5,900 electronic contacts over that secret phone, including calls or texts before and after Jonathan fatally shot Robert that August evening in Tehachapi, Smith said. One of those calls, he noted, was an 80-minute conversation over the burner starting about noon while Sabrina was calling and texting Robert.

"There's only one reason she's doing that: because if law enforcement ever looks into the phone records, she thinks all they're ever going to find is: 'I called my husband over and over again,'" Smith said. "But she failed to mention to Detective Meyer that she did that while talking to the man who killed her husband."

Hours later, Jonathan went about making their dreams come true, the prosecutor said.

"He stood outside the shop and prayed about what he was about to do," the prosecutor said, "but he felt that murder was inevitable based upon the purpose, the plan that Sabrina and him had about the future."

From then on, he said, their focus on God's purpose for them never wavered. They spoke after the murder, with Sabrina worried only about Jonathan's well-being—and the timely disposal of evidence—and during the night when Sabrina was supposedly so overcome with grief that she collapsed on the porch.

"She told Emily, 'The best is yet to come,' Why is the best to come? Because this was the plan. This was anticipated," said the prosecutor. "How do you move from the death of her husband and raising two kids to immediately adoring a young, sexy guy? Because it's the plan."

A plan, Smith argued, sweetened by more than $300,000 in life insurance and the promise of millions more in a settlement from the railroad, but one that relied on them to keep their wits in the face of mounting pressure from police.

"You are also able to hear their descent into paranoia," said Smith, pointing to the wiretaps. "They are seeing things that aren't even there. Why do you do that? Because he killed somebody and you know law enforcement is going to look into it."

Sabrina responded to the heat, he said, with "lies, lies, lies. That's all we heard." For a time, it seemed to work, Smith argued, leading up to Sabrina telling Jonathan that "everything's fine," after Meyer told her the investigation had hit a dead end.

"Everything is fine because they haven't found them out," the prosecutor said. "But everything's not fine. If you're an appropriately acting widow, everything is not fine. If they're at a dead end, you have a completely different response. Why is everything fine? Because Jonathan Hearn and Sabrina Limon didn't think law enforcement knew what they were doing at this point. She did not want the murder of her husband solved. You can tell from these calls."

Everything was fine, he argued, because their plan was working.

"In this case, you heard a lot of testimony about Robert. Everybody loved Robert. You heard it from countless people," he said. "But two people saw him as an impediment, as something in the way of a future. And one of those persons testified because he shot and killed him. The other one is the one who put it in motion and she sits here in the courtroom today."

Richard Terry walked from the counsel table to the podium. It was a few feet across the courtroom, but he treated it like a slog.

"A long road, it takes a lot out of you," he told the jury. "I've done a lot of these. At this point, what I'm going to suggest: breathe in, breathe out."

Counsel and jury now oxygenated, Smith began his summation. Defense attorneys at this juncture of a trial always suffer a disadvantage. This would be Terry's only opportunity to address the jury; Smith would later be afforded a rebuttal argument. Terry would remind the jury of this, so listen closely. You won't hear from me again.

"You are the judges of the facts of the case," he told panel. "Your job is not to come in here and make moral judgments about Sabrina Limon and her relationship with Jonathan Hearn or her relationship with her own husband."

Facts, Terry said, that certainly placed his client in a bad light at times. "You've heard about her flaws. You've heard about the mistakes she made in her life," he said. But these facts and flaws, he said, must be put into a larger context.

"The issues in this case are relatively simple in a lot of ways," he said. "Did Sabrina Limon solicit and conspire with Jonathan Hearn to kill her husband? Whether Sabrina Limon knew Jonathan Hearn killed her husband, whether or not she failed to report that to the police."

There were secrets in this case, according to Terry, but they had to do with sex, not murder. Sabrina resisted opening up her personal life, and he argued that other witnesses in the case had, too.

"All of them, or a lot them, were very guarded about their involvement in this type of relationship," he said. "A lot of that probably had to do with we have TV cameras in here filming everything that's being said, and they're worried about their image in the public and public perception of who they are and their morality."

Similar to them, Terry argued, Sabrina "didn't want to disclose her sexual life to police." Part of that was because of a double standard for women. "If the man is having a lot of sex, the view is he's a stud," said Terry. "And, believe me, I've heard this one all too often in this case relating to my client: If she's a woman, she's a slut or a whore. How many times have we heard the term 'slut shaming'?"

Terry acknowledged that it was reasonable to claim, as the prosecution did, that Sabrina was hiding her affair with

Jonathan because she had conspired with him to kill Robert.

"Is it also reasonable that that Miss Limon was trying to protect her image and the image of her husband?" he asked. "She didn't want to sully her husband's name—ever—on the stand. She admitted that Robert was a good man and was a good husband and a good father, that he loved his children and he loved her. It doesn't mean he was a perfect man. None of us are. He was as flawed a human being as the rest of us. He had his demons he was dealing with also, as we all do."

His flaws, like hers, did not send Sabrina into a conspiracy to murder him, Terry argued, pointing to the wiretaps and police interrogations as proof of why Sabrina was as stunned as anybody to find out about Jonathan's actions.

"How many times did she say, during the interview with police, 'It can't be him. It can't be true. It's not him. He wouldn't do that'?" asked Terry. "She wanted to believe that Jonathan could not have done this. He was a firefighter. He was, by all appearances, a man of deep faith. How many times did we hear him praying on those intercepts? How many times on the text messages between the two of them did they talk about getting on their knees and praying and talking to God?"

Jonathan, the attorney said, "fulfilled a need in her for something that was lacking" after she and her husband opened their marriage. "She didn't believe that Jonathan was even capable of this. She didn't want to believe that Jonathan was capable of this to the point of almost deluding herself."

Yes, Sabrina called and texted Jonathan at critical points in the case—the day Jonathan scoped out the murder scene in May 2014, the day he actually killed Robert—but Terry argued, "That was their normal communication, something they did on a daily basis."

Terry took issue with Eric Smith's suggestion that Sabrina wasn't acting like an "appropriately acting widow" after Robert's murder. "I honestly don't know what that is," he said. "I know what Mr. Smith's view is. I can't say what a normal response would be. Nobody can. Everybody responds in a different way to the loss of a loved one. And when you feel like you're drowning, sometimes you grab on to any life preserver that you can."

In her case, that was Jonathan because she was "struggling to deal with her husband's death," said Terry. "The one anchor was Jonathan. She was dependent on him, much like she was when Robert was living, dependent on Robert. Jonathan was the thing keeping her going."

Moving on to the alleged poisoning plot, Terry argued that not only did the prosecution have no evidence that Sabrina was involved, what information it did produce made no sense. Why, he asked, would Jonathan even be on the internet for a banana pudding recipe? "If Sabrina was in on it, the easiest thing would have been to ask her: 'What's your recipe? Can I have it so I can make it just like you do?'"

There was no evidence Jonathan ever poisoned a dog, no reports of dead or missing dogs presented, and the suggestion that he made a double batch of pudding—for Sabrina's family, one tainted version for Robert, both of which put in Sabrina's refrigerator—flew in the face of logic.

"What mother would ever expose her children to the possibility of being poisoned? Who knew who would have access to it?" said Terry. "If Rob found it, how do we know he wouldn't eat it right there and then?"

As for allegations they felt poisoning would fool investigators because Robert had a previous health problem, Terry urged the jury to look at Robert's BNSF medical records. "You will not find one incident where Robert Limon sought medical treatment while he was on the job for BNSF. Not one report."

Nor was there evidence that she knew Jonathan was checking out the crime scene when they spoke on the phone in May, said Terry. He acknowledged that Sabrina had told police that she had told Jonathan about Robert's workplace in Tehachapi around that time. But this call, he argued, blurred together with all the others, two lovers talking constantly.

"Remember: Sabrina is really lousy with dates. She couldn't remember exact dates if her life depended on it," said Terry. It was a curious statement from her own lawyer; her life did depend on it.

Terry then returned to the central theme of the case: only Jonathan ties her to the murder. "Is there any evidence, other than Jonathan Hearn's testimony, that says Sabrina knew what he was doing? That he was going up to Tehachapi to kill her husband?" he asked. "They presented no evidence that Sabrina knew for certain what Jonathan was up to. Her testimony was that he was tired after work, that she was busy, that she went to church that day, see her mom, get the kids ready."

As for why she was on the phone with Jonathan at the same time she was contacting her husband, Terry chalked it up to multitasking. "We've all done this. I know I have."

Terry urged the jury to remember, always, that Sabrina was having an affair, an affair she desperately wanted hidden. Everything she said and did, from the Valentine's Day card to the statements in the wiretaps to the snow globe for Christmas, spoke to her misguided love for Jonathan, not her complicity in the murder of her husband, the attorney argued.

"Mr. Smith says (this evidence) shows that she was planning on getting rid of her husband and starting her new life with Jonathan Hearn. That is one way of looking at it. It is certainly reasonable," said Terry. "It's also reasonable that Sabrina believed she was in love with Jonathan, as she's testified, and she was living a fantasy with Jonathan, that she bought into the fantasy maybe a little too much."

Instead, the evidence, like Jonathan's morbid to-do list, pointed only to Jonathan as the killer. "*He* asked God to kill Rob Limon," said Terry. "And I guess Jonathan decided he was going to play God and kill Robert Limon. *He* decided to kill him so *he* could have Sabrina for himself, so that Robert is out of the picture, so that *he* could live that fantasy that he and Sabrina had talked about, but *he* wanted it."

Sabrina, Terry said, merely fell prey to Jonathan's powers. "Sabrina can be somewhat manipulated by the men in her life, or at least influenced by the men in her life, including her own husband," said Terry. "She is not a strong person on her own, and she can be managed. And Jonathan needed to maintain that control over her. So she didn't stop and think about him as a possible person who did this to her husband."

What she failed to see was the evil that lurked within, he said. "What would it take, ask yourself, for somebody to be willing to kill another man to have their wife and being able to live with that?" said Terry. "What kind of sick individual would even consider that as an option? I don't know what snakes are in his brain, but ladies and gentlemen, the bottom line is, would any of us be willing to kill another human being just because somebody asked us to? I would hope not. I would hope we're better than that. But Jonathan Hearn certainly isn't."

Terry reminded jurors of Jonathan's demeanor while testifying. "That man sat up on that witness stand and described how he went about killing Robert Limon in cold blood as if he was discussing how he brushes his teeth in the morning," the lawyer said. "He is cold, calculating, thoughtful, plans ahead. Is that Sabrina from what you've seen?"

And he is the only reason, Terry argued, that Sabrina ended up in this courtroom. The DA only charged her after Jonathan got a deal. "To save his own hide, he came in and spun his story so that he would have a day out of prison in the future and take away her life," said Terry. "They made a deal with a coldblooded killer so that they could get her."

He urged the jury not to be a party to this injustice. "I'm asking you to do your job—no more, no less—to examine all the evidence in this case, to question it all, to discuss it thoroughly among yourselves, to try to reach a just and right decision in this case. Mr. Hearn's already taken away Robbie and Leanna Limon's father. Don't let him take away their mother, too."

A different Eric Smith returned to the podium, a more impassioned Eric Smith. "There have been two shiny objects the defense has used in this case," he began. "One is sex. Sex, sex, sex! One is the children and emotion."

While his counting was off—it was actually three objects—Smith spoke with a force he hadn't shown all trial, unleashing an attack on Richard Terry's summation.

"Ridiculous!" he said of the suggestion Sabrina lied about her affair out of fear of slut shaming. "Dale Smith told Detective Meyer all about the open relationship. Jason and Kelly talked all about what was going on." For that matter, he said, the swinging years ended in 2008.

"How does 2008 have anything to do with this case?" he asked incredulously. "Why do we have to hear Dale Smith testify about something in 2008?"

And why, he asked, did the defense have to call Sabrina's children and ask if they missed their mother?

"For them to come here and testify to things that adults could have testified to is unseemly and beneath this trial," Smith said. "But that's what they did because they wanted to give sympathy. That's the only reason for it. 'Do you miss your mom?' Of course, she misses her mom. But that's not what we're here for. We're here for: Did Sabrina Limon commit the crimes?"

He highlighted a jury instruction issued by the judge to not let bias, sympathy or public opinion influence their decision.

"That is what the defense has tried to do. The defense just did it. 'Don't take away their mom?' This is a court of law! You're supposed to come here and apply reason to facts. You're not supposed to sit up there and say don't take away their mother. That is directly in contravention of a jury instruction. That's not what you're here for. It's not supposed to be said. The trial is an objective look at the facts. The trial is an objective look at: Did Sabrina Limon commit this crime? That's it. That's it!"

What Robbie and Leanna want "has no significance," he said. "But there are three victims of what happened in this case. That's Robert, that's Robbie and that's Leanna. They are victims in this case. But you must put out of their mind what their desires might be."

The facts, that evidence, proved that Sabrina and Jonathan put in motion a plan to replace Robert with Jonathan, he said.

"This is not a case of he said/she said; this is a case of he said/she lied," said Smith. "Everything that Jonathan Hearn testified to is corroborated by the evidence, by cell records, by items seized, by phone context. And what are you left with? Sabrina Limon. That's what you're left with. Based on her testimony, she lied to law enforcement at every turn. I don't even know how that's up for debate. There are so many lies in there, it's unbelievable."

He said she lied about her affair, lied about being controlled by Jonathan and lied about thinking she was living in a fantasy world. "It's not a fantasy if you're doing an action," Smith said. "It's a plan if you're doing an action."

He ended by highlighting a single statement from Sabrina from the hours and hours of recordings. It was a moment from her last interrogation with Det. Meyer. As he dramatically recreated for her the final moments between Robert and Jonathan, she told him: "I didn't even wanna—I just wanted to know if he suffered. And he said he didn't suffer. I didn't know details."

At the time, Meyer didn't catch it. He said later, "I'm in there by myself. I'm thinking about the next question. And there's guys watching in on the interview. They didn't text me, either."

But they caught it later and the significance hit them like a bolt. Nobody had told Sabrina how long Robert may have lingered, only that he'd been shot, because nobody knew.

"Who are we talking about in that audio?" asked Smith. "She just wanted to know that he didn't suffer. And *he* told her that he didn't suffer. That's it. That's her statement! That's what she asked Jonathan Hearn. She just wanted to know if he suffered. He said he didn't suffer. Sabrina Limon knew Jonathan Hearn killed her husband."

And so, concluded Smith, she should be held accountable for Robert's murder. "She took him away from the family. She's the one that set it in motion," he said. "She did this with Jonathan Hearn and that's why we're here. That's why we've been here for weeks on end, because crimes such as these demand that everybody be held accountable."

28.

After brief talks the afternoon of Oct. 3, the panel returned the next morning for its first full day of work. At 10:15 a.m., after less than two hours, jurors sent a note to the judge. They wanted to see the last piece of physical evidence introduced by the prosecution, the sparkly snow globe that Sabrina gave Jonathan for Christmas 2013.

The judge conferred with attorneys for both sides and neither had any objections. It was delivered in its brown paper bag to the jury room. The request was a head-scratcher. What relevance did this have for the jury?

There wouldn't be much time to ponder.

Four hours later, jurors sent a second note. They wanted a read-back of testimony from the afternoon session of Sept. 19, day seven of the trial. That was a busy day with Det. Meyer on the stand giving testimony and introducing recordings. In the 1:30 p.m. to 3 p.m. block requested by the jury, prosecutors played the video of Sabrina's interview with Meyer in Bakersfield, the one that had caused so much angst for Sabrina and Jonathan to the point she rescheduled it after discussing it with Jonathan. The prosecution also played the wiretap recording of Sabrina talking to Jonathan from the car on the ride home with her sister. After passing the scene of her husband's murder, Sabrina said of the session, "Everything's good," even though no killer had been identified. Prosecutor Eric Smith held this statement up as consciousness of guilt.

The judge met again with the lawyers, who saw no problem with the jury re-hearing this portion of the trial. The court reporter went into the jury room and read the testimony and, presumably, the transcript of the recordings.

A final note came 20 minutes later. It asked if the attempted murder charge related to the poisoned-pudding plot or, "Does it include the actual murder?"

After speaking with lawyers, the judge gave two one-word answers: "Yes," it related to the pudding; "No," it had nothing to do with the actual murder.

The last note of the day came at 4:10 p.m.: "We have completed all the verdict forms signed by the foreperson."

In just over one day of deliberation, the jury had decided the fate of Sabrina Limon.

The next day, Oct. 4, the judge began the court session with a warning. He noted that at Sabrina's preliminary hearing in February, held before a different judge, "there was an outburst from spectators in the courtroom." Several people from the side of the audience section for Robert Limon's family and friends applauded when the judge ordered Sabrina tried for murder.

Judge Brownlee looked at the audience in his court. "That will not happen today," he said. "Whatever the jury decides, everyone present has to sit calmly and quietly listen to the verdict. This is in the spirit of the state of California and you will conduct yourself accordingly. Understood?"

Dozens of people nodded yes in the audience.

"Okay," the judge said, "let's bring them in."

The bailiff escorted the jurors into the jury box. They appeared grim-faced, but otherwise betrayed nothing. Sabrina, wearing a purple blouse and dark jacket, stood and watched them.

"We have all 12 in the box. Good morning, everyone," the judge said.

"Good morning," they responded nearly in unison. Normally, the panel gave a cheery response to the judge's greetings. This morning, they were subdued.

"Nice to see you all back," the judge said. "We received a note yesterday at 4:10 p.m. that we have completed all the verdict forms signed by the foreman, which appears to be (juror) number seven. Madam forewoman, is that correct?"

"That's correct," she said.

"Did you have the opportunity to date and sign the verdict form?"

"Yes, I did."

"Good, would you fold that in half and hand that to our bailiff."

The jury forms went to the bailiff who carried them to the clerk, who in turn handed them up to the judge. The judge leafed through the forms one by one—six for each count—making sure everything was filled out correctly. All eyes were glued on his face for any hint of what the forms said; his face said nothing.

Sabrina appeared terrified. Her mouth open, she looked at the judge, looked at the jury, looked down, looked up. She then pursed her lips and looked at the judge again as he leafed through the final page.

"The verdict form does appear to be in order," said Brownlee, handing them to the clerk. "Madam clerk, please."

The clerk stood and read from the forms.

"Superior Court of California, County of Kern, Metropolitan Division, the People of the State, plaintiff vs. Sabrina Limon, defendant," she began and read off the case number.

"First count, we the jury impaneled to try the above entitled cause find the defendant, Sabrina Limon, guilty of a felony, to wit, murder of Robert Limon."

Richard Terry reacted first. Stone-faced until now, he furrowed his brow, turned his head to the left, tipped his head down and shook his head no.

Sabrina made no immediate reaction. She then pursed her lips and shook her head slightly. After Terry patted her shoulder, she dropped her head and seemed to whisper something to herself as if praying.

Eric Smith and Det. Meyer at the prosecution table stared straight ahead and showed no reaction.

But for a collective exhale, the spectators remained silent.

The clerk continued reading the verdict form, saying that the jury determined that the murder was in the first-degree and "found it true that it was done with premeditation and deliberation."

On the second and third counts, the jury found her guilty of conspiracy to commit murder and solicitation of murder, finding to be "true" the "overt acts" that Sabrina used a burner phone to avoid police detection, told Jonathan where Robert worked and what his schedule was the day of the murder before Jonathan fatally shot him.

Sabrina now began breathing more heavily; Terry pulled off his glasses and rubbed his eyes.

On the fourth count, attempted murder in the pudding plot, the clerk read, "We the jury find the defendant, Sabrina Limon, not guilt of a felony, to wit, attempted murder of Robert Limon." She was also found not guilty of the act of poisoning.

In its factual determinations, the jury found it "true" that Jonathan purchased the arsenic but "not true" that he mixed it with pudding and delivered the dessert to Sabrina, or that Sabrina put it in Robert's lunch before calling him and telling him not to eat it.

The reading of the verdicts ended with count six. "We the jury find the defendant, Sabrina Limon, guilty of a felony, to wit, accessory."

Sabrina began quietly weeping. She dabbed her nose with a tissue.

The judge said, "Madam forewoman, is that the true and correct verdict as to each count?"

"It is," the forewoman said.

"Mr. Terry, would you like the jury polled?"

"Yes," Sabrina's lawyer said.

One after the other, nine women and three men each said, "Yes."

"You have now completed your jury service in this case," the judge told the panel. "On behalf of all the judges of the court, please accept my thanks for your time and efforts."

As Terry whispered to Sabrina, the judge told the jurors their names and addresses would remain private, but that they may talk to the lawyers and anybody else now.

"Thank you for your service," the judge said, "You're now excused."

Sabrina struggled to her feet and watched as the jurors walked into the jury room at the back of the court.

A sentencing date was set and the judge had a few words for the lawyers. "Counsel, you have my sincere thanks for putting on an excellent case. We'll be in recess."

Sabrina broke down into tears. She was shackled and led back to jail.

Prosecutor Eric Smith embraced Robert Limon's sisters.

On the plaza outside the courthouse, the reaction to the verdict fell along family lines.

"I'm excited. I'm relieved," Robert Limon's sister, Chris Wilson, told reporters. "It's just been a long three years and it's time to put this behind us and move on. It'll never bring my brother back, but it will bring justice, and that's what we've been looking for."

Sabrina's sister, Julia Cordova, bristled at the response from Robert's family. "How anybody could be celebrating during this time is sickening to me," she said. "It's those kids, Robbie and Leanna, they're going to suffer for the rest of their life for this."

The verdict, she said, defied common sense. "A coldblooded murderer? They believed him? It's just absurd to me." Her sister, she insisted, "didn't do this, I know that. She's an amazing mother, an amazing person."

Inside the courthouse, Smith was quiet and appeared spent as he met with reporters.

The trial went as he had expected—and as he had hoped. "It is the end of a long road," he said quietly. "It is basically getting two people, the two individuals involved in Robert's death, convicted. And that's done now."

He acknowledged the media attention and live streaming of the proceedings "was a little nerve-wracking at first," but that faded. "Everything else, it's just another trial."

"It's all about justice for the families. That's what we're here for. It has to do with them being able to move on to have closure," he said. He then smiled. "I'm not a hugger, but I hugged a lot of people today."

There would be no smiles from Sabrina's attorney. "It's hard to fathom how they found her not guilty of attempted murder but involved with the murder," he told the *Bakersfield Californian*.

Days later, in another interview, he still didn't understand the verdict. "As a defense attorney, those convictions haunt you," he told KBAK-TV. "You do everything humanly possible, do everything in your power to try to convince the jury of your client's innocence, and despite your best effort, the jury still convicts."

He grumbled about the courtroom camera the judge allowed over his objections. "The witnesses are sitting there at home watching the stuff, which affects the testimony you can get from them," he said, though he didn't single out any particular witnesses. And he said he had no regrets about putting Sabrina on the stand. "We would have been in the same position now of regretting now of not putting her on the stand."

Then he returned to the jury, those nine women and three men who "sided with him"—Jonathan Hearn. "I would have liked to have had more males on the jury," he said. "I would have liked to have an even split, which is what I would have preferred or at least a larger percentage of men."

With jury selection conducted in privacy, little was known about the panel. Their occupations, education and other biographical material was sealed by the judge, as were their ages and hometowns. From the audience section, they appeared to skew a little older—middle-aged and beyond—and were a friendly lot. During courtroom breaks, they chatted with each other in the hallway about their children, grandchildren and weekend activities. Every greeting from the judge got an enthusiastic "good morning" or "good afternoon" in return.

The only juror to speak out publicly was Priscilla Phillips, juror number six, who described a decision-making process that was more difficult than the swift pace of deliberations might have suggested. Phillips told KGET-TV reporter Olivia LaVoice that she was "wasn't quite sure" Sabrina should ever have been charged with first-degree murder. "But I believe she was the mastermind behind the whole thing."

She said the panel rejected the charges related to the poisoning because of reasonable doubt. "While I thought that it was possible she did it, there was no evidence to prove that she did it," said Phillips. And jurors were more responsive to Richard Terry's appeals to their emotions than prosecutor Eric Smith would have wanted.

"I had a hard time not crying," Phillips said of the day the children testified. "My heart broke for those children," she said. "We talked about the kids and what it was going to do to them to find their mom guilty. We talked about how horrific that was going to be for them."

As for the characters of the two key players, Jonathan Hearn struck her as "very intelligent book wise, but very naive streetwise. I felt bad for him. I felt bad for everybody involved. I thought it was such a waste of a promising life."

Sabrina was another matter.

"She didn't help herself," said Phillips. "I'm sure that was part of the reason why a lot of us women were on there, so we could have empathy with her, but I never had that for her. I didn't sympathize with her. We live in a world where it's too easy to get up and walk away. I never felt a connection with her."

In the end, Phillips said, "The biggest thing I kept circling back to were the statements they made that Rob Limon would rather be dead than divorced. I don't believe anyone asked him that question."

On Thursday, Nov. 16, 2017, Jonathan Hearn returned to court for his formal sentencing. It was a different Jonathan on display. Gone were the dark suit and ties, replaced by a turquoise scrubs-like uniform over a long-sleeved T-shirt with "Kern County Jail" written across the collar.

Gone, too, was the intellectual, detached demeanor.

Robert's sister, Chris Wilson, spoke for the family. With her sister, Lydia Marrero, next to her for support, Chris stood less than 10 feet from Jonathan and fought back tears as she told Judge John Brownlee of a "roller-coaster ride of emotions" over the last three years.

"There's been tears of sadness, tears of pain, tears of anger, followed by the bitter sweetness of justice," she said in a wavering voice. "The pain of heart has diminished with the honesty and admission of guilt from Mr. Hearn."

At the defense table, Jonathan began to weep, dabbing his nose with a tissue.

"We do not struggle with Mr. Hearn's plea deal," Cindy said. "He has spoken and testified to the truth and that has brought accountability to all parties involved. Through all of these emotions, I have come to a place of forgiveness for Mr. Hearn. Forgiving is not okaying the actions of Mr. Hearn. I will never forget. But I will heal through forgiveness and that justice has been served to our brother."

It was a short speech, and as she returned to the audience section with other friends and family of Robert's, Jonathan broke down. He gasped and sighed and wiped tears. He then stood, the shackles on his handles jingling. He turned to his left and looked at the Limon family through wet eyes and said: "I have sinned."

He sniffled and continued, "I am aware that for my crimes, anything short of death is really merciful. For my sin, I truly do deserve much worse. I have wept and struggled, searching for adequate words to express my repentance. It seems like saying, 'I'm sorry,' to you all will never be enough. So speaking on borrowed and undeserved breath, I offer you my broken-hearted and genuine apology, knowing that it cannot compare to the grief that I have caused all of you."

For the next 20 minutes, he apologized to everyone—to the judge, the court staff, the detectives, even the journalists—for exposing them to "my evil," saving his most emotional apology to those closest to Robert. "I'm sorry for the grief that I caused to Robert's mother, that broke her heart," said Jonathan, "and to the two children whose dad I took away from them. I'm so sorry."

Noting that he once was a fire instructor, he said that his life had now become "a syllabus for a tragic lesson," saved only by a higher power. "It was only as I confessed and acknowledged my sin that I was shown forgiveness and grace," he said. "It was that assurance of love, your honor, that grace and forgiveness, as I knelt there, crying and shivering in that jail cell three years ago, that compelled me to speak the truth."

He would have confessed earlier, he said, but for the advice of his lawyer telling him to let the legal process run its course. He apologized for making the families wait so long to hear the truth from him.

"When I receive the sentence, just beyond those doors is a cold and discouraging chamber of captivity, of bondage, despair and hopelessness. It is there where I will be building a life, though, not of my self and my own will, but of Christ and his will, the one who has delivered me," he said. "By the grace of God, I am what I am."

By prior agreement, Jonathan Hearn received his sentence of 25 years and four months for his guilty plea for voluntary manslaughter.

Convicted of the more serious charge of first-degree murder, Sabrina Limon faced a harsher sentence than Jonathan, up to life without the possibility of parole. Her sentencing was delayed, however, after she hired a new attorney to guide her through the post-conviction process: Sharon Beth Marshall, who already had played a brief supporting role in the case. She represented Karen Lynn Hudgins, Sabrina's friend who got into a scuffle with Kelly Bernatene. Karen pleaded no contest to a single count of misdemeanor battery.

It would be up to Marshall to formally seek a new trial for Sabrina. In the meantime, Sabrina's family wrote letters of support to the judge while Robert's family braced for another grueling day in court, this time facing down Sabrina, for whom they have expressed no forgiveness. "She's a wicked woman," said Lydia Marrero. "What she did was very evil. I don't know how else to explain it."

It may all have come down to a little glass ball. Of all the evidence the jurors had at their disposal, from a silencer to a bottle of arsenic, it was that snow globe they wanted to see again. This evidence had been presented by the prosecution to prove Sabrina's free will in an affair that led to murder, that she was not under a man's power, that she was no Bathsheba.

But this gift from Jonathan's Silver Lakes lover symbolized something else. Inside the snow globe was a second globe, a metallic planet Earth—a shiny silver world surrounded by glitter and water, sealed off from outside by glass.

It was a fantasy world. And one that could be so easily shattered.

Pictures

Questioned by lead Det. Randall Meyer, Sabrina Limon made what would later be alleged as a highly incriminating slip-of-the-tongue so quick and subtle that Meyer didn't catch it at the time. (Kern County Sheriff)

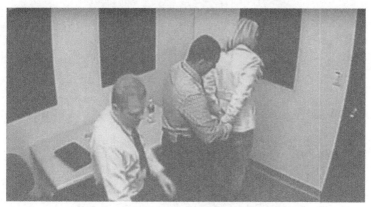

Sabrina Limon is hauled off to jail after her statements in two rounds of interrogation failed to convince detectives she knew nothing about the plot to murder her husband. (Kern County Sheriff)

Kelly Bernatene went from Sabrina Limon's best friend to accuser after discovering Sabrina's affair with killer Jonathan Hearn. (Photo by Henry A. Barrios, The Californian)

At trial, Sabrina did not make a good impression on jurors even as they worried about what woud happen to her two children if she was convicted. (Photo by Henry A. Barrios, The Californian)

A security camera captured Jonathan Hearn driving to and from the murder scene several times before he summoned the nerve to gun down Robert Limon. (Kern County Sheriff)

After reaching a plea deal with prosecutors, Jonathan Hearn testified against his former lover, Sabrina Limon, implicating her in the murder plot. (Photo by Henry A. Barrios, The Californian)

*For More News About Michael Fleeman
Signup For Our Newsletter:*

http://wbp.bz/newsletter

*Word-of-mouth is critical to an author's long-
term success. If you appreciated this book please
leave a review on the Amazon sales page:*

http://wbp.bz/boda

AVAILABLE FROM FRANK C. GIRARDOT, JR AND WILDBLUE PRESS!

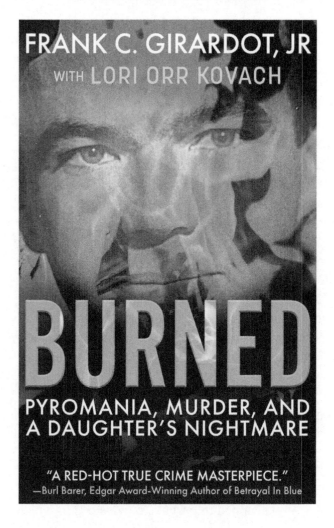

BURNED by FRANK C. GIRARDOT, JR

http://wbp.bz/burneda

Read A Sample Next

Chapter 1: Fire Season

Anyone who says there are no seasons in California hasn't been there.

In the Golden State, seasons are not things that rely on weather alone. The four seasons aren't necessarily tied to celestial movements or planetary alignment, either. Like a traffic jam on a Sunday morning that seems to have been caused by nothing, California seasons just happen and, like the freeways, seasons have names—just not spring, summer, winter or fall—like a quartet of hippie children.

Just as they know the difference between the San Diego, Santa Monica and Hollywood freeways, natives—and longtime residents of Southern California—know the difference between rainy season, hay fever season, June gloom and fire season.

The Southern California skyline—dominated by a mountain range alternately called the Santa Monicas, the San Gabriels or the San Bernardinos—holds the clues. Typically, those clues are the opposite of what one might think. When the air is cold and the Los Angeles or San Gabriel rivers thunder below their snow-capped sources carrying giant boulders and snapped tree trunks down steep mountainsides and into the vast cement canyons of the basin, it's rainy season.

No one knows how to drive in the rain. And most vehicles are not prepared for it. Think, for example, how day after day of 100-degree heat can affect skinny rubber wiper blades. It dries them out. And eventually when it rains, no one in L.A. who has a car that's more than two years old can see out the windshield. Think also about all that oil and dust that's collected on the freeway. It hasn't been washed away for months. None of this stops an Angelino from doing 80 miles per hour between destinations and inevitably getting in an accident because he or she couldn't see or couldn't stop fast enough on slick pavement. And that leads to hours and hours of extra time on the road for commuters.

In short, rainy season can shut down L.A. Too much water too fast and freeways simply flood. Sometimes, the mountains of dirt that create a barrier between the freeway and an adjoining neighborhood simply collapse in a slide that can shut down roads for days, if not weeks. And it's not just the freeways that are affected. Suburban neighborhood streets built atop flattened paths in the foothills before the advent of modern engineering can revert into ancient creeks moving mud-laden cascades along their way to ancient beaches that were formed over millions of years as the streams and arroyos of prehistoric L.A. carried their cargo of silt to the sea.

The docile brook that is the Los Angeles River and an urban canoe destination for hipsters can become a raging torrent that has been known to wipe out entire homeless encampments on its banks.

Rainy season is followed by hay fever season. In late winter and early spring, gray fields and brown hills become colorful impressionistic paintings. Green grass, orange California poppies, purple and blue lilacs and yellow wild mustard fill the skies with pollen and dust that produce epic amounts of allergies and wonderment.

Hay fever season usually lasts until the first heat wave— or at least until the jacarandas lose their flowers. Then spring is over.

At the end of spring, there's this weather pattern that some in L.A. call June gloom. It's the time of year when every day is a cliché. Some might say it's the movie "Groundhog Day" in real life. The beginning is usually marked by stories of black bears lounging in the swimming pools of foothills homes or rummaging through garbage cans in the early morning. Watch enough weather reporters on TV, you'll learn the phrase "coastal eddy" and you'll just get sick of its companion phrase, "night and morning low fog along the coast clearing in the afternoon when temperatures will reach the 70s." It's pretty much what you'll hear for week after week ad nauseum.

Then the unbearable, suffocating and oppressive heat kicks in. You'll know the change has arrived when every home in the neighborhood is shuttered and all you can hear at high noon in some suburbs is the whine of air-conditioner compressors doing their best to keep Angelinos comfortable.

Fire season typically announces itself with catastrophe. As the skies clear and daily temperatures rise, all of those flowers, grasses and weeds that were so magnificent around Easter have turned to dry tinder. At the entrance to the Angeles National Forest above the San Gabriel Valley, there's a dial that looks like it could be the spinner from "Wheel of Fortune." A ranger is responsible for letting visitors know the daily fire danger rating. Usually, the ranger will turn a dial on the wheel to one of the pie slices that range in color from green to bright red as a way of visually explaining what should be readily apparent to anyone with half a brain.

The fire danger slices are coded "low-moderate," "high," "very high," "severe," "extreme" and "catastrophic."

Even the bears, deer and mountain cats have a sense of the change in conditions; the weaker of the species will take great risks at the beginning of fire season. In a fire, the more seasoned predators such as bears and red-tailed hawks will hunt weaker prey seeking to escape the blaze. Other animals, including the cats, will hunker down in dens and wait it out.

To the public not traveling in the forest or encountering the wheel of misfortune, the National Weather Service will use local media and law enforcement bulletins to post red flag warnings and fire weather watches to "alert fire departments of the onset, or possible onset, of critical weather and dry conditions that could lead to rapid or dramatic increases in wildfire activity."

There is also a sliding scale for the severity of those of warnings. A red flag warning usually means that if a fire occurs in the foothills or mountains around L.A., the result will be extreme. One step below that is the fire weather watch, which means fire danger is high, but manageable.

Before any catastrophe, fire season has its signs—even if they are only present for a few hours, they are apparent: low humidity, strong winds and clear skies. During fire season, departments around California place additional firefighters on duty, staff more fire engines and keep equipment sharp and ready to roll.

Like anything and everything in Southern California, nothing really follows the rules. One day it's foggy and cool and the next, residents of a foothills community peppered with fancy real estate are fleeing a fast-moving and out-of-control brush fire.

Live in L.A. long enough and you'll understand it. But knowing when there's an advantageous change in the weather takes an expert: someone like a firefighter—or an experienced arsonist. Someone who watches for the change and can smell it in the air.

Glendale, a Los Angeles suburb nestled in the foothills between Pasadena—home of the famed annual Rose Bowl—and the San Fernando Valley found itself at the emergence of the 1990 fire season, the intersection of the dangerous weather pattern and an arsonist bent on destruction. The result—a catastrophe—was the $50 million College Hills Fire, which claimed 46 homes and damaged 20 others. There were injuries, but fortunately no one was killed.

While the foothills above L.A. burned, a predator lurked at the outskirts of Glendale, snapping photos and watching his prey flee.

The Pillowcase Pyro was in his element. He'd been doing this for years.

Chapter 2: Verlin Spencer

South Pasadena, Calif., could be Anytown, U.S.A. After all, the fabled Route 66, called the Mother Road by its admirers, cuts through its center just as it did (winding from Chicago to L.A.) through St. Louis, Oklahoma City, Amarillo, Gallup, Flagstaff, Kingman, Barstow and San Bernardino.

On the surface, South Pasadena is a town not all that different from Winslow, Ariz., or Galena, Kan., other spots on America's Main Street. There is a family-owned corner drugstore with a working soda fountain, parks, tree-lined streets and a public library that is open most days of the week.

A boutique grocery store still employs a staff of butchers and sells penny candy in bulk. The South Pasadena High School football team fills its stadium on Friday nights during football season and Homecoming Week is nearly a holiday.

South Pasadena residents are civic-minded. They care about their quality of life and working together, and were able to prevent the building of a massive freeway that would have sliced the tiny community of 30,000 residents in half. The construction would have completely changed the nature of a mostly unchanged suburb.

While South Pasadena shares a longstanding connection with its sister communities on Route 66, it also has something that makes it unique—it's just a few miles from the financial center of Los Angeles and less than a dozen miles from Hollywood. In fact, that proximity has made South Pasadena a somewhat familiar backdrop in dozens of movies. South Pasadena's civic landmarks can be found in films as diverse as "Step Brothers" and "Halloween."

In spite of its gentle nature, the community hasn't always had it easy.

On May 6, 1940, South Pasadena was the site of one of the nation's first mass school shootings. The memory is only now fading, but the scars may never heal.

Tragedy happened because Verlin Spencer, the South Pasadena/San Marino Middle School principal, went on a shooting spree that morning. He said he couldn't control himself. Years later, he claimed he didn't even remember what happened. But there were some pretty good reporters back in the day who took notes.

So, when Spencer set out to kill those who had wronged him, he made good on the promise. By day's end, five were dead and one seriously injured. It wasn't like folks didn't see it coming. Spencer was somewhat of a crackpot and a very weird-looking dude. Thin-faced, Spencer kept his hair close-cropped on the sides, but maintained a wave on top that covered his receding hairline. He was also a potential molester who dosed himself daily with a combination of drugs including potassium bromide, which was used by doctors in the early half of the 20th century to suppress erections.

The genteel standards of journalism in 1940 didn't really allow reporters to reveal what Spencer's actual problems were. His proclivities were only hinted at. One can guess a doctor, acting on medical and pharmacological knowledge we would now consider barbaric, got Spencer to suppress his sexual impulses via chemical castration.

Apparently, the bromides and barbiturates also eliminated Spencer's sense of right and wrong. His plan to kill several co-workers at the school began early in the morning. Before leaving for work, Spencer dashed off a letter to his wife, telling her he had been fired from his job as principal and couldn't stand to live any longer. According to news accounts at the time, the note was also his will, which read: "I Verlin Spencer being of sound mind. This is my last will and testament and leave all my property to my wife Polly. This will become null and void if she spends more than $200 on my funeral expenses."

Spencer, 39, exhibited no outward signs of mental illness. Born in 1902, he had a normal childhood and graduated from a teacher's college in Colorado before entering Stanford and later, the University of Southern California.

In what would become a standard line in just about every news story on a mass shooting or serial killer in the 20th century, Spencer's hometown newspaper, the Greeley, Colo., Republican noted: "Former classmates of Spencer in Greeley were dumbfounded at the story of the tragedy in California. They described Spencer as a good student of the studious, non-athletic type of kindly, genial disposition and excellent reputation."

Anyway, on the morning of May 6, Spencer arrived in the school district's administration office and asked for a meeting with three co-workers. When the group was seated, Spencer pulled a pistol from his belt and began firing. Killed in the office were South Pasadena school Superintendent George Bush, 56; John Alman, 52; and Will Speer, 55. After shooting the men, Spencer got up, walked from the room, calmly closed the door and pointed his gun at Bush's receptionist, Dorothea Talbert. She thought the gunshots she heard were backfires from a student's car.

"He was leaning against the doorway. He said nothing to me at all. After he fired at me the first time, it seemed that he was waiting to see what the effect of it was," Talbert recalled. "He held the gun up close to his eyes. After he fired a second time, I fell."

Talbert survived, but two of Spencer's co-workers at the junior high were not as lucky. After driving the few blocks from the administration building to his school, Spencer got out of his car and tracked down teacher Venner Vanderlip, who was teaching the school's wood shop class. Spencer lured him from the classroom by saying he needed help with a student who had been hurt. Vanderlip followed Spencer into the hallway and was shot to death.

Before leaving the school grounds, Spencer encountered longtime art teacher Ruth Sturgeon, who was about to retire. He shot her once in the head. She slumped dead at her desk, where a note on her calendar read, "26 days to go."

Spencer then found his way back to his car, awaited the arrival of police and when they had him cornered, he held a shotgun to his chest and pulled the trigger.

Unfortunately, Spencer survived. He was sentenced to state prison and released in 1970 on a technicality after 30 years behind bars. He moved to Hawaii and was never heard from again.

South Pasadena's next tragedy would also be a mass murder. A mad man's killing of four innocents who died in a hardware store on a crisp fall evening nearly went unnoticed—much to the dismay of their killer.

http://wbp.bz/burneda

**AVAILABLE SOON FROM DEBORAH VADAS
LEVISON AND WILDBLUE PRESS!**

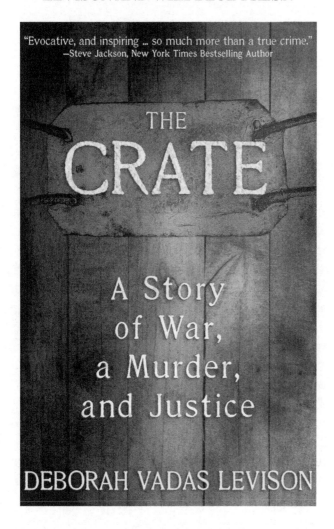

THE CRATE by DEBORAH VADAS LEVISON

http://wbp.bz/cratea

Read A Sample Next

Chapter One

NATURALIZATION

Even in my darkest nightmares, I'd never imagined the words my brother would whisper in my ear.

My family and I had arrived at the hotel minutes earlier. Already the suite lay in a state of chaos, so that when my cell phone rang it took me a few moments to trace the sound and find the device, buried under boarding passes, sunglasses, and baseball hats on the kitchenette counter. I answered with one hand and loaded bottles of Gatorade into the refrigerator with the other.

The kids were arguing, staking their claims for pullout couches and cots in the spacious living area surrounding the kitchen, jostling for the best view of the TV.

"Hang on, I can't hear," I yelled into the phone, slamming the refrigerator door. "For God's sake, can someone turn the air conditioner down? It's like the Arctic in here." I turned around to see the boys poised for a pillow fight, and braced for the inevitable howls. Fourteen-year-old Jake would never allow himself to be bested by his eight-year-old brother, Coby.

Jordyn, our oldest, was seventeen. Coolly, she snatched the cushion out of Jake's hand before he could strike.

I turned my attention back to the phone. A familiar number shone on the screen. "Hey, Pete."

My brother Peter's voice came through muffled by the racket in the room. Still, he sounded strained, and a wisp of apprehension fluttered over me.

"Are Mum and Dad okay?" I shouted over the noise. My parents were eighty and eighty-four, increasingly frail, and with mounting health concerns. They lived in Toronto, hundreds of miles away, and I constantly imagined the worst.

"They're fine, Deb," my brother said, somber, with no hint of his usual chipper tone. I drew back a heavy curtain and unlatched the glass door, seeking the quiet of a balcony. In front of me lay a gorgeous screened lanai furnished with a large wooden dining table and chairs. Another world shimmered outside here on the deck in Florida: bright, mild, calm.

"Now I can hear you better," I said into the phone. "What's going on?"

"Everyone's okay," Peter repeated. He paused. "How about you guys? When do you leave for Florida?"

I glanced around. Beyond the table stood a row of recliners on an open-air balcony that wrapped around the lanai. I pulled a second door closed behind me and walked barefoot to the iron railing, gazing out on a magnificent, unobstructed view of blue Gulf waters.

"We're here! Just checked into the hotel. I'm looking at the ocean now, actually. Are you at work?" That might explain the tension in his voice, I thought; my brother's medical practice involved harried hours of examinations followed by long evenings of dictation, often leaving him stressed and exhausted. He still had a block of patients to see, he confirmed.

I continued, "I know you hate the heat, but it would be nice for you to get away from the hospital for a few days and relax. You sound like you're on edge. When did you last swim in the ocean?" I chattered on, my unease dissolving as I basked in the sunshine and told my brother about our trip.

My husband, Craig, our kids, and I had arrived in Fort Myers that afternoon with Jake's travel team, Xplosion, for an elite baseball tournament that would pit us against some of the best high school ballplayers in the country. Initially, I had not wanted to stray out from under the luxurious green and leafy canopy surrounding our New England home, where the woods near our house beckoned, shady and cool, just like those in which I'd spent my childhood in Canada. I dreaded the prospect of Florida in July; "hot, thick, and humid" constituted my least favorite climate.

Peter paused again before answering my question. "The last time we were at the ocean? Probably when we came down to visit you last fall."

"Oh, that's just the Sound." I referred to Long Island Sound, the swirling gray bathtub of fresh and saltwater that rings the north shore of Long Island and the southern shores of Westchester and Connecticut. To my surprise and delight we'd found, though, an hour's drive from our home to the corner of Rhode Island, the open Atlantic rippling outwards in an endless spread of mint jelly, and dotted along the coast, quaint seafaring villages with weathered wooden piers like wrinkled fingers pointing out to sea. The discovery of this maritime scenery helped soften my docking in America.

I'd felt ambivalent about the whole move. Torontonians typically are not a migratory species. For the most part, those who hatch in Toronto nest there, attend college somewhere close, and settle in the suburbs for the long haul. That life, I had imagined for myself, too. When we moved away, I felt guilty, selfish for leaving my parents. They'd been immigrants themselves. Surely when they landed in Canada in 1956 they assumed that their family would huddle there together forever. When Craig and I left with two of their grandchildren, we effectively took away half of their family.

I'd cried when we all sat down at my parents' kitchen table to break the news. My mother had nodded slowly and said, "Anyvay. You have to do vhatever is best for your family." My father stood up quietly and walked out, but not before I saw that his eyes were wet.

But still, the company that Craig worked for, Trans-Lux, had offered him a good job and we were flattered that they seemed willing to go to great lengths to move us to the States. The tight economy in Toronto in the mid-nineties meant that another, equally good job might not be so easy to find. I'd left my own job in public relations to stay home full-time with Jordyn, a toddler then, and Jake, a baby. In the end, Craig and I agreed: We'd be a Swiss Family Robinson of sorts. We would embark on a year-long adventure, and after that we would come home. One year, we gave ourselves.

Trans-Lux sent a team of movers, and I watched as they packed our tidy little life into boxes and onto a moving van bound for the border.

Craig had wanted to live in or as close to New York City as possible since he would be working on Wall Street for three weeks out of each month, while the fourth week would be spent in Norwalk, Connecticut, the headquarters of Trans-Lux. To Craig, New York held all the allure of Oz: a furious pace, vast business opportunity, endless entertainment, and a spinning kaleidoscope of humanity that appealed to his adrenaline-junky personality.

I had no interest in living in Manhattan. Even though metropolitan Toronto bustled just as much, I perceived New York to be dirty and dangerous. I wanted more living space, not less. I hated traffic jams and parking hassles. And I wanted a stroller-friendly front porch, fresh air, and lots of green grass for our kids. We expanded the home search progressively north of New York City, moving along the Hutch to the scenic Merritt Parkway in Connecticut. As the numbers on the exit signs increased, the property prices decreased.

Eventually, our real estate agent brought us to Trumbull. Our agent had pegged Craig as a huge sports fan. When she pulled up in front of Unity Field, the town's main baseball complex, the sun appeared from behind the clouds and shone down, brilliantly illuminating a banner at the entrance. The sign read, "*Welcome to Trumbull, home of the 1989 Little League World Champions.*" Craig practically drooled. I could almost hear a chorus of angels burst into song. *Well, that's that*, I thought. *Here's home.*

In 1996, when my husband and I and our young family first arrived in Connecticut, I'd heard some new friends say to their kids, "Let's have a catch." The phrase rolled around in my head. You "have" a headache or you "have" an appointment, I thought. My dad never said to me, "Let's have a slalom" when we went skiing. But having a catch seemed to be what people in Fairfield County, Connecticut, did on their wide, manicured lawns.

We found a sprawling, if dated, house on a flat acre of land with towering oaks and spacious rooms. Bigger than anything we could afford in Toronto, Craig said. Great bones, I said. Surely, with some modern finishes, we could turn a profit in the twelve months we planned to live there before flipping the house and returning home to Canada. It felt, as we say in Yiddish, *bashert:* fated, meant to be.

And it seemed safe, this little town. A keep-the-front-door-open, leave-your-car-unlocked, let-your-kids-play-outside kind of town. Where all sorts of townsfolk, Jewish or not, drove to the local temple every Monday night to play Bingo. We signed on the dotted line.

Somehow, as we settled into a warm and welcoming community, a wide circle of friends, and a comfortable routine of school, work, and family life, that one year stretched into two, then five, then ten. In 2010, we had been in the States for fourteen years.

In that time I had morphed into an all-around Trumbullite: Suburban mom, carpooling in a minivan and hosting cookie-baking play dates and sleepovers, birthday bashes and after-sports pool parties for the kids and their friends. And publicist, earning media for an eclectic clientele throughout the Northeast. And journalist, interviewing movers and shakers around the state for a local paper. And volunteer, member of this committee and that, fundraiser for this project and that, room mother for this class and that.

I transformed from *alien* to *citizen* on April 8, 2005, my husband by my side, both of us eager to obtain dual citizenship, to vote, to give our children opportunities that came with being American. I didn't want to be an alien. I wanted to belong. I pledged allegiance to the flag of the United States of America, learned the words to the Star Spangled Banner, and celebrated Thanksgiving with all its trimmings ... a holiday that in Canada, as Jews, we'd ignored.

Gradually, and without meaning to, I dropped my Canadian identifiers, shedding *"aboot"* for "about," "Mummy" for "Mommy," "pop" for "soda." I understood what the kids meant when they asked for my "pocketbook," not purse, so they could buy "cotton candy," not candy floss, or a "candy bar," not a chocolate bar. *Runners*? Sneakers. *Duotang*? Folder. *Eaves troughs*? Gutters. *Garburator*? Garbage disposal. I took care not to ask for homo milk, and soon I became accustomed to buying it in jugs rather than bags. I lost track of Canadian exchange rates and Members of Parliament and stopped loading up on Canadian-brand groceries during visits to the place I still called home. And I gave birth to a third child, an American.

I connected more to being Jewish than I had earlier in life, an aspect of my persona that I had minimized as my parents worked hard to assimilate. Perhaps my own marriage and motherhood had provided the impetus, or perhaps my yearning for a sense of community had propelled me along. Whatever the reason, trying on Judaism for size reminded me of standing in a dressing room surrounded by dozens of rejects, zipping the one thing that – at last! – fit perfectly.

And I embraced baseball.

After years spent on the bleachers at Unity, I'd finally figured out the game. I'd come a long way from the days of yelling "SLIDE!" to a runner headed for first, or referring to the dugout as a penalty box. I could recite the rules, use the lingo, follow the plays. I shouted "Give it a ride!" to the batter or "All right, one, two, three!" to the pitcher. I felt comfortable speaking *baseball;* it was yet another language I had learned.

Craig and the kids seemed thrilled to be here in Florida, and now, standing in the mild breeze on the terrace, I felt excited, too. During school vacations, three or four times a year, we invariably returned to Toronto to visit our families – a marked contrast to this rare junket due south. Here, we'd swim in the sea and bask on the beach. In downtown Fort Myers, we'd treat the kids to ice cream cones, browse the surf shops. Jordyn would try on straw hats. Jake and Coby would ask for necklaces with a shark's tooth. Something for everyone.

It would be a great vacation.

"You should come down for a few days," I urged my brother on the phone. "A change of scenery would do you good. It's a pretty hotel."

I leaned on the railing and gazed out at the tops of swaying palm fronds. The surf rippled, crystal clear and glistening in the late day sun. Gulls circled in the sky. Sailboats and ships floated across the horizon. Pastel colored umbrellas polka-dotted the coastline and little kids with plastic shovels dug for shells in the sand. I tilted my face upward to catch the sun's rays. *Ahhhh.*

Over the phone, my brother suggested I sit down. Slowly I lowered myself to the edge of a chaise lounge.

"Something's happened," Peter's voice dropped low.

The needles of anxiety returned to prick at me. "Peeps. For God's sake. What is it?"

"There's been a murder ... at the cottage."

http://wbp.bz/cratea

AVAILABLE SOON FROM ANNE K. HOWARD AND WILDBLUE PRESS!

HIS GARDEN by ANNE K. HOWARD

http://wbp.bz/hisgardena

Read A Sample Next

1.

The monster stirred inside him. Most times, he could tame it. Keep it hidden. Silence its screams. But tonight, the beast demanded release.

She lifted her head up. "You're taking too long. I'm done."

He pressed her head back down. "You're done when I say you're done …"

She wriggled beneath the firmness of his grip. "No!" she protested, forcing herself up from his lap. She stared him straight in the eyes—defiant and unafraid. "That's all I'm doing for you, Devin."

His calloused fingertips nervously tapped the upholstered backbench and his spine tingled with an odd mixture of excitement and fear. The beast was rising. There was no going back. Not now. Not ever. "Rape her," the monster instructed. "Rape the whore!"

*

It had been a long night of hustling for Nilsa Arizmendi and Angel "Ace" Sanchez. Maybe it was the hot weather, but the regular johns were being especially cheap and irritable, and Nilsa was forced to negotiate smaller fees. Ordinarily, she charged $30 for a half hour, but tonight's tricks were turning a maximum of only $20 and some demanded blowjobs for a measly 10 bucks. Like shrewd customers at a turn-of-the-century street market, the johns knew that the vendor in question was desperate for cash.

Ace loitered around the corners of New Britain Avenue, where his girlfriend worked. He stared glumly at the filthy surroundings, trying not to think about Nilsa's activities. He did not like their lifestyle. In fact, he despised it. But how else could he and Nilsa score drugs? The couple's shared habit was not cheap. In July 2003, they were each smoking about 20 to 30 pieces of crack per day and shooting up a bundle-and-a-half of heroin, which translated to about 10 to 15 bags on the streets. Sometimes, Nilsa used up to three bundles of heroin a day, depending on the amount of crack she smoked. It was a nasty cycle. The crack got Nilsa and Ace ramped up and wired and the heroin brought them down. They needed both to survive.

Without the drugs, sickness set in. Being drug sick was terrible—worse than having the flu. In the darkness of their motel room, the childhood sweethearts huddled together in sweat-soaked sheets, shivering with nausea and chills. Every joint and bone ached as invisible bugs furiously crawled beneath the surface of their skin. In between fits of vomiting, their bowels loosened and the bed became soiled. Nilsa kept the curtains drawn and placed the Do Not Disturb sign on the outside door handle for days at a time. The room was a mess. Their lives were a mess. Besides the incessant and all-consuming craving for heroin, she felt shame.

"This shit has to stop," Ace thought as he watched Nilsa emerge from the back seat of an old man's car. She walked toward him, tucked her tie-dyed T-shirt into her dungaree shorts and offered a faint smile. Normally 140 pounds, the 5'2", dark-haired woman was now only skin and bones. "I'm tired," she said. "Let's go home."

On the walk back, Nilsa briefly disappeared and scored a blast of crack at Goodwin Park in Hartford. She returned to Ace and attempted to take his hand. He pulled away. "I'm done with this shit. You gotta go to rehab, Nilsa. We both gotta go."

She acted like she did not hear him. It was usually the best way to avoid a fight.

But tonight, Ace would not let up. "I'm done with the fucking drugs," he mumbled, running his hand through his greasy dark hair. Normally, he kept it long, but a few days before, he had cut it short. "Done with the hustling. Fuck. Fuck this shit."

Their shadowy figures forged into the night, softly illuminated by the neon lights of outdated motels. Rolling hills of forest stood far in the distance, strangely comforting and yet somehow sinister. When Nilsa's high wore down, they started to quarrel. This time, Ace would not take no for an answer. They both had to go to rehab in the morning.

Nilsa was reluctant. She had been in and out of rehab for years and it never did her any good. Still, she loved her four children and desperately wanted to be done with the drugs and get clean forever and for good. Overhead, the night sky opened and a warm drizzle began to fall. The blue rock watch on Nilsa's frail wrist ticked into the early morning hours. They walked southbound along the pike, past Cedar Hill Cemetery containing the corpses of Connecticut's affluent class, including legendary actress Katharine Hepburn, and then a smaller cemetery containing the remains of lesser-known citizens.

Ace gently elbowed Nilsa. "You gonna start singing?"

She sometimes sang Christian hymns that she learned in childhood as they walked along the pike. It passed the time and gave them both a sense of comfort in the midst of all the pain. She smiled beneath the foggy moonlight. "You want me to?"

"You know I like your voice," he replied.

Her smooth, clear voice chimed like a bell into the darkness of the night:

O Lord my God, When I in awesome wonder,
Consider all the worlds Thy Hands have made;
I see the stars, I hear the rolling thunder,
Thy power throughout the universe displayed.

By the time they reached the parking lot of the Stop & Shop in Wethersfield, Ace had persuaded Nilsa to agree to the plan. Nilsa was worthy of a long and healthy life. After all, Ace needed her. Her mother needed her. Her children needed her. She vowed to never turn another trick again or inject poison into her veins. The party was over and fuck her if it had not been the party from Hell.

Nilsa eyed a lone vehicle parked in the far corner of the store's lot. "That's Devin's van."

"Let's get back to the motel," Ace said.

"I'm just gonna say hi."

Nilsa walked across the lot to the beat-up blue van owned by their mutual acquaintance, Devin Howell. They had met Howell a few months before. At the time, he was pumping gas at the Exxon gas station on the corner of Broad Street and New Britain Avenue. The rain was heavy and Ace and Nilsa were soaking wet as they approached Howell's van and asked for a ride to their motel room on the Berlin Turnpike in Wethersfield. "We'll give you five bucks," Ace said.

Howell had to go to Lowe's to price out some supplies for an upcoming job. He was driving in that direction anyway, so it was not a problem to assist two near-strangers who appeared down on their luck. "Yeah, sure. The door's unlocked."

Nilsa and Ace squeezed into the bucket seat on the passenger side. Nilsa used her street name, Maria, when she introduced herself to Howell. As they drove to The Almar Motel, Howell told the couple in his mild Southern drawl that he had a lawn-care business. Ace glanced over his shoulder at the back of the van. The space was large, with a long bench sofa littered with lawn service tools and clothing. The stench of body odor pervaded the vehicle's interior.

When they arrived at the motel, Ace and Nilsa invited Howell into their room to hang out. Howell brought some beer and marijuana. Nilsa and Ace offered to share a little crack, but Howell refused. He was a weed and booze guy. Together, the three got high on their poisons of choice. Howell told them that he was living in his van and he often parked it at the Stop & Shop parking lot in Wethersfield. He left the motel less than an hour later. As he drove back to the Stop & Shop lot to bed down for the night, he glanced at the open ashtray and saw that a $20 bill rolled up inside of it was gone. "No fucking good deed goes unpunished," he cynically thought. Ace and Nilsa had ripped him off.

In the months that followed, the occasional contact with Howell proved beneficial to Nilsa and Ace. The couple had lived on the Berlin Turnpike for the last 18 months or so, first at The Elm Motel and then at The Almar. Their daily routine involved walking from the motel on the pike to the familiar section of New Britain Avenue in Hartford where Nilsa turned tricks, about 1½ miles from The Almar. Ace had not worked a job for seven or eight months and he no longer had a vehicle of his own. Especially in the cold weather, Nilsa and Ace relied on acquaintances to spot them walking along the busy roadway and offer a lift. Occasionally, they had money for a cab, but that meant less money for drugs.

Howell also proved useful in assisting Nilsa and Ace to cop drugs. He did not mind driving them to local dealers living 15 to 20 minutes away. He would not get high with them when they scored. He seemed content to do them a favor by giving them a ride in exchange for a few dollars. All told, Howell served as the couple's makeshift Uber driver on about five occasions over the course of one month.

At approximately 2:45 a.m. on July 25, 2003, Ace watched Nilsa's skeletal form traipse across the empty parking lot. It was hard for him to believe that this was the same woman whose weight had sky-rocketed to 180 pounds when she was last released from federal prison—all beefed up by the cheap, starchy food. Nilsa stopped at the van and appeared to talk to Howell, who sat in the driver's seat. Then she walked around the van and got into the passenger side. Howell turned on the engine and slowly drove away. It was the last time Ace would see Nilsa alive.

*

When Christ shall come, with shout of acclamation,
And take me home, what joy shall fill my heart.
Then I shall bow, in humble adoration,
And then proclaim: "My God, how great Thou art!"

Nilsa "Coco" Arizmendi, Jan. 29, 1970–July 25, 2003
Rest In Peace

http://wbp.bz/hisgardena

See even more at:
http://wbp.bz/tc

More True Crime You'll Love From WildBlue Press

A MURDER IN MY HOMETOWN by Rebecca Morris

Nearly 50 years after the murder of seventeen year old Dick Kitchel, Rebecca Morris returned to her hometown to write about how the murder changed a town, a school, and the lives of his friends.

wbp.bz/hometowna

THE BEAST I LOVED by Robert Davidson

Robert Davidson again demonstrates that he is a master of psychological horror in this riveting and hypnotic story ... I was so enthralled that I finished the book in a single sitting. "—James Byron Huggins, International Bestselling Author of The Reckoning

wbp.bz/tbila

BULLIED TO DEATH by Judith A. Yates

On September 5, 2015, in a public park in LaVergne, Tennessee, fourteen-year-old Sherokee Harriman drove a kitchen knife into her stomach as other teens watched in horror. Despite attempts to save her, the girl died, and the coroner ruled it a "suicide." But was it? Or was it a crime perpetuated by other teens who had bullied her?

wbp.bz/btda

SUMMARY EXECUTION by Michael Withey

"An incredible true story that reads like an international crime thriller peopled with assassins, political activists, shady FBI informants, murdered witnesses, a tenacious attorney, and a murderous foreign dictator."—Steve Jackson, New York Times bestselling author of NO STONE UNTURNED

wbp.bz/sea

Printed in Great Britain
by Amazon

19305508R00183